AFGHAN ENDGAMES

South Asia in World Affairs Series

T. V. Paul, Series Editor

AFGHAN ENDGAMES

STRATEGY AND POLICY CHOICES FOR AMERICA'S LONGEST WAR

EDITED BY
HY ROTHSTEIN AND JOHN ARQUILLA

Georgetown University Press
Washington, DC

FOUNDATION®
BOOKS

Delhi • Bengaluru • Mumbai • Kolkata • Chennai • Hyderabad
Pune • Thiruvananthapuram

Published by
Cambridge University Press India Pvt. Ltd.
under the imprint of Foundation Books
Cambridge House, 4381/4 Ansari Road, Daryaganj, **New Delhi** 110 002

Cambridge University Press India Pvt. Ltd.
C-22, C-Block, Brigade M.M., K.R. Road, Jayanagar, **Bengaluru** 560 070
Plot No. 80, Service Industries, Shirvane, Sector-1, Nerul, **Navi Mumbai** 400 706
10 Raja Subodh Mullick Square, 2nd Floor, **Kolkata** 700 013
21/1 (New No. 49), 1st Floor, Model School Road, Thousand Lights, **Chennai** 600 006
House No. 3-5-874/6/4, (Near Apollo Hospital), Hyderguda, **Hyderabad** 500 029
Agarwal Pride, 'A' Wing, 1308 Kasba Peth, Near Surya Hospital, **Pune** 411 011
T.C. 25/ 2731 Lukes Lane, Ambujavilasam Road, **Thiruvananthapuram** 695 001

This edition is published by Cambridge University Press India Pvt. Ltd. by arrangement with Georgetown University Press, Washington DC, USA

First South Asia Edition 2013

ISBN 978-93-82993-02-5

This book was made possible in part by a research grant from the US Department of Defense. All statements of fact, opinion, or analysis expressed are those of the authors and do not necessarily reflect the official positions or views of the US government or any US government agency. Nothing in the content of the book should be construed as asserting or implying US government authentication of information or agency endorsement of the authors's views.

Published by Manas Saikia for Cambridge University Press India Pvt. Ltd. and
printed at Bhavish Graphics, Chennai

To the memory of
General Wayne A. Downing

CONTENTS

ACKNOWLEDGMENTS

This book began as a research project funded by the Office of the Secretary of Defense. We would like to thank Ben Riley, a principal deputy in the office of the Assistant Secretary of Defense for Research and Evaluation, for his generous support and encouragement. His agile mind and keen insights have done much to guide and advance this work and other undertakings of ours over the years. We also want to thank Nancy Ann Budden, director of the Defense Counter Terrorism Technology Office, who has an uncanny ability to recognize fresh ideas and ensure that they are drawn to the attention of the appropriate authorities in Washington—and elsewhere.

At Georgetown University Press, Don Jacobs and the entire staff worked swiftly and exceptionally efficiently on our behalf, with patience and never-failing good grace. Here at the Naval Postgraduate School, our colleague Rebecca Lorentz coauthored one of the book's chapters, but also worked tirelessly to help with the editing of the entire manuscript. It is hard to see how we could have stayed on track—much less on schedule—without her clear vision and organizational skill.

It is also apparent to us that we have enjoyed blessings beyond count in the form of our contributors—an all-star cast of experts across the range of fields relevant to solving the strategic riddles of Afghanistan. To each of them we offer our frank admiration and humble thanks.

Finally, we acknowledge with profound respect and deep gratitude the extraordinary sacrifices of all the veterans of the war in Afghanistan. We have visited with and listened to many of them, always coming away with fresh perspectives and a determination to keep on fighting for policies and strategies that will honor their service with success, and bring an end to the long suffering of the Afghan people.

PREFACE

In most wars the outcome is often predictable long before the fighting stops. The fate of the Axis powers in World War II was foreseeable as early as 1942, with the defeat of the Germans at Stalingrad and the Japanese at Midway, yet the conflict raged on until 1945. Similarly, 1968 was the watershed time in the Vietnam War; by then it was clear to many that the United States would not defeat the insurgents. Still, American forces fought on for several more years and Saigon did not fall and become Ho Chi Minh City until 1975. This pattern of knowing the outcome long before the war ends has held as well when guerrillas have been beaten, from the Kenyan Mau Mau and the Malayan insurgents of the 1950s, and in many irregular wars ever since.

The current conflict in Afghanistan, however, has broken the mold. After more than a decade of hard fighting, either side could still win. For the insurgents, "victory" would most likely come in two phases: First there would be the withdrawal of foreign forces; then the Taliban would come back into power. For the American-led coalition, winning seems as hard to define as it has been to achieve. The favored outcome of a strong, legitimate central government presiding over a period of peace is not likely to emerge. But the thwarting of Taliban aims, the defeat of local al-Qaeda elements, and the rise of some form of effective governance may all be well within the realm of possibility.

The chance of gaining a successful outcome can be maximized by adjusting the allied coalition's strategic aims; and determining the range of options that might be pursued through such a shift is the goal that animates our study. The prospects for strategic adjustment, even this late in the war, have generated much interest in the Office of the Secretary of Defense, particularly on the part of Ben Riley, a senior official who encouraged us to bring together the best analytical team possible. We have assembled some of the finest minds in the fields of military history and strategy, anthropology, ethics, and communications to take a fresh look at the war in Afghanistan.

The first task undertaken was to dispel the popular myth of Afghan invincibility and its corollary: that Afghanistan itself is a forbidding "graveyard of empires." From the ancient Greeks to the British in the nineteenth century, foreign control has been a common occurrence in Afghan history. But if not a graveyard, Afghanistan has nevertheless become something of a charnel house during the past three decades of near-constant warfare. Well over a million Afghans have died, most at the hands of Russian occupying forces in the 1980s. But the civil war that followed their departure eventually escalated to become very bloody as well. With all this suffering in mind, it seems clear that the primary goal of a winning strategy should be to find a way to stop, or sharply stem, the killing. Thus, each of the alternatives developed in this book has been designed to save Afghan lives.

The range of solutions considered covers a spectrum from complete, speedy withdrawal to "doubling down" on existing commitments. In between these extremes, there are variations that include staying indefinitely, but with very small forces, and encouraging neighboring states to take more prominent roles—put less delicately, to end their "free riding" at American expense—to tamp down the violence in Afghanistan.

In his June 2011 speech on Afghanistan, it seems that President Obama tried to "thread the needle" between competing views about staying the course or withdrawing. The president correctly noted that the Taliban and al-Qaeda had been weakened by the surge of additional coalition forces. But he also intimated that the cost of the war was undermining America's economic recovery, and called for modest, deliberately timed force reductions. While some will argue that the speed of the ongoing drawdown is too slow, others will oppose troop reductions on the grounds that they jeopardize prior gains. Missing from the president's speech, and from the larger American strategic discourse, was a reaffirmation of US objectives and a realistic appreciation that the greatest impediment to progress is the Afghan government itself—the very institution that we so arduously support. Also, the manner in which troops are used is far more important than their sheer numbers—another important factor too long neglected in American war councils. We hope that insights can be gained from *Afghan Endgames* that *do* speak to these matters, whether in public debates or in policy discussions taking place behind closed doors.

Beyond military concerns about losing hard-won gains, the urge to remain in Afghanistan may also be driven by broader ethical obligations that accompany the later phases of all foreign wars. Thus, at this point the requirements of *jus post bellum* (justice in the postwar period) come to the fore. Short of the obligation to prevent the outbreak of a genocidal bloodbath at war's end, there may be no ethical requirement to stay until a strong, legitimate central government is ensconced. Instead, there is a specific duty to protect those who fought on our side and would be at risk of Taliban retaliation for having done so. Indeed, this ethical obligation extends as far as welcoming them to resettle in the United States, much as Hmong and Montagnard fighters were welcomed in the wake of the Vietnam War.

The risk of renewed bloodletting aside, another factor to consider about an American exit from Afghanistan is the effect it would have on the emergence of Afghan civil society. It may be that the whole nation-building enterprise in Afghanistan has been structured backwards. Instead of expanding outward from the core in Kabul, a more networked, from-the-edges-inward approach could prove more appropriate. Further, keeping a large number of foreign forces in Afghanistan, as the coalition has for so many years, might actually be inhibiting the growth of an indigenous progressive movement that is neither pro-Karzai nor pro-Taliban, but which carves out its own independent path.

A central theme running throughout *Afghan Endgames* is that there are inevitable costs and risks that accompany each possible strategic variation that might be tried. Our goal has been to ensure that each perspective is thoroughly presented and thoughtfully analyzed with these factors in mind. Beyond this, we have striven to search out the degrees to which the various alternative strategies relate to each other. What we have found is that there is more complementarity than competition among and between them. Indeed, this has led us to see the possibilities for synthesis across the competing ideas; but it has also contributed to our own distinct views.

Thus, we look at the Afghan endgame as one in which, regardless of strategic preference, American presence will surely draw down. But looking through the lens of alternative strategies enables us to see the value of making swift, sharp, force reductions, and even of pursuing the goal of full withdrawal in a timely manner. At the same time, respect for concerns about the American reputation in the world suggest to us the need to engage, right now, in a "battle of the story" about the reasons for withdrawal and the likelihood of our return should the bad old days come once again to this troubled land.

In addition to the issue of force levels, debate about which constitutes only one small part of comprehensive strategic thinking, we also conclude that the goal of establishing strong, central democratic governance is not achievable by the path that has been pursued for the past decade. Instead, something with more nuance will be called for, probably along the lines of civil society networks that aim first at repairing the fabric of Afghan society at the district and provincial levels, only later moving on to the center in Kabul, if practical.

Our thoughts also go to the problem of Pakistan, an ambivalent ally whose territory the enemy enjoys, for the most part, as a haven from allied forces. A range of views about the role of Pakistan unfold in this volume. For us, though, two things seem very clear: The Afghan War can be won—in the sense of sharply reducing violence and replacing it with agreed-upon order—from inside Afghanistan; and putting pressure on Pakistan to "do more" may actually play into al-Qaeda's deep game, the aim of which is to destabilize the world's sole Muslim nuclear power. Another important insight is that a sharp reduction of coalition forces—along with a renewed focus on operations solely within Afghanistan—will ease tensions with Pakistan, encourage productive involvement by neighboring states, and may even prompt India to curtail activities in-country that are viewed with suspicion by those in power in Islamabad.

It is against this backdrop, at this crucial time, that we offer *Afghan Endgames,* in the hope that this book will stimulate and elevate the public discourse about a conflict whose outcome will likely have a profound shaping influence on the course of world affairs in the twenty-first century.

We must not be afraid of Afghanistan and would profit by letting it be the master of its own fate. Maybe it is not the most attractive solution for us, but I feel that I am right in asserting that the less they are able to see us, the less they are likely to hate us . . . we will have a much greater chance of getting the Afghans on our side if we abstain from any interference in their internal affairs whatsoever.

Lord Roberts of Kandahar,
Commander of the Kabul and Kandahar field forces,
Second Anglo-Afghan War, 1879–80

PART I

Overview

CHAPTER 1

Understanding the Afghan Challenge

Hy Rothstein and John Arquilla

More than a decade into the American intervention in Afghanistan, the status quo there is untenable. The overthrow of the Taliban in 2001–2 had near universal support and was briefly the top foreign policy priority of the United States. But Afghanistan's importance was downgraded during the Bush administration's first term because of the invasion of Iraq in 2003. It became the "other war" within policymaking circles and our commitment to this campaign became unclear. Interest in Afghanistan was revived later in the decade when it became a matter of central emphasis for President Obama, its salience underscored by the near doubling of US troops in-country to one hundred thousand since he first took office.

Even now, however, one could argue that the level of commitment to the war has been a winding road and remains so. All recognize that Afghanistan is the place from where the 9/11 attacks on America were plotted. If the country reverts to Taliban control it may once again become a major node in the al-Qaeda network. This outcome, which would mean that US and allied efforts in Afghanistan have been in vain, would be seen as unacceptable by the American public and leaders across the political spectrum.[1]

Thus the stakes are high in Afghanistan, but it is no simple matter to identify effective and realistic endgame strategies, in large part because of the problematic results of the Afghan campaign over the past decade. The striking initial American victory in the fall of 2001, which drove the Taliban and al-Qaeda from power with less than two hundred Special Forces soldiers working with a few thousand friendly tribesmen, was followed by almost nine years of policies and actions on the ground that resulted in deteriorating security conditions. Each new approach taken by the United States and its International Security Assistance Force (ISAF) allies did little to thwart al-Qaeda and the Taliban.

In the early years of the war, the various initiatives pursued seemed to rely primarily on wishful thinking, assessing good prospects for success just because we so desperately desired to see a secure, democratic state emerge in Afghanistan. Whereas most would now say that this maximalist political goal is beyond reach, the deteriorating security situation began to change for the better in the summer of 2010. By December the momentum, in some key areas, shifted from the Taliban to coalition forces for the first time since early 2002. The consolidation of these gains remains a significant challenge since the Taliban continues to demonstrate resilience and adaptability.[2]

In unveiling his strategy in a December 2009 speech at West Point, President Obama said: "I have determined that it is in our vital national interest to send an additional 30,000 US troops to Afghanistan. After 18 months our troops will begin to come home." In one arduously prepared, highly anticipated speech that was supposed to outline a new strategic approach in Afghanistan, the president simultaneously proffered two contradictory policies: escalation and withdrawal. Even a cursory examination of the projected withdrawal timeline revealed troubling inconsistencies. The drawdown of troops from the 2009–10 surge began in July 2011 as President Obama promised, but is following a slow path to returning simply to presurge levels. Significant numbers will remain until 2014—and some presence will likely continue indefinitely.

In announcing the specifics of the troop drawdown, Obama added that the US mission in Afghanistan would "change from combat to support" by 2014. "We won't try to make Afghanistan a perfect place. We will not police its streets or patrol its mountains indefinitely."[3] Presumably, the residual forces that remain for years to come will focus on hunting terrorists. Republican reaction to the current drawdown and the longer-range plan has ranged from tepid and qualified support to opposition, setting the stage for Afghanistan strategy to be a major issue in the 2012 presidential election cycle.[4]

Coinciding with the drawdown of US troops, Obama announced that the United States supports political reconciliation and incorporation of Taliban groups into the Afghan government if they are willing to break with al-Qaeda.[5] However, the phased withdrawal of US and ISAF combat troops has sown seeds of distrust with our Afghan allies, and it has likely emboldened the Taliban and al-Qaeda, despite the military pressure that they are under. Thus it is not clear how successful these political negotiations can be. At some level our enemies in Afghanistan believe that time is on their side, knowing that most US military and allied forces will eventually leave and that the American people are increasingly opposed to the war.[6] It is against this dark backdrop that fresh strategic alternatives must be developed.

Thinking Strategically about Afghanistan

Given the continuing importance of Afghanistan, the fragile and reversible progress only recently achieved after a decade of engagement there, the waning commitments from ISAF allies to remain in Afghanistan, and the increasing political and budgetary pressure on US policymakers, it seems imperative to explore alternative policies and strategies that might succeed in bringing the war to an acceptable close. Should recent successes be reversed or should our current goals in Afghanistan become untenable or too expensive to achieve, the adoption of new approaches will be inevitable. Our firm belief is that a range of acceptable outcomes exists, and accordingly, a variety of strategic approaches might be applied successfully, albeit under varying conditions. It is with this purpose in mind that we have brought together some of the best minds among American strategists to craft and consider possible new paths.

Throughout history, across time and cultures, strategists have almost always insisted that any blueprint for victory must start with a reasonable approximation of what that outcome would look like. The great British strategist, B. H. Liddell Hart, called the process one that "looks beyond the war to the subsequent peace."[7] The goal of US strategy in Afghanistan has been mostly consistent since 2001 and remains to disrupt, dismantle, and eventually defeat al-Qaeda and deny terrorists the use of safe havens in either Afghanistan or Pakistan. This strategy necessitates developing Afghan capabilities sufficient to prevent the return of the Taliban to power.[8] The challenge of reaching this goal, given the tight constraints imposed by our domestic politics and a wary public that is skeptical after ten years of war, is daunting. Ample evidence suggests that the American public is no longer willing to pay the high cost of an indefinite commitment to achieve this goal. To be fair, nailing down a realistic goal is not as easy as pundits and armchair policymakers and strategists suggest. Policies and strategies are built on what is known, which is often, and for long periods, very little. What is actually attainable changes as more becomes known.[9]

Clausewitz recognized this dimension of strategy in his discussion about the disabling affects of *friction, chance, and uncertainty* in war.[10] With this observation in mind, our view is that policymakers would be wiser to start with a range of acceptable outcomes rather than a single, fixed, desired endstate. While it would be optimal to take such an approach from the outset, our view is that identifying and working from a range of alternatives can still be useful in informing policy and ultimately strategy, at any stage of a conflict, should circumstances change significantly.

Bernard Brodie once affirmed, "Strategy is nothing if not pragmatic.... Above all, strategic theory is a theory for action."[11] But the counterinsurgency (COIN) doctrine that is currently being pursued in Afghanistan may be fatally flawed. To start with, it is enormously costly because it seems to include everything. For example, the coalition seems to pursue democratic nation-building in a traditional culture on one day, then focuses on improving highways and hydroelectric dams the next, followed by trying to capture or kill Taliban and al-Qaeda fighters on another day. But in Afghanistan there is no self-evident connection between democratic nation-building, economic development, and successful counterinsurgency. If the essence of strategy lies in making choices under constraint, the American approach is certainly inefficient and possibly ineffective, considering its difficulty in being supported and sustained over the long term. And for the Afghan people, who may not need or want modernization or democracy, the desire may be for something far more basic: an end to rampant killing and terror.

Strategy, and perhaps we really mean grand strategy, is the bridge that relates power to political purpose. It uses all instruments of statecraft with political purpose in mind. Grand strategy is neither power nor purpose. It simply connects the two.[12]

Arguably, the counterinsurgency strategy in Afghanistan does not adequately serve the purpose of being "connective tissue," since its political purpose seems to have expanded beyond defeating al-Qaeda to neutralizing the Taliban and building sufficient capacity in the Afghan state to secure its future and US interests.

Even though President Obama has reiterated his determination to fight the "good war" in Afghanistan, there exists grave doubt among both the Afghan and American people about the legitimacy of the government of Hamid Karzai and therefore the overall cause. This lack of a righteous cause, perceived or real, is not trivial. Furthermore, at some level the Afghan people know that the Taliban will still be around long after coalition forces have returned to their home countries.

Constraints Imposed by the Region, Its Neighbors, and Afghan Culture

The evidence is clear that elements within the Pakistani state have covertly supported the Taliban and provided safe haven to al-Qaeda operatives throughout its ongoing fight with coalition forces. At the same time, Pakistan has arrested dozens of al-Qaeda leaders and tacitly permitted the United States to conduct drone strikes within its territory. This situation seems inexplicable to many Western observers. The reality is that these policies reflect the national security agenda of Pakistani leaders as they understand their interests; so, Pakistan's strategic goal in Afghanistan is to eliminate Indian encirclement by manipulating Pashtun ethnic nationalism while maintaining the dependence of the United States on Pakistan for security cooperation.[13]

Accordingly, stabilizing Afghanistan requires the formation of a legitimate state capable of controlling and developing its territory without threatening its neighbors—especially Pakistan. Pushing the Taliban out of power in 2001 had the effect of reducing Pakistani influence in Afghanistan by putting in power a group of people who sought closer relations with India, Pakistan's long-standing enemy. Relations between India and Pakistan have been strained by historical and political issues defined by the violence that accompanied the partition of British India in 1947.[14]

Pakistan's goal in the past and at present is to bring Afghanistan under its influence in order to preclude India's establishment of a second front along the Afghanistan-Pakistan (AFPAK) border. India, a country eight times Pakistan's size in population and economic resources, would gain a strategic advantage if it were able to cultivate a friendly regime in Kabul. Accordingly, Pakistan benefits by supporting Pashtun extremists who would undermine a nationalist government that might accept Indian influence in Afghan affairs. Supporting insurgent forces in Afghanistan is a very rational policy choice for Pakistan.

The serious constraints faced by Pakistan, a key player in any US plan, and a nation simultaneously confronting grave terrorist threats of its own, limits the degree of cooperation that can be expected from that country. In fact, Pakistan's strategy of "cooperation" with the United States is one of the primary causes of contemporary terrorism directed at Islamabad. Reactions to recent events, such as the CIA contractor killing three Pakistanis in Lahore and the US commando raid that killed Osama bin Laden, illustrate the rage, embarrassment, and resulting tensions that characterize the fragile and turbulent relationship between the United States and Pakistan. Now more than ever, there is a real risk that drawing Pakistan deeper into the Afghan conflict might spark an internal social revolution—perhaps the true objective of al-Qaeda's "deep game." A way ahead must be found, therefore, that concentrates on the possibility of winning the war in Afghanistan mostly from *inside* Afghanistan.

Yet there are other limitations to what can realistically be achieved that come from within Afghanistan itself. These limits, such as they are, have been imposed by a number of factors, some clearly recognized, others underappreciated or simply too difficult to deal with. A few known factors that limit options are the challenges posed by local warlords, a fragile Afghan security apparatus, inadequate national revenue, booming opium production, and a weak central government of questionable legitimacy.

Even in light of the successes that began in 2010, America's Afghan strategy must be prepared for shocks that can reverse the momentum. A deficit in strategic thinking categorized the first eight years of the war to the point where vague and irrelevant military and political theories, when pursued in the field, resulted in actions that undermined the war effort, empowered the Taliban, and raised the overall level of violence. The Afghan people, after more than thirty years of constant warfare, may simply want the shooting to stop and to be left alone.

Considering a Range of Acceptable Outcomes

The identification of acceptable outcomes consists largely of recognizing and understanding the art of the possible. What one wants and what is possible necessitate the development of a pragmatic understanding of the social, cultural, and political behavior of the communities that are waging this war. Washington would prefer Afghanistan to be a country that is governed in accordance with the will of its people, its population prospering from a system of free and fair trade. It would also be a country where the rights of its women were respected. This reflects an ideal outcome.

But does this outcome accurately reflect our true national security interests? We suggest that waging war anywhere, and in Afghanistan in particular, can and should have more narrowly defined national security interests, which may allow for the emergence of a range of alternative acceptable strategies and outcomes. Our most vital interests in Afghanistan are, first, to keep terrorists from using that country to plan and launch strikes against the United States and its allies, and second, to keep insurgent groups from using Afghanistan to destabilize Pakistan.

President Obama reaffirmed this at West Point in 2009, when he said: "Our overarching goal remains the same: to disrupt, dismantle, and defeat al-Qaeda in Afghanistan and Pakistan, and to prevent its capacity to threaten America and our allies in the future."[15] These basic security interests should be the starting point from which multiple acceptable outcomes, and the respective strategies associated with them, are crafted.[16]

Centrality, Legitimacy, and Stability

Tying together notions about the centrality of governance, legitimacy, and ultimately stability in Afghanistan is the key to develop winning strategies. We consider the measure of "centrality" in Afghanistan to lie somewhere on a continuum between a strong, centralized state to something much more decentralized, more confederated, and "edge-like." Our basic measure here is of the degree to which the functions of governance are conceived, administered, and directed from the national capital. Centrality can also be assessed in terms of the subnational entities—states, provinces, districts—and how their administrations are chosen, whether from the center or locally, and the degree to which they have some kind of autonomy of action. Countries like China and Vietnam would thus be considered very centralized, whereas the United States, with its federal system allowing much power and discretion to the states themselves, would fall somewhere in the middle range of centrality. Afghanistan has traditionally featured decentralized governance. In theory, acceptable political outcomes from an American perspective can lie anywhere on this continuum.

By legitimacy we mean the acceptance of the government by the people. Most democracies, taking the pulse of their people with regular, fair voting, naturally enjoy high levels of legitimacy. But to be legitimate a government need not be democratic. The authoritarian monarchy in Saudi Arabia, for example, has a moderately high level of social acceptance, and we would thus consider it to have substantial legitimacy. The persistence of Vladimir Putin's rule in Russia seems also to feature classical authoritarian tropes, yet the Russian people continue to support the kind of governance with which he has come to be associated.

On the other hand, there are many nondemocratic rulers who stay in power only on the basis of *force majeure*, a phenomenon most commonly seen in many African countries, some of which eventually lose their ability to govern through coercion, as happened to dictators in Tunisia, Egypt, and Libya during the "Arab Spring" of 2011, and which also led to an uprising in Syria. These sorts of authoritarian states, we reason, have low levels of acceptance, and round out the "legitimacy spectrum."

Our insight is that the effort of the past decade to create a centralized, democratic, relatively modern state in Afghanistan has been too single-minded in focus. While we do not reject the very possibility of such a move ever occurring, our view is that good policy demands an examination of the potentially acceptable outcomes that might emerge from ending up somewhere else on the "centrality" continuum. Good strategy can only flow from good policy alternatives.

We have been too slow in recognizing the fact that extending the reach of the central government is viewed by most Afghans as an attempt to reshape their society in a way they do not want. It is thus hardly surprising that the insurgency became so virulent between 2002 and 2010. Afghanistan has historically been relatively stable when power resides at the local level and is apportioned out among the tribal leaders. More importantly, legitimate central governance has always been based on dynastic and religious sources, not on democratic elections. It does not

FIGURE 1.1. "Centrality" Continuum

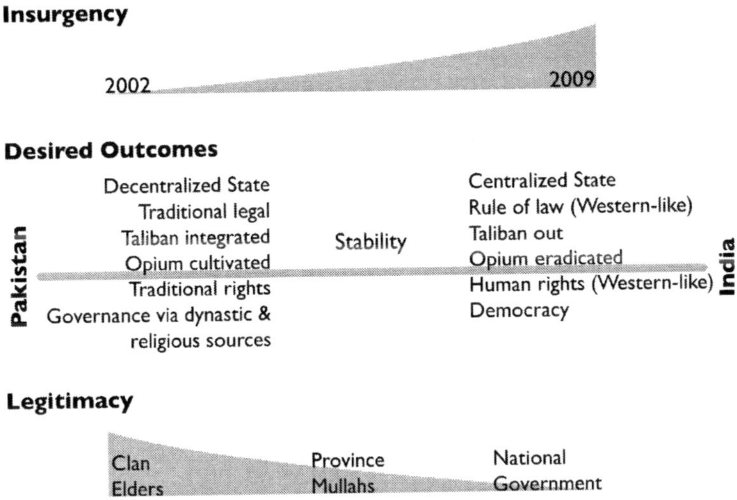

help that the government in Kabul ranks next to Somalia near the top of the UN list of corrupt regimes.[17] Figure 1.1 illustrates the importance of identifying where on the "centrality" continuum stability can be found.

The United States has mostly supported policies aimed at achieving outcomes indicated on the right-hand side of the "centrality" continuum depicted in figure 1.1. Unfortunately, this type of governance is for the most part alien to Afghans and therefore not legitimate. For Afghans, legitimate governance lies much closer to the left side of the "centrality" continuum. In fact, leaders put in place through democratic elections have tended to be viewed as illegitimate by most Afghans. Additionally, Pakistan's policy supports a position much closer to the left of the continuum, while Indian policies support a position much further to the right. Therefore, it should not be a surprise that the insurgency has intensified as a direct result of not adequately considering where on the "centrality" continuum US policy should lie.

Some Dynamic Relationships and Their Attendant Propositions

Since "stabilization" is clearly a core value to be cultivated under any of the possible strategic paths, it is important to think about what this concept means, in practical terms, as not all stable solutions are "created equal." For example, installing a strong authoritarian ruler might ensure stability, but it would be of a very brittle sort, and his fall could quickly lead to chaos. On the other hand, a decentralized system of governance might have more trouble preventing outbreaks of disorder and violence, but which would function reasonably well in terms of its ability to *restore* the societal equilibrium once it had been disturbed.

Decentralization carries additional challenges of its own. The Taliban may oppose local governance in the same way that they now oppose Kabul. This challenge would be exacerbated by a lack of competent administrative capacity at the local level. Poorly administered local governance creates vulnerabilities that are exploitable by insurgents. Also, the current Afghan power brokers would likely resist any move toward decentralization because such a shift would undermine their status, authority, and ability to profit from corruption.[18]

Decentralization may also make it more difficult for the United States to achieve the minimalist acceptable outcome of keeping terrorists from using Afghanistan to plan and launch strikes against itself and its allies, and to keep insurgent groups from using Afghanistan to destabilize Pakistan. Exerting positive control over decentralized organizations is simply a more difficult and complex undertaking.

On the other hand, a decentralized political order is much more likely to be supported by the population. Whereas fighting the Taliban will probably be necessary under any political arrangement for some time, a political solution that reflects the natural preference of the people will go a long way toward eliminating insurgents and ultimately achieving US political goals.[19]

The matter of foreign military presence is also another factor that is likely to loom large for a long time to come. Here the key concept in play may be "time." It seems that the larger the foreign troop presence, the shorter the time the foreign mass public will be willing to live with the intervention. This is certainly the case with the American public today; but it was also true, to a great degree, of the Soviet society's response to the heavy investment in troops made by Moscow during the 1980s. Conversely, it may well be that a very light foreign military footprint stretches out the time that its parent society is willing to live with such a venture. The relationship may not be strictly linear, but it seems worth considering that the smaller the presence, the longer the time for engaging the enemy may be allowed.

This issue of "staying power" is related to the question of risk. A heavier investment in troops may shorten the time allowed to fight but increase chances of winning outright, whereas a smaller force, with more time, may prove unable to repress enemy forces and the terrorism and insurgency they foment. But the foregoing may pose a false dichotomy, as it could be that the true key is in the concept of operations employed.

The wrong doctrinal approach, pursued by large numbers of troops, is bound to fail, at ruinous cost. The best example of this is the half-million-plus troops the United States sent to Vietnam. A good doctrine can succeed, even with small numbers, as seems to have been the case in El Salvador in the 1980s and in the Philippines today, where 55 and initially 160 troops, respectively, were employed alongside host-nation security forces to counter rising, violent insurgencies.[20] Therefore, in the Afghan case, making troop reductions without clearly identifying the varying paths to acceptable political outcomes will not, by themselves, result in good strategies.

Finally, any discussion of "staying power" in Afghanistan must consider what seem to be the essential elements of the Taliban's strategy—playing for time and dominating all things local. A strategy that empowers local leaders and clearly demonstrates that the United States will keep a limited presence in Afghanistan (perhaps akin to our commitment to South Korea, where American troops still serve, nearly sixty years after the fighting ended there) undermines our enemies' belief that time is on their side and that they can control all things local.

Yet another dynamic tension is in play with regard to the matter of the enemy enjoying "haven" on sovereign Pakistani territory. It is clear that US and allied forces cannot invade Waziristan, for this would almost surely spark Pakistani opposition, perhaps even a social revolution in Pakistan. Even the relatively lighter touch of the Predator bombing campaign causes problems and does not seem, by itself, to have war-winning potential. The same can be said of the US commando raid during which Osama bin Laden was killed, which sparked much Pakistani outrage. Thus a key point here might be to consider how the Taliban and al-Qaeda might be defeated in Afghanistan by operations conducted mostly *within* Afghanistan, coupled with new efforts to cut the flow of weapons and money into Afghanistan that insurgents need to continue operating. In Iraq, the insurgency was tamped down without ever having to go into or strike on the sovereign territory of Syria or Iran. It might be that a similar sort of result could be achieved in Afghanistan.

Structure of the Study

Our goal is to explore strategic alternatives in order to be prepared for every possible scenario that may emerge, even this late in the war. With this in mind, our study breaks down into three parts that cover background, comparative strategies, and ethical and social considerations.

In addition to this introductory chapter, Part I includes a range of historical, cultural, and operational perspectives, all of them quite fresh. Victor Davis Hanson, for example, contravenes the widely accepted view that Afghanistan is the "graveyard of empires," noting that, in ancient times, this country was conquered by Alexander and kept under stable Greek rule for two centuries thereafter. Aside from submitting historical evidence of Afghanistan's "conquerability," Hanson also draws insights from the Greek concept of operations—a skillful blending of military repression and co-optation of local tribal leaders—that have considerable applicability today.

Thomas Barfield takes a more social and cultural perspective on the conflict in Afghanistan today, noting that the rise and persistence of the Taliban echoes an urban/rural pattern of divisiveness first observed by Ibn Khaldun in the fourteenth century. He also reflects on the nineteenth-century "Great Game" between Russia and Britain in central Asia, which ended with the two empires leaving the Afghans as a buffer between them. Further, he observes that the continuing salience of religious rule in Afghan minds, and a social predilection for something other than a strong central government, runs sharply counter to the preferred American outcome. Indeed, his line of argument suggests that efforts at centralization are likely to prove highly problematic.

Hy Rothstein closes out Part I with an operational assessment of the fighting based on his extensive firsthand observations of the war over the course of the past decade. He keys on the tensions between coercion and persuasion, and how misapplying US counterinsurgency doctrine led to faulty prosecution of the war until 2010. He finds that (at least in military terms and in selected areas) the campaign against the Taliban, as it unfolded in 2010, was the first period of clear success since the Taliban and al-Qaeda were driven out of power and influence in late 2001. In spite of the recent success, however, Rothstein is doubtful that the positive effects, achieved at great cost, are sustainable given current and likely future conditions in Afghanistan and in the United States, unless a different plan is adopted.

Part II consists of a thorough exposition of the range of strategic options available at this point in the war in Afghanistan. It begins with Andrew Bacevich, who focuses his analysis on what is commonly called "grand strategy." That is, he considers the place of Afghanistan in overall American foreign policy and national security strategy. Noting that the United States lost in Vietnam but still won the Cold War, Bacevich considers the possibility that the larger American goals of making the world less permissive of the rise of terrorist networks may still be achieved, even if the Afghan campaign is wound down without the Taliban having been decisively defeated. He notes also that other great powers have made similar decisions to draw back from interminable commitments and have prospered, while others, like the Soviet Union, whose forces stayed in Afghanistan too long, suffered catastrophic consequences.

Frederick Kagan provides counterpoint to Bacevich's views with his assessment of what would be necessary to achieve an outcome that would see a strong, legitimate central government emerging in the wake of war. As one of the principal architects of "the surge" in Iraq, Kagan supports the larger investment in troops and a longer time commitment as preconditions for pursuing this US-preferred outcome. He is well aware that war is not simply a numbers game, and embraces a range of innovative tactics to go with the renewed commitment to the campaign. Kagan also assesses whether the American public and its elected leaders would support such an approach. But his bottom-line assessment is that giving up on Afghanistan would both allow the threat posed by al-Qaeda to rise yet again, and would hand our enemies an enormous propaganda victory whose ripples would spread around the world.

Edward Luttwak finds a middle course between Bacevich's and Kagan's arguments. First, though, he offers a sharp critique of the existing strategy in Afghanistan. Then he outlines his alternative concept of operations. He seeks to employ a kind of "strategic leverage" that will induce China, Iran, Russia, and India to engage more actively in the process of keeping a lid on the problems posed by unrest in Afghanistan. Luttwak's approach is minimalist in nature in that the US contribution is mostly in developing the plan and providing advisors to assist in its execution. The US force structure and resources required for such a campaign are quite small, and the timeline for engagement is open-ended. Luttwak's strategy also calls for cultivating tribal allies who can provide order, if not the kind of modern central governance we prefer.

Part II ends with Scott Gartner and Leo Blanken's novel approach to thinking about a sustainable Afghan security structure. First they explore just how to assess our strategic performance in the war in Afghanistan. Is effectiveness appropriately measured by the miles of paved roads? Schools opened? Gains in public opinion? Or are they more focused on violence levels? Then they move on to consider a possible end state in which violence recurs regularly, but a societal security structure emerges that allows for an orderly equilibrium to reemerge in the wake of each bout of conflict. It is a very different sort of "victory" that they envision, and one that poses tough challenges to know how well or poorly one is doing. But it is an approach that must be considered and that may offer the best hope for development of a practical policy stance toward the "Afghan problem" that can be sustained over the long term.

Part III consists of a range of other perspectives that look at Afghanistan through the lenses of just-war ethics, information strategy, civil and uncivil society, and finally our concluding effort to synthesize the various lines of thought and argument advanced in this volume into a distinct, yet multifaceted, approach to the endgame in Afghanistan.

Russell Muirhead begins by bringing together the strategic possibilities discussed in Part II by considering their ethical implications. Beyond the justice of the cause in Afghanistan and the importance of fighting justly, Muirhead considers how the relatively recently developed ethical category of "post-war justice" bears on the endgame in Afghanistan. The crucial question in the background of his analysis is whether it would be just to end up with an illegitimate government, if doing so were accompanied by an end, or a near-end, to the fighting.

Muirhead argues that postwar justice does in fact require that ISAF and the United States do what is in their power to leave a *legitimate* state behind. But he differentiates between a legitimate state and a democratic state or a state that fully protects individual rights, which some ideas of postwar justice seem to require. Against this, Muirhead argues that the obligations of postwar justice are minimal, and focus on stability and legitimacy rather than on democracy and individual rights. Furthermore, Muirhead draws our attention to the specific duties that the United States has acquired over the course of more than a decade of fighting: We have important moral responsibilities to the groups and individuals who have taken enormous risks to aid the war effort, and it is imperative that these responsibilities not be neglected as the conflict comes to an end.

Robert Reilly considers the manner in which a number of crosscutting concepts bear upon the war in Afghanistan. He keys in particularly on the whole matter of "influence strategy," the attempt to convince the Afghan people—including the Taliban, their sympathizers, and people who simply feel caught in the middle—to move toward peace. This is a society that has been at war constantly for more than thirty years, implying at least the possibility that a well-crafted message, thoughtfully disseminated, might induce all parties to consider peace. He explores how the differing end states along the legitimacy/centrality spectrum might affect the crafting of our information strategy, as well as the manner in which our fixation on a single preferred outcome has sharply constrained influence operations. In an echo of Fred Kagan's concern about handing al-Qaeda and the Taliban a big propaganda victory, Reilly offers an approach that aims at improving the situation on the ground by doing better in the "battle of the story."

Another key issue area considered in this section of the book is the role of networks of nonstate actors, the subject of Jade Rodriguez and Rebecca Lorentz's chapter. They explore both the role of civil society nongovernmental organizations (NGOs) and the influence of "uncivil society" criminal networks. The Taliban, too, is viewed through this network level of analysis. Important issues that Rodriguez and Lorentz consider from a fresh point of view include the notion that "corruption," so easy to condemn, may actually hold the potential for creating stable societal solutions. They also differentiate between NGOs and private contractors, exploring the tensions between the two, and between them and governmental actors. Finally, they hold out the hope that a civil-society-oriented approach—particularly one that aims at reaching out to Afghan youth—might operate in a decentralized way while actually improving the prospects for central governance. It is an intriguing concept.

Afghan Endgames concludes with our overall assessment of the strategic alternatives and larger considerations regarding the campaign in Afghanistan. Our goal is not simply to argue against the current plan, but instead to lay out the range of possible paths ahead and the conditions under which they ought to be pursued. For there are workable, alternative futures that might arise, whether the United States stays the course, leaves, does something in between, or is confronted with some sort of shock to the political, military, or economic environment that necessitates drastic strategic recalibration. The art lies in identifying the differing strategies best suited to coping with any and all eventualities.

Beyond this we also consider such overarching factors as allied force drawdowns (made more swiftly, and perhaps deeper, given the death of bin Laden), the likelihood that some form of negotiations will rise, and the persistent, perhaps growing risk that Pakistan will be destabilized by a continuing conflict. But to be clear, we also assume that any strategic adjustment that is ultimately made will almost surely necessitate at least a nominal US presence—likely measured from a few thousand to several thousand troops, at a minimum—to protect our investment and watch after overall American interests in this region, at least for the near-term future.

Additionally, there are those observers who argue that a punishing counterterrorism effort, rather than patient counterinsurgency, may be the best way to get the Taliban to the bargaining table or to defeat them outright. So far, despite the significant casualties in their leadership ranks, both the Taliban and al-Qaeda have been quite resilient.[21] Therefore, the argument that somewhere in the future is a "tipping point" at which enough killing will finally turn the tide, if we just keep it up, is unpersuasive to us. Many other activities must be successful for this kind of counterleadership effort—in some respects a latter-day version of Vietnam-era "body counts"—to mean anything to the outcome of this struggle for Afghanistan. Indeed, it is new concepts of operations that lead to the detection, disruption, and defeat in battle of the foot soldiers of the insurgency—rather than just their nominal leaders—that are more likely to cause the kind of attrition that saps the enemy's will to keep on fighting.

Strategic diversity must be considered a virtue. In light of the uncertainties the United States and its allies face in Afghanistan and Pakistan, it makes sense to proffer and vigorously debate a range of alternative strategies, even this late in the war. Strategic adjustment is almost certainly going to be necessary, given domestic political, regional, and international dynamics. This makes it all the more important to consider various strategic alternatives and their costs and risks now, in a period of rough "stasis," rather than during the next major crisis, a time when attempts to hold a thoughtful discourse are most likely to founder.

Notes

1 For instance, President Obama said, "The goal that we seek is achievable, and can be expressed simply: No safe haven from which al-Qaeda or its affiliates can launch attacks against our homeland or our allies." Council on Foreign Relations, "Essential Documents: Obama's Remarks on Afghanistan," June 22, 2011, www.cfr.org/afghanistan/obamas-remarks-afghanistan-june-2011/p25333.

2 The White House, Office of the Press Secretary, "Overview of the Afghanistan and Pakistan Annual Review, December 16, 2010," www.whitehouse.gov/the-press-office/2010/12/16/overview-afghanistan-and-pakistan-annual-review [accessed April 21, 2011].

3 Council on Foreign Relations, "Essential Documents: Obama's Remarks on Afghanistan," June 22, 2011, www.cfr.org/afghanistan/obamas-remarks-afghanistan-june-2011/p25333.

4 House Speaker John Boehner (R-OH) responded to Obama's June 22, 2011, announcement of the troop withdrawal by saying, "It's important that we retain the flexibility necessary to reconsider troop levels and respond to changes in the security environment should circumstances on the ground warrant. It is my hope that the President will continue to listen to our commanders on the ground as we move forward. Congress will hold the Administration accountable for ensuring that the pace and scope of the drawdown does not undermine the progress we've made thus far." Senator John McCain (R-AZ) said, "I am concerned that the withdrawal plan that President Obama announced tonight poses an unnecessary risk to the hard-won gains that our troops have made thus far in Afghanistan and to the decisive progress that must still be made. This is not the 'modest' withdrawal that I and others had hoped for and advocated." Both quotes cited from *The Hill*, June 23, 2011, http://thehill.com/blogs/congress-blog/foreign-policy/168201-congressional-reaction-to-troop-withdrawal-from-afghanistan.

5 Obama said, "We do know that peace cannot come to a land that has known so much war without a political settlement. So as we strengthen the Afghan government and security forces, America will join initiatives that reconcile the Afghan people, including the Taliban. Our position on these talks is clear: They must be led by the Afghan government, and those who want to be a part of a peaceful Afghanistan must break from al-Qaeda, abandon violence, and abide by the Afghan constitution." Council on Foreign Relations, "Essential Documents: Obama's Remarks on Afghanistan," June 22, 2011, www.cfr.org/afghanistan/obamas-remarks-afghanistan-june-2011/p25333.

6 Polling shows a decrease in overall support for the war and an increase in support for significant troop drawdowns. For example, a CBS News poll on June 8, 2011, showed that 64 percent of people surveyed wanted to decrease troop presence whereas 51 percent felt that the United States should not be involved at all. A CNN poll validated these percentages and found that only 36 percent of Americans supported the war whereas 62 percent opposed the war.

7 B. H. Liddell Hart, *Strategy* (New York: Praeger Publishers, 1967), 336.

8 The White House, Office of the Press Secretary, "Overview of the Afghanistan and Pakistan Annual Review, December 16, 2010," www.whitehouse.gov/the-press-office/2010/12/16/overview-afghanistan-and-pakistan-annual-review [accessed April 24, 2011].

9 BG(Ret) Huba wass de Czege, "Systematic Operational Design: Learning and Adapting in Complex Missions," *Military Review* (January–February 2009): 4.

10 Carl von Clausewitz, *On War*, trans. Michael Howard and Peter Paret (Princeton, NJ: Princeton University Press, 1976), 85–86.

11 Bernard Brodie, *War and Politics* (New York: Macmillan Publishing Co., 1973), 452.

12 Colin S. Gray, *Modern Strategy* (New York, NY: Oxford University Press, 1999), 17.

13 David Barno, Andrew Exum, and Matthew Irvine, *Beyond Pakistan—A Regional Security Strategy for South and Central Asia*, June 2011, www.cnas.org/files/documents/publications/CNAS_Beyond-Afghanistan_BarnoExumIrvine_1.pdf [accessed June 21, 2011].

14 Barnett R. Rubin, "Afghanistan and Pakistan," https://wacphila.org/education/msfrc09_afpak.pdf [accessed June 21, 2011].

15 The White House, Office of the Press Secretary, "Remarks by the President in Address to the Nation on the Way Forward in Afghanistan and Pakistan, December 1, 2009," www.whitehouse.gov/the-press-office/remarks-president-address-nation-way-forward-afghanistan-and-pakistan … [accessed April 24, 2011].

16 See The White House and Stephen Biddle, Fotini Christia, and J. Alexander Thier, "Defining Success in Afghanistan: What Can the United States Accept?" *Foreign Affairs* (July–August 2010): 50.

17 Thomas Johnson, "Counterinsurgency in Afghanistan: Snatching Victory from the Jaws of Defeat," in *Operationalizing a Comprehensive Approach in Semi-Permissive Environments: NDC Forum Paper*, ed. Christopher M. Schnaubelt (Rome: NATO Defense College Research Division, June 2009), 187.

18 Ibid., 53

19 Ibid.

20 Hy Rothstein, "Less Is More: The Problematic Future of Irregular Warfare in an Era of Collapsing States," *Third World Quarterly* 28, no. 2 (2007): 279, 284.

21 Matthew Rosenberg and Julian Barnes, "Al Qaeda Makes a Comeback," *Wall Street Journal*, April 6, 2011.

CHAPTER 2

A Familiar Western Experience in Ancient Afghanistan

Victor Davis Hanson

The ancient Greek and Macedonian experience in areas that are now incorporated within modern Afghanistan offers eerie parallels to the current, American-led NATO efforts there to defeat the Taliban and foster consensual government under Hamid Karzai. Ancient Greek speakers had little trouble initially overrunning the country and scattering tribal enemies. In time they were able to establish a rich infrastructure and founded new cities on Hellenic principles, largely in the plains and major crossroads. However, tribal insurgent forces were never completely defeated nor were the highlands and mountain areas well pacified. For a relatively small population of soldiers and military colonists to transform Afghanistan into a stable Western kingdom, constant infusions of military manpower, capital, and settlers were necessary to resist local insurgents, to win over often friendly tribes and provincials, and eventually to create a Hellenic presence that might ensure stability and quiet in the region at large. Those aims were largely achieved for two centuries, until the benefits—a buffer zone for the Seleucids from tribal incursions, access to trade with the Orient, proximity with a rich India, and exploitation of rich farmland— of such a distant outpost of Hellenism were not considered worth the rising costs in blood and treasure. If present-day Western forces enjoy the use of a sophisticated military technology unknown to the Greeks and Macedonians, those advantages seem neutralized by the zeal of contemporary Islam that unites and galvanizes tribal Afghanistan in a way unknown in the fourth to second centuries BC. And if Alexander and his successors resorted to violent means to put down insurrections, such savage methods are now contrary to the norms of constitutional societies in the West, and would erode public support for the war far more than restore it through inflicting punishment on an enemy.

"Ancient" Afghanistan

Present-day Afghanistan in antiquity covered the loosely demarcated regions of Sogdiana in the far north and Bactria in the center. It also incorporated various smaller portions in the west of Media, Parthia, and Aria, as well as some of the provinces to the south known in antiquity as Parapamisadae, Drangiana, and Arachosia. Until the arrival of Alexander the Great, the general area was little known to Greeks. And it was only loosely confederated into the Persian Empire and administered by Iranian-speaking satraps and tribal chieftains loyal to the Achaemenid King. All that changed with the final defeat of Darius III at Gaugamela in northern Iraq and the subsequent arrival of Alexander himself the following summer, 331 BC—an ancient moment somewhat analogous to the American invasion of Afghanistan in reaction to 9/11.[1]

We have no continuous historical narratives for what would become a subsequent two-century Greek presence in ancient Afghanistan. Afghanistan was not a central concern of the Greek historians, and few Greeks had visited the region and even fewer returned with accurate information. The result is that the chronology and details of Alexander's Afghan legacy remain largely hazy and in dispute. The evidence that does survive is drawn from passing mention in extant and well-known sources on the years of Greek presence (330–120 BC); fragments of lost histories (e.g., Pompeius Trogus, Isidore); occasional anecdotes in Hellenistic and Roman literature (for example, in Justin, Pliny, and Strabo); numismatic catalogues, mostly beginning in the nineteenth century, drawn from thousands of unearthed Greek gold, silver, and bronze coins; and some material remains brought to light by sporadic archaeological excavation. Yet, despite the fragmentary record, we can at least agree on a roughly two-century period of Greek-speaking rule that began with the sudden arrival of Alexander the Great shortly following his victory over Darius at the battle of Gaugamela, and ended with the gradual breakup of an independent Graeco-Bactrian Empire somewhere around between 146 and 120 BC.[2]

Various general questions arise about the Greek experience in the ancient region now known as Afghanistan that are relevant to contemporary Western efforts to once more change hearts and minds in attempts at nation-building. These commonalities will resonate through a brief survey of these two centuries of early Western occupation and control. One, why did Greeks and Macedonians covet such a far off and apparently inhospitable region, more than three thousand miles away from their own homes in the southern Balkans? Two, how did such a comparatively small number of westerners conquer ancient Afghanistan and hold it against a wide variety of numerically superior foes? Three, why and how did a Western-state presence come to an end in the second century BC? Four, to what degree did the Greek-speaking occupiers of Bactria leave behind any lasting Western legacy? And five, to what degree are any of the answers to these questions relevant to the ongoing American efforts in Afghanistan following 9/11.[3]

Two Centuries of Greek and Macedonian Invasion and Occupation

Westerners attempted to conquer, occupy, exploit, and transform ancient Afghanistan against the near impossible demographic, geographic, political, and logistical odds.

The Entry of Alexander the Great (330–323 BC)

Almost no westerners had been to ancient Afghanistan before the latter half of the fourth century BC, when Alexander the Great reached Bactria amid the apparent breakup of the eastern provinces of the Persian Empire. And Alexander's original interest in Bactria per se was only incidental: The Macedonian general had set out to capture the rogue satrap Bessus, who had fled from what is today Iraq with much of his imperial Persian treasury northward to his home. Bessus had initially accompanied, but soon kidnapped, the defeated and fleeing king Darius III. Upon reaching Afghanistan, internecine bickering among the surviving Persian satraps broke out. Bessus, satrap of Bactria—along with the Persian commander Nabarzanes, Satibarzanes, the satrap of Areia; and Barsaentes, satrap of Drangiana and Arachosia—soon murdered Darius in hopes of stopping Alexander's pursuit. The assassination seems to have been organized by Bessus, who soon crowned himself King Artaxerxes V in hopes of reconstituting the eastern Persian Empire under his own leadership, based in this more remote but familiar and defensible northeast sanctuary.

In pursuing Bessus into his native region, Alexander initially wanted mostly to end challenges to his acquisition of the collapsing Persian Empire, and to recover what he had not yet acquired of the Achmaenid treasury—and had no idea of the subsequent problems that an occupation might entail. As part of that aim, Alexander planned to leave secure provinces at his rear, and to use the supplies of the region to support a push farther east into the Punjab. Indeed, Alexander's own subsequent three-year sojourn in Bactria, Sogdiana, and the areas around Kabul and Helmand Province are the only well-recorded periods of the long Greek-Macedonian presence in the region, largely as a result of four extant traditional sources of Alexander's eastern conquests.[4]

Alexander's entry into the region inaugurated the most vicious and brutal period in his brief ten-year military career in Asia. He had never experienced a level of danger commensurate to what his army faced from constant tribal insurgencies that seemed almost immune to the charges of his heavily armed phalanx. His fury and exasperation arose partly because the death of Darius had fragmented Persian resistance and dispersed it to areas far from the well-traveled and accessible Babylon and Persepolis. His interest grew partly because he was now no longer ostensibly a Macedonian foreign conqueror and destroyer, but the successor to Darius and thus the political and religious leader of millions of nonwesterners, including tribes in ancient Afghanistan; and he seems to have been surprised and bewildered by the challenges posed by the terrain, tribes, and climate of the far northeastern portions of the empire. It was in Afghanistan where his heretofore devastating tactics of shock battle were not able to vanquish enemies, who were careful to avoid phalangites and redefine the face of battle in terms more advantageous to local conditions.

As a result, nothing in Asia before or after Alexander's presence in ancient Afghanistan matched the level of violence he unleashed. He began systematic and constant executions of civilians and entire villages. Widespread dissatisfaction and conspiracies arose among his own disaffected troops, who, with the death of Darius, were confused about whether they were still foreign conquerors or now de facto legitimate successors to the Persian ruling elite. In the confusion Alexander executed his most trusted lieutenants amid a comprehensive effort to co-opt former Iranian officials and tribal leaders by granting limited autonomy and embracing local customs. Nonetheless, the result of such savagery was that a small Macedonian elite came to control tens of thousands of square miles of hostile territory for the next two centuries.[5]

After burning Darius's capital at Persepolis in June 330, Alexander headed north through Iran toward the Caspian Sea. Once he arrived in the Persian province of Hyrcania, Alexander defeated most identifiable local resistance. He recruited into his army some fifteen hundred orphaned Greek hoplite mercenaries that had been mustered in the now-defunct imperial Persian army and then won over the satrapies of Hyrcania and Parthia, as well as Tapuria.[6]

Then, after putting down the Mardians, a very warlike tribe, and allotting them to the satrap Autophradates, Alexander headed back southward into Parthia and Aria. There he recruited more local officials and at this point entered from the west into what is now formally Afghanistan. Alexander found that the combination of ravaging cropland, targeted slaughter, and the taking of hostages had proved successful in subduing the Mardians and other tribes. If he could not go up into the highlands, then indigenous tribes would have equal difficulty ejecting Alexander from the far richer valleys.[7]

Bessus was by then ensconced at home eastward and to the north in Bactria—soon to be trapped between Alexander's advancing forces in the west and the mountainous border with India in the east. Alexander put down some uprisings in areas he thought were conquered and stabilized, executed rebellious satraps and many of their forces, and then headed through Drangiana up the Helmand Valley to Kabul. We are unsure of his exact route on his way over the Hindu Kush into Bactra, the capital of Bessus's home satrapy of Bactria; we know only that he planned to cut Bessus off completely from both the west and south. Throughout his whirlwind march, Alexander employed flying columns of fast-moving cavalry and lightly armed troops, and in total probably had at his disposal no more than forty thousand to fifty thousand troops.[8]

Alexander began to protect his lengthening lines of communication with a series of fortified compounds and camps in which he installed both Macedonians and former Greek mercenaries to establish new military colonies. It was ironic, but to his ultimate advantage, that thousands of both mercenary and patriotic Greeks who resented Macedonian imperialism had enlisted in Darius's army over the last decade. Most hated Alexander as much as he did them. These adventurers now found themselves far from home, out of work, and surrounded in a hostile eastern landscape without many options other than dealing with Alexander and his western retinue. So over the next year Alexander turned his former enemies to his own side and founded settlements of Greek speakers from Artacoana to Arachosia, near modern-day Kandahar, to ensure the fealty of his Persian administrators, and as bases to provide protection from roving nomads.[9]

But at some point in this drawn-out sojourn Alexander's own Macedonians grasped that their king was probably not going to head home after capturing Bessus, and thus the odds of their own prompt and safe return to Greece and Macedonia were diminishing, especially as forced marches through inhospitable climate and terrain increased. If Alexander's army had entered Afghanistan solely to pursue Bessus, it soon learned that, even after his death, getting out would be far more difficult than getting in. Conspiracies of all sorts among Alexander's army soon broke out, predicated on the general fear that their once-beloved commander had "gone native," surrounding himself with effete former Persian officials, as he adopted the dress and mannerisms of an Eastern potentate. In reaction to this growing dissension, an increasingly violent and paranoid Alexander began a series of retributions that, in turn, fueled more cycles of the internecine violence, which was an instability that the outnumbered Western invaders could ill afford.[10]

In short order Alexander executed on charges of treason his most trusted and experienced lieutenant, Parmenio, and his son Philotas, as well as several of their suspected adherents. As Alexander's old lieutenant Antipater famously put it, "If Parmenio plotted against Alexander, who is to be trusted? And if he did not, what is to be done?" In the subsequent two years before he left Afghanistan, Alexander would himself, in a drunken fit, spear his loyal general and friend Cleitus, and then go on to execute six hundred Macedonian pages on charges of conspiracy. He would be forced to divide his subordinate commands among a wider variety of generals, in constant worry that the growing insurgent war was leading to outright insurrection from his own, disaffected Macedonian commanders. Indeed, much of the subsequent intrigue, coups, and massacres that would plague Greek Bactria for two centuries began with the example established by Alexander himself.[11]

In his final pursuit of Bessus during spring 329, Alexander reached the area around Kandahar in February. There he destroyed most of the villages and farms on the northern slopes of the Hindu Kush. After capturing Bessus—who was betrayed by his fellow satraps—Alexander quite capriciously wiped out the Branchidae, who were supposedly of Greek ancestry and had, in fact, offered belated allegiance to the new king. Even with the end of the last Persian resistance, there came the realization that the indigenous tribes of Afghanistan were not willing to accept Alexander's westernized rule without proof of his martial invincibility. Thus began another round of bloodletting in a manner not seen since his invasion of Asia Minor five years earlier. In short order Alexander wiped out the entire male population of seven cities on the Jaxartes River and enslaved the women and children, including, most notably, the large Persian settlement of Cyropolis. Perhaps seven thousand civilians in all were executed there.[12]

After defeating an opportunistic attack from northern Saka tribesmen, and then suffering a defeat of his own forces in Marcanda, Alexander leveled most of the settlements of the Zeravshan Valley that had either joined or aided the rebellious and soon-to-be-executed satrap Spitamenes. In early spring 328, Alexander then went north of Bactria, along the Oxus River toward Marcanda, to put down another rebellion by the Sogdian tribal chieftain Ariamazes. By summer 328, a successful Alexander had crucified Ariamazes and liquidated his family, destroyed much of the infrastructure of the province, founded six new fortified Marjah cities, and had gone on to do much the same to the west in the nearby region of Margiana. A year later, by spring 327, Alexander quelled the last resistance in Sogdiana by storming some recalcitrant enemy citadels and then left Bactria and Sogdiana for good that summer, effectively ending his brief conquest and occupation of what is now Afghanistan.[13]

After three years of constant fighting, Alexander left behind a relatively pacified province, predicated on the superiority of Macedonian infantry and heavy cavalry in conventional battle, and on promises not to interfere too greatly with the prestige and influence of obedient provincial officials and wealthy landowners. Alexander had perhaps welcomed over twenty thousand new Greek-speaking colonists from the west and dispersed them among eight to twelve new cities. He had killed thousands of tribal enemies. And yet his generals also trained an indigenous army of thirty thousand *epigonoi*—local youths who were outfitted as Macedonian-style phalangites. Alexander established a fortified line along the Oxus River to protect Bactria from nomadic raids from the north. The innately productive agriculture of Bactria, combined with the veneer of Greek governance and technology, would make Bactria and its environs a prize in the wars of succession following Alexander's death.[14]

How, then, in a mere three years had Alexander's relatively small forces turned the region into a Macedonian province some thirty-six-hundred miles from Pella? His successful strategy from the beginning marked a sharp contrast from his prior method of occupation and administration of the more accessible and civilized western and southern regions of the conquered Persian Empire. In ancient times, like the modern era, Afghanistan proved far harder to subdue than Iraq. Unlike his past experience elsewhere, Alexander did not inherit a relatively docile population, which might transfer allegiance to him on the defeat of Persian imperial forces, or, alternatively, resist in conventional set battles in relatively open terrain. Instead, Alexander found that ancient Afghanistan was not only hostile to the successor of Darius but had caused Darius himself untold problems; tribes there resented not only Macedonians but any foreign presence, and the Bactrian cavalry forces vastly outnumbered Alexander's own horsemen. Thus Alexander would have to systematically ravage territory, wipe out entire villages, and enslave conquered peoples in a dirty war to which his conventional troops were not accustomed. From the moment Alexander arrived in the regions now known as Afghanistan, he was engaged in constant warfare directed against remnants of Persian forces, his own rebellious Greeks and Macedonians, indigenous tribal peoples, and nomads from across the Oxus. Apparently, the notion that supposedly conquered tribes would spring back to resistance as Alexander passed on was a new experience for the Macedonian king. He could not equate the relatively easy task of initially defeating tribes with the far more difficult challenge of making them either subservient or at least quiescent.[15]

Although Alexander had promised a new "brotherhood of man," such utopianism was predicated on his naïve assumption that millions would peaceably shift their allegiance to the Macedonians, once the Achmaenids were defeated in a small number of dramatic conventional battles and he had shown his own eagerness to unite, at least superficially, east and west. That did not happen in this part of Asia, and the once matchless Macedonian army in Bactria and Sogdiana soon found itself bogged down by an insurgency that did not confront it in open battle. In almost every case of rebellion, the Macedonians were successful in putting the insurgents down; but, again, such efforts required a level of systematic violence rarely seen in past wars, either in Greece or Asia. Alexander's favored tactics were the taking of hostages, focused slaughter of entire recalcitrant villages, and the burning of infrastructure, along with the destruction of trees and vines.[16]

Second, aside from the use of systematic violence, Alexander installed both Persian and Bactrian tribal leaders as local administrators, apparently to lower the profile of the conquering Macedonians—in a manner well familiar to contemporary Western forces in Afghanistan. Yet it was a general truism that almost every Persian-speaking grandee Alexander enlisted, either as satrap or as an allied tribal chieftain—Arsaces, Autophradates, Catanes, Dataphernes, Satibarzanes, Spitamenes, Tyriepsis—at one time or another revolted against him, both during and after his occupation of Bactria and Sogdiana. Long before the American frustration with Hamid Karzai, Alexander the Great encountered outwardly sympathetic local leaders who predicated their loyalty solely on perceptions of his own strength and the general proximity of his army. Their allegiances were fluid, and they depended on the degree to which Alexander's military seemed unconquerable and, in particular, capable of punitive deterrence in short order. In such a vast landscape, a perception of Western omnipotence was not always possible, given that the Macedonians did not have the manpower to supplant local populations, and angry locals soon sensed that their resources were being drawn off to subsidize Macedonian military operations elsewhere that were largely of no concern to themselves.[17]

Alexander founded a number of new military colonies to serve as bases of operations to convince locals to remain loyal to the Macedonians. These smaller military forts and the cloning of new "Alexandria" city-states of sorts—such as Alexandria-of-the-Caucus, -Archosia, -Aria, -Eschate, -Oxiana, -Tarmita—had a twofold purpose. One, the introduction of Greek-based community organization and technological expertise in matters of architecture, town planning, and agriculture might enrich the region at large and convince local tribes of the material advantages of putting up with their Greek overseers. Two, such Greek-speaking communities could furnish local manpower to Macedonian military commanders and serve as bases to help keep down the local population, especially the more remote tribes in the mountains. We have no idea how many Greek and Macedonian soldiers and settlers eventually settled in ancient Afghanistan during the lifetime of Alexander, but it may well have been somewhere approaching forty thousand, establishing the foundations for a two-centuries-long Western community.[18]

Fourth, and most controversially, Alexander initiated a number of practices designed to assimilate his own troops with those of local residents. Such protocols ranged from the trivial one of adopting traditional Bactrian and Persian dress and custom to the more fundamental one of conducting mass mixed marriages as well as the recruitment and training of local warriors in traditional Macedonian military practice. Note here that such apparent "nation-building" and counterinsurgency strategies provoked a fierce reaction from the Macedonian rank and file, who felt that the conquering Hellenic Alexander was becoming Asiatic rather than the conquered Asians becoming Hellenized. To implement these multicultural protocols, Alexander had to execute or murder his most trusted but recalcitrant generals—Parmenio, Philotas, and Cleitus—and liquidate six hundred young pages on charges of conspiracy, butcher thousands of Greek veterans, and kill or deport a number of former supporters, most prominently the philosopher Callisthenes. The entrance into ancient Afghanistan, and the subsequent infighting over the proper way to wage a dirty war against a multitude of tribes, nearly destroyed the unity of Alexander's army itself. Such strife and internecine warring among westerners would become the pattern of subsequent Macedonian occupation and eventually would do as much as native opposition to undermine stability. Macedonians, for good reasons, thought that they could easily defeat Asians in battle, and when they could not, they quickly turned on each other in frustration.[19]

Seleucid Bactria, 323–250 BC

With the death of Alexander in 323 BC, the Macedonians did not leave Afghanistan, even though the ostensible aim of their original invasion—the capture of Bessus—had long ago been achieved. They had discovered that, despite the rough terrain and the great distance from Greece, the region was wealthy from its rich, though limited, farming landscape whose production could be increased with western agricultural practices and improved irrigation. The new Macedonian settlements also kept nomads out of the northern borders of their inherited Asian empire growing to the south and west. The region enjoyed a lucrative location on the trade routes to China and India. And it offered military advantages to Hellenistic successor kings, both by its proximity to India with its wealth in manpower and elephants, and as a source of valuable Bactrian horsemen that may have numbered, in theory, nearly thirty thousand. If originally most Greek speakers had been coerced into serving in ancient Afghanistan, many in the Hellenistic provinces of Asia soon understood that they could find more prosperity in Bactria than was possible back in Greece and its environs.[20]

After the unforeseen death of Alexander in 323, successor generals immediately fought each other for the dismembered regions of the old Persian Empire in Asia. The resolution of spheres of influence in Asia among Antigonus, Ptolemy, and Seleucus required more than twenty years of constant fighting until the Battle of Ispus in 301 BC established the outlines of the new, emerging kingdoms of the Hellenistic world. Bactria and its environs, circa 312 BC, fell to

Seleucus. He saw ancient Afghanistan as a rich source of supplies and manpower for his near-constant efforts to secure a Hellenistic Asian hegemony.

In the seventy-five years after the death of Alexander the Great, the Greek-speaking population of ancient Afghanistan grew, but so did the internecine fighting of Hellenistic generals over the province. The Western community had not only to fear nomadic northern invaders and insurgencies among natives, but also large invasions of Macedonian armies and the Seleucids' own huge requisitions of food, manpower, and horses for the near-constant fighting elsewhere to the south in Greek-run Asia.

Over twenty thousand Greek veterans rebelled against their Macedonian overseers, causing Perdiccas, the first claimant to Alexander's Bactria as regent in Babylon, to put down the revolt. He ordered his lieutenant, Pithon, to massacre scores of the rebels, and the eventual toll may well have climbed to more than three thousand. Apparently, the threat of a Greek revolt overshadowed the clear advantages of incorporating so many Greeks into Macedonian nation-building in a distant land. Pithon's stern measures brought short-term relief, but they were suicidal for the long-term Western occupation of the region.

After the deaths of Perdiccas and Antipater, the Asian provinces again saw non-stop fighting between Antigonus, Cassander, Eumencs, Lysimachus, Ptolemy, and Seleucus in a series of climactic battles between 316 and 301. By 312 BC, Seleucus had assumed tenuous control of Aria, Bactria, Margiana, Sogdiana, and most of ancient Afghanistan. He soon wisely called off a war against India, consolidated his rule, and then defeated Antigonus in 301 at Ispus in eastern Turkey. That victory brought all of Alexander's Asian holdings under one rule, inaugurating the so-called Seleucid Empire of some thirty million subjects spread over 1.5 million square miles of territory.[21]

During the rule of Seleucus I (312 BC–281 BC) and his son Antiochus (281–261 BC), constant fighting for the right of succession ceased for a brief period. Peace held with India and over a half century of relative calm ensued. In Afghanistan the early Seleucid era was characterized by a renewed expansion of Greek settlements and investment in infrastructure and agriculture (cf. the founding of Aï Khanum on the Oxus). Alexander's military forts along the Oxus River were rebuilt and fortifications in Maracanda were strengthened to protect the northern borders of the empire from nomad invasions by Scythian tribes.

Bactria in essence was aligned with the empire as a vast military outpost to protect the northeastern flank of Seleucid rule—perhaps analogous to the Soviet attempt in the 1980s to integrate Afghanistan into the lives of its communist republics, or analogous to the American effort to promote democracy in Islamic nations in the Middle East. The result was that trade from India and China across Afghanistan increased, and the Seleucids began minting an enormous amount of new silver coinage based on the Attic Greek standard of weights and measures. The general peace, a monetized economy, and increased Eastern trade brought yet another new influx of Greek colonists, inaugurating the so-called legendary era of the "thousand cities of Bactria."[22]

The Greek sense of general prosperity, however, began to erode almost immediately with the assassination of Seleucus in 281 BC. A period of dynastic wars followed in which his son Antiochus sought to preserve the empire. While distant Bactria and its environs were largely free from war, once more rival Hellenistic generals began to draw manpower, horses, and food from the northern provinces to field forces fighting in far distant theaters from Asia Minor to Egypt. These pressures apparently explain the revolt of the Bactrian satrap Diodotus, a Greek-speaking native of the region (285–c. 239 BC) who sought to sever ties with the Seleucids. Sometime in the decade between 255 and 246 BC, following the death of Antiochus II, Diodotus carved out an independent Greek-Bactrian empire that was to endure for over a century.[23]

The Independent Kingdom of Greek Bactria (250–246 BC to 140 BC)

Thirty years after the establishment of an autonomous Graeco-Bactria, the Seleucid king Antiochus III invaded Bactria as part of a larger effort to restore the Seleucids' century-old Asian Empire in the northeast. By 212, with a huge army of well over one hundred thousand infantry and cavalry, Antiochus had entered Armenia, Media, and Parthia to end their independence from the empire. And by 210–209 he had crossed into Bactria, now ruled by another Greek-speaker from Asia Minor, Euthedemus, who had sometime earlier taken the kingdom away from the heirs of Diodotus, aligned it loosely with other breakaway satraps in Parthia, and now argued to the invading Antiochus that he was not so much a rebel as an opponent of prior Bactrian rebels under the Diodoti. Note that relatively small numbers of Western troops were once again fighting each other in conventional battles while far greater numbers of indigenous tribes no doubt welcomed the internecine carnage.[24]

In the initial battle at Tapuria on the Arius River, the huge army under Antiochus won a hard-fought victory and routed Euthedemus's mostly mounted forces, who retreated to his heavily fortified capital at Bactra. Euthedemus then rallied his Greek-speaking military elite who fought in the style of traditional heavy Macedonian horsemen. There were also phalangites in close formation, supported by native Bactrian cavalry who saw more advantage in having local westerners rule them than in being subjects again to a distant Seleucid king. For the next two years (208–206 BC), deadlock set in—brought about by Euthydemus's wise use of the vast network of fortified camps and military colonies—that finally led to negotiations with Antiochus. The Seleucid king apparently appreciated the vital role that even an autonomous Greek-speaking kingdom might continue to play on his northern flank by keeping at bay nomadic tribes, and so agreed to an alliance between Euthedemus and the Seleucid Empire. Such a pact once more secured the flank of Antiochus and provided him with supplies for a subsequent successful invasion eastward into India. While peace was eventually restored, the general upheaval could only have endangered the tenuous Greek-speaking hold on the region.[25]

Under the joint rule of Euthedemus (who died between 200 and 190 BC) and his son Demetrius (who disappears in the historical record after 180 BC), the now permanently autonomous Bactrian kingdom secured its borders and began minting its own coinage again at an unprecedented rate. The region enjoyed a new prosperity brought on by secure trade routes from the east and an expansion by the successors of Demetrius to the east, including the establishment of a Greek-speaking affiliated kingdom in northwestern India.[26]

At some subsequent point—again the literary record is almost nonexistent—after warring with the Euthedemian monarchy, Eucratides (who ruled from c. 175 to 145 BC) assumed control of the Bactrian kingdom—perhaps after the death of Demetrius. During his twenty-five years in power, Eucratides would soon prove to be the most successful and illustrious of all the major monarchs and provincial rulers during the two-century life of the Greek-speaking ancient Afghanistan; his rule was characterized by a new eastern capital at Eucratidia, opulent coinage, and consolidation of warlords and tribes surrounding Bactria into an autonomous kingdom.

In a now familiar pattern, Eucratides's achievement was quickly followed by the breakup and disintegration of Bactria during a series of nonstop invasions by nomadic northerners and in-fighting between various Greek-speaking leaders. Eucratides's incessant warring had drained the kingdom, especially his efforts to absorb parts of western India. The assassination of Eucratides, either by his son or a rival, set off yet another chain of internecine Bactrian fighting, which allowed Parthia to annex western Bactria and nomads from the Eurasian steppes to descend from the north, often identified as the Asii Pasiani, Tochari, and Sacarauli. Sometime around 140 BC, ancient Bactria, under its last monarch Heliocles, came to an end as an independent and autonomous Greek-speaking kingdom.[27]

Military Lessons, Ancient and Modern

The verdict on the Greek and Macedonian occupation remains ambiguous because Westerners both succeeded in ancient Afghanistan for two centuries and yet ultimately failed in turning the country into a permanent outpost of Hellenism.

Why Was Afghanistan Important to Westerners?

Why did Alexander and his successors so covet a tribal Afghanistan that was distant and landlocked, with difficult terrain and an often harsh climate? It was apparently unsuitable for Greek speakers, who preferred to fight on temperate level plains in heavy columnar formation, who were comfortable with the outdoor assembly and commerce of the formal city-state, and who focused much of their cultural life around a far different Mediterranean, olive-based agriculture? Entry into Afghanistan was predicated on a fluke—the retreat of the claimant to the Persian throne, Bessus. Had he fled elsewhere, Alexander might never have entered the badlands of Afghanistan. On arrival the Macedonians found the weather to be foreboding and soon snow fell; the people were backward and savage, especially in their abhorrent practice of raising dogs to devour their dead and even the ill and feeble. Curtius noted that the Macedonians were entering a region where there was "an absence of all civilization."[28]

Nevertheless, with improved irrigation techniques, the well-watered plains of ancient Afghanistan were capable of a rich agriculture in grains, grapes, and deciduous fruit trees—even though arable land in ancient Afghanistan probably, as today, comprised no more than 10 to 15 percent of the entire land area. Farming, then, was the source of Greek wealth in Bactria. Such profits could be well marketed, given Bactria's location on the main trade routes from China and India. Once the word got out that Bactria offered prosperity, thousands of Greek speakers flocked in—many of them were mercenary soldiers in the surrounding region looking for pay. Strabo at least could summarize Greek-controlled Bactria as extremely productive, largely because of the "excellence of the land," which was the source of the region's power.[29]

Immigrants over the next two centuries also coveted even richer opportunities in western India and the Punjab to the east. Thus Bactria was prized as a supply depot and jumping-off point for eastern invasions. Once the old Persian Empire in the east was reconstituted by the Seleucids, ancient Afghanistan also proved to be a necessary bulwark against nomadic tribes that might threaten the growing Greek presence in southern Iran and northern Iraq.

Indeed, the multifaceted role of the Seleucid Empire—its original rule over ancient Afghanistan, its subsequent rivalries and warring, and its constant requisitions—largely explains why Greek speakers continued to immigrate to Afghanistan. The monarchy often paid high prices for mercenary Bactrian cavalry, Indian elephants, and Greek-speaking phalangites, and ensured a relatively profitable route of trade and travel from mainland Greece and Macedonia. During the ascendance of Seleucid influence in Asia, the Greeks in Bactria thrived. In turn, with the steady decline of the Seleucid Empire amid Armenian, Parthian, and Roman pressures, the Western presence in Bactria was also doomed.

The interest in the regions around ancient Bactria is both similar to and different from the current, decade-long Western presence in Afghanistan since October 2001. Despite conspiracy theories about nefarious American desires to build and control a supposed new oil pipeline across Afghanistan, or to exploit untapped exotic mineral finds or to eradicate the opium trade, the United States' aims were not colonial but entirely strategic, predicated on the global situation following the al-Qaeda attacks of September 11, 2001, that killed three thousand Americans. Again, bin Laden, in some sense, was our rogue Bessus who prompted an invasion that otherwise probably would not have occurred.

So, like Alexander the Great, the American military initially went into the region with relatively small forces and solely for punitive purposes. That desire to eradicate the Taliban sanctuaries for radical Islamic terrorists is perhaps analogous to Alexander's pursuit of Darius and later renegade satraps in search of "security." And, like Alexander and his successors, America and its allies have stayed far longer than anticipated and have found themselves engaged in nation-building activity that transcended military operations and were far harder to stop than start. But unlike the case of the Macedonians and their successors, there arose little formal Western interest in permanently occupying Afghanistan.

If ancient reports praised the "thousand cities of Bactria," the modern media dwell mostly on the wretchedness of Afghanistan: its backward material conditions and endemic corruption, its harsh landscape, its remoteness from globalized civilization, and the great divide between Western secular life and fundamentalist Islam. The differing attitudes toward the region involve not so much the human and natural challenges across the centuries for Westerners posed by Afghanistan—they are, in fact, eerily similar—but the far different ancient and modern responses to them.

Whereas the Macedonians and the Greeks saw profit and material advantage in ancient Afghanistan, current Westerners see little but hardship and sacrifices in blood and treasure—despite the recent discovery of huge deposits of natural resources. The ancients envisioned their occupation as permanent, the moderns see it as transitory; the one saw Bactria as uniquely suited for further imperial operations, whereas in the present Afghanistan is seen as unfortunately positioned between a treacherous and manipulative ally in Pakistan, an outright enemy in theocratic Iran, and opportunistic and predatory neutrals in China and Russia. The result is that the Macedonian message was essentially "stay, build, and prosper"; the American message is "finish the job, leave, and end the expense." In terms of military morale, it is difficult to assess across the centuries whether the better soldierly incentive accrues from the idea of building a permanent civilization or of establishing just enough stability to be able to return home.

How Was Afghanistan Won and Controlled?

Alexander and his successors were faced with two general truths for nearly two centuries, realities that remain mostly constant even today for foreign occupiers of Afghanistan: They were vastly outnumbered and their presence was always contested to some degree. We do not know the population numbers of either the ancient regions composing modern Afghanistan or the size of the Greek-speaking Bactrian veneer. At present the population of Afghanistan is roughly twenty-seven to thirty-one million. By the end of 2010 there were about ninety thousand American military troops stationed in the country, along with nearly fifty thousand NATO allied soldiers—in addition to tens of thousands of aid workers and reconstruction facilitators.

In other words, aside from the Afghan army, there is currently present about one Western soldier for every two hundred Afghans. To use arbitrary but reasonable ancient numbers, if Afghanistan in 200 BC numbered about three million in population, and there were about thirty thousand Greek-speaking soldiers under arms, then the ratio of Westerners to locals would have been 1:100, which suggests that even in antiquity relatively small numbers without much technology were able to control a vast landscape.

In turn, those numerical disparities prompted a general policy somewhat familiar to contemporary Western practice in Afghanistan. When possible, surge Western troops into troubled areas, co-opt local tribal leaders into joining with the foreigner, and eradicate those recalcitrant tribes or factions that are impossible to subdue and are uninterested in arguments appealing to their own self-interest.

Pacification for long periods was accomplished on three broad fronts: military, political, and economic. Militarily, the Greeks and Macedonians sought first to ensure conventional military superiority that would result in control of the richest farmland, large cities, and accessible plains. In the ancient context, this meant the superiority of spearmen fighting in the close formation of the phalanx, supported by heavy lance- or spear-bearing cavalry. Other than the occasional ambush, there is not a single instance of native Bactrian or Sogdiana tribesmen defeating a phalanx of heavily armed spearmen—in the same manner than no Afghan force has ever been successful in defeating a modern Western counterpart in conventional battle. Substitute phalangites and heavy cavalry for conventional American motor-assisted brigades, Special Forces teams, and airpower, and the respective strategies of counter-insurgency seem roughly similar.

Most of the Western heavy cavalry and phalangites were stationed in a series of fortified forts in the larger cities, leaving the mountainous regions alone. In addition, the Greeks and Macedonians also sought to form smaller raiding and mounted patrols whose tasks would be like our era's night raids: the sudden entry into tribal villages, which were designed to kill the leaders of insurrection and keep the enemy off-guard. Often, such operations resulted in what would appear to modern sensibilities as wide-scale atrocities, and are analogous to modern predator missions that assassinate suspected terrorist leaders without a great worry over collateral damage. And finally, all the successors of Alexander integrated their militaries with local forces, either drafting young Bactrians to undergo formal training as phalangites, or outsourcing military operations to local sympathetic or bought-and-paid-for provincial officials. In 2010 the American- and NATO-trained Afghan army numbered about 130,000 and is scheduled to double in size by 2013.

Politically, Westerners in antiquity again were ingenious in their efforts to win over a large population through a tripartite strategy. First, Greeks and Macedonians adopted local customs of dress and manners to avoid gratuitously offending locals, or even reminding them of their subservience. When we read in the historical record of ten thousand Bactrian horsemen, under Euthedemus, such participation suggests a sizable indigenous landed nobility that was in service to the Greek-speaking monarchy in Bactria. Second, except for occasional expeditions, the high mountain provinces were relegated to satraps of varying degrees of loyalty. And third, intermarriage, integration, and assimilation were commonplace to such a degree that it is difficult to know, by the second century BC, which Hellenic-named leaders of independent Bactria were even native Greeks. In any case, the Greek veneer was always pretty thin, leading Strabo to scoff that eventually there was not much difference in customs and characteristics of the Bactrians and Sogdians from those of the nomads to the north.[30]

Economically, the Greeks were faced with a paradox. They had stayed in the regions of ancient Afghanistan to prosper; in the ancient context of zero-sum economics that usually meant at the expense of local residents. Yet the influx of Greek-speaking immigrants brought and created wealth (coined money), which was soon to be evident in large, new cities and improved agricultural production. The key for the Greeks was not merely to thrive, but to demonstrate that they prospered by increasing the overall riches of Bactria itself, rather than at the expense of local tribesmen. Throughout two centuries there is clear evidence of a steady growth in coined money in Bactria, reflecting both the monetization of the economy, when the stored bullion of the old imperial treasury were melted down into coined money, and the improvement in agriculture. Finally, the presence of the Seleucid Empire meant that Bactria had found ready export markets not so common under Achmaenid rule, namely, the sale of grains and horses, and the renting of phalangites and horsemen to Seleucid armies.

Other than in matters of colonization and immigration, current American policy seems to be following the ancient paradigm in surprising fashion. The United States spends at least $100 billion a year in Afghanistan, its allies spend perhaps roughly half that number in aggregate. In addition, NGOs, charities, and direct foreign aid from dozens of nations contribute billions of dollars more aimed at improving the material conditions of rural Afghans, as a mechanism for turning them against the Taliban.

How Was Afghanistan "Lost"?

Somewhere around 140 BC, the independent Greek-speaking kingdom of Bactria and its associated rule over surrounding provinces came to an end. We know this from the archaeological record of destroyed cities and settlements, the precipitous drop in gold and silver coinage, and the sudden absence of references in the literary record to Bactrian monarchs. What happened?

Three general developments ended Western rule. First, near-constant civil warring attenuated the already small populations of Greek speakers. Seleucus was forced to fight almost nonstop between 323 and 301 to control Bactria—and was himself assassinated in 281. The later usurper, Diodotus, fought a conventional war against the Seleucids to establish an autonomous ancient Afghanistan. His line was destroyed by the interloper Euthedemus, who was in turn attacked by Antiochus III, who sought to reincorporate Afghanistan back into the Seleucid Empires. Euthedemus's royal line was ended by Eucratides, who sought to expand Bactria, but who himself was assassinated by rivals. The constant infighting among the ruling Western cadre finally so weakened the Greek-speaking presence that opportunistic rivals from Parthia and India, along with northern nomads, were able to carve up the kingdom. If the Roman colonial motto had been "divide and rule," the Bactrians' was the inverse: "rule and divide." In any case, in ancient Chinese sources Bactria was considered "feeble" at the time of the late-second-century-BC nomadic invasions.[31]

In addition, the fate of Bactria was intertwined with the Seleucid Empire, whose rulers facilitated lucrative trade with the region, provided a conduit westward with Hellenism, and offered a stream of fresh Greek-speaking colonialists and mercenaries. Yet under the rule of Antiochus II (261–246 BC), there were already clear signs of imperial overstretch within the vast empire; not just Bactria revolted, but also Cappadocia and Parthia, who saw opportunity as the Seleucids became bogged down in a long war with the Ptolemaic kingdom in Egypt and challenged by the Attalids in northern Asia Minor.[32]

After the establishment of Bactrian autonomy, a rival but weakened Seleucid Empire nevertheless proved to be more of an advantage than a danger, but unfortunately, the entrance of Rome into Eastern Mediterranean affairs cut off the monopoly of East-West trade enjoyed by the Seleucids. By the early second century BC, Romans had ended Seleucid influence in Greece and much of Asia Minor. And by the time of the ongoing collapse of Bactria (e.g., 145–125 BC), the once vast Seleucid Empire was on the way to becoming little more than a rump state of a few cities in Syria.

Finally, ancient Afghanistan—Bactria, Sogdiana, bordering regions in Media, Parthia, and Aria, and areas of Parapamisadae, Drangiana, and Arachosia—had never comprised a coherent whole. Once a regional consensus surfaced that Bactrian manpower and wealth were on the wane, rivals in Parthia, India, and regional nomads from the north and China simply carved out their own spheres of interest.

The demise of the Greeks and Macedonians in Bactria suggests that contemporary Afghanistan, despite its remoteness, tribal organization, and harsh climate and weather, is subject to the interested politics of an enormously wide region—not surprising for a landlocked region without ports and subject to overland logistics across a variety of provinces. In the ancient context that meant creating both alliances with and deterrence against the satraps in eastern Iran and the Indian kingdoms bordering the Hindu Kush. There also were never enough Westerners in Afghanistan to endure civil strife among such small communities, whether fighting against the Seleucids or staging a series of coups to wrest control from Bactrian monarchs. There was simply no margin of error that might allow intra-Greek rivalries and fighting, given the enormity of the landscape of ancient Afghanistan and the fierce nature of its multitude of tribes. Translated to the modern era, the ancient example suggests that the fate of the American effort in Afghanistan hinges on ending Pakistan's stealthy effort to aid and offer sanctuary to the Taliban, as well as finding ways of keeping Iranians from subverting American efforts—while keeping the Western alliance intact and committed to the NATO effort.

Westerners rarely experience coups anymore or play the "great game" in Afghanistan as colonial rivals. Nevertheless, dissension among the NATO ranks has weakened Western unity with idiosyncratically restrictive rules of engagement and announcements by the Netherlands and Canada, among others, of impending complete withdrawals.

Moreover, in the United States between 2009 and 2011, there was little domestic support for planned American troop increases. Ten years of on-again/off-again fighting have eroded American public support for what is now—a decade after September 11—considered an optional war in a distant region that has almost nothing to do with our original intent of punishing al-Qaeda, especially after the killing of bin Laden in May 2011. Our own differences are not exactly similar to a Diodotus attacking the Seleucids or Euthedemus in turn overthrowing the Diodotids, but a lack of continuity in American policy and practice has similarly translated to confusion about our ultimate aims and abilities. Four American commanders have been in charge of the war since January 2009. And without focus, Afghanistan becomes a remote theater, far from the immediate interests of Westerners. For all the Roman braggadocio of winning back the fallen legionary military standards (the golden *aquilae*) snatched by the Parthians after the terrible Roman defeat at Carrhae in southeastern Turkey (53 BC)—their version of a 9/11-like national disaster—the

Romans eventually came to accept noninterference in Parthia's far-eastern interests, allowing Parthian rivalries, coups, and civil strife to weaken their rivals far more than their own legionary expeditions.

What Became of the Greek Legacy?

In chronological terms, how does one define "legacy," given the endlessness of history? Is Hellenic success confirmed by two centuries of a westernized Bactria, or is failure proved by the relative absence of anything Western after 100 BC? By 160 BC, Greeks no doubt were struck by the amazing ability of Westerners to have planted durable colonies and a Hellenicized culture in a remote and rugged Afghanistan that had already lasted more than 150 years—and was then in its most impressive era of construction and expansion under Eucratides. Yet within another hundred years (e.g., 60 BC) the Greeks in Bactria were mostly the stuff of memory, with only a few surviving architectural remains and perhaps some isolated Greek-speaking settlements fused with local tribes.

Collapse was ensured with the absorption of the Seleucid Empire by Parthia and Armenia in the east and Rome in the west, ending the lifeline of Bactria to its Greek and Macedonian roots. The nomadic invasion from the north by the Sakai and others drove the Greek-speaking survivors into the mountains of ancient Afghanistan where they either perished or were absorbed into native tribes, leaving only the mythical stories of a lost Greek elite. Almost all of the cities that Alexander himself had founded and that were expanded by his successors under both Seleucid and an autonomous Bactrian control had more or less ceased to exist well before Roman imperial times.[33]

The historian Frank Holt ended his long comparison with the Americans and ancient Greeks in Afghanistan with an admittedly theatrical picture of an extinct, Greek-speaking Bactria submerged by the savage customs of the native Bactrians:

> Not in the palace, but in the theater, there appeared the most significant sign that the first European attempt to transform Afghanistan had ultimately failed. Where once Alexander's and Seleucus's settlers had assembled by the thousands to keep alive their ancestral arts, where practiced actors had donned their masks and recited the lines of classical poets, a new kind of tragedy now unfolded on a stage littered with the human wreckage of an awakened population. The natives needed no Greek theaters, so they piled upon its stage and front row seat the scattered remains of their unburied dead, whose bodies were otherwise in the way. As if the Greeks had never come, the Devourer dogs were growling again over the bones of the Bactrians.[34]

The Use and Abuse of Ancient History

As we have seen, the two-century occupation of ancient Afghanistan offers lessons for Westerners who are as foreign to the region as were Greek speakers of the past. Respect for local custom and practice, mastering tribal politics and exploiting their fissures, the use of overwhelming force against recalcitrant areas, targeted assassinations, navigation through the labyrinth of regional politics, expansion of local wealth, enlistment of locals for provincial government with a sense of political autonomy, avoidance of Western rivalries—all these strategies remain almost constant two millennia later. Greek Bactria was a kingdom that was run largely successfully by heavy infantry and cavalry from cities and forts without need to occupy the mountainous regions that were home to fiercely independent villages and tribes.

Nonetheless, there are also important differences. The Greeks and Macedonians were preindustrial. The military forces of Greek-run Bactria lacked the communications, transportation, and weapons of modern NATO forces, all of which can become force multipliers to traditional warfare—and likewise demand careful scrutiny of any comparisons with phalangites and horsemen. Alexander had to send flying columns to hunt down an insurgent leader rather than dispatch a Predator drone missile into his living room. The rules of war may not be changed by technological revolution, but the processes and delivery systems have quickened nearly beyond imagination.

When we talk of an ancient globalization reaching Asia, brought about by the Hellenizing Seleucids, we mean roughly a thin veneer of Greek-looking cities, Greek-speaking Asian courts, and Greek literature and science among a small elite operating far from Athens or Asia Minor. Modern globalization, in contrast, can be endemic at all levels of society. Instant cell phoning, the Internet, videos, DVDs, and jet travel have far greater potential to bring westernization, in holistic fashion, to non-Western regions. But whether such insidious technological diffusion will aid NATO forces in bringing changes to the Afghan attitude toward women, education, or religious tolerance remains to be seen. Present-day westernization surely is a far more potent force that the Hellenization ushered in by Alexander the Great. Again, whether it can help to erode support for the Taliban and its influence is uncertain.

Ancient Afghanistan also enjoyed a multiplicity of religions. While there are records of religious distrust between Westerners' worship of Olympian gods and related sects and an indigenous Zoroastrianism, the tension is not analogous to the present fervor of radical Islam, a politico-religious ideology that purports to transcend much of Afghanistan's traditional tribal and geographical divides in order to blame the West for the general misery in the Muslim world. Ancient Bactrian reaction to the successors of Alexander was primarily cultural and political; modern resistance ostensibly revolves around the Islamic zeal of the Taliban and al-Qaeda.

It is also popular in some quarters to label the NATO effort as colonial or imperialist. In truth, there is no present attempt to occupy Afghanistan permanently in the manner of the successors of Alexander the Great. In modern terms, Afghanistan is viewed as a liability to be reduced, not an opportunity to be exploited. The Western attitude toward Afghanistan is more akin to the rank and file of Alexander's army (who, upon the capture of Bessus and recognition of some of the savage customs of the Bactrians, simply wished to pack up and go home) than to the successors who saw opportunity in settling amid Bactria's fertile, though limited, plains.

Also, the popular culture of the West is quite different across the millennia. Between antiquity and the present is the shadow of a fierce antiwar, anti-interventionist popular creed among Western populaces that has not forgotten the legacies of nineteenth-century colonialism, two world wars, and the Cold War. When George W. Bush delivered to the Middle East his "Brotherhood of Man" speeches proclaiming a shared and universal human desire for freedom, few Western intellectuals rallied in the manner of their ancient counterparts, who had trumpeted Alexander's similar purported idealism. Western public opinion would tolerate neither triumphalist talk of "civilizing" Afghanistan nor resort to a level of violence analogous to the methods used successfully by Alexander the Great.

In sum, ancient and modern Afghanistan offer similar physical and human challenges to would-be Western occupiers, present or past. The key is whether the technological advantages of the contemporary West and its sophisticated counterinsurgency strategies can trump a far greater popular skepticism in Europe and America about the morality and practicality of its own mission. The answer to that dilemma will determine whether David Petraeus and his successors can create a westernized Afghanistan in the age of globalization that lasts longer than what two millennia ago was constructed for nearly two centuries by the Greeks. So far, the United States is experiencing even more difficulty in its first decade of occupation than did Alexander the Great and his successors.

Notes

1 For the rough area of ancient Afghanistan—a term that probably did not come into common usage until the seventeenth century—see F. Holt, *Thundering Zeus: The Making of Hellenistic Bactria* (Berkeley: University of California Press, 1999), 10–11.

2 For the ancient sources about Bactria, see F. Holt, "Discovering the Lost History of Ancient Afghanistan," *Ancient World* 9 (1984): 3–10. Scholars often used the terms "Greek Bactria," "Greco-Macedonian Bactria," "Seleucid Bactria" or "Hellenistic Bactria" to reflect: (a) that the Macedonians under Alexander and his successors claimed they had established a continuous outpost of Hellenism in ancient Afghanistan; (b) a great number of Greek mercenaries and traders from the city-states accompanied, fought against, and later joined the Macedonian generals; (c) most Macedonians in the armies of Alexander the Great and the successors nevertheless claimed to share many of the same customs and religion as the Greeks, and some spoke various dialects of the Greek language.

3 For the distinction—ethnic and linguistic—between Greek and Macedonian, see J. Rohm, ed., *The Landmark Arrian: The Campaigns of Alexander* (New York: Pantheon, 2010), 333–36 (written by E. Borza). We know that literate Macedonians wrote in and usually spoke some dialect of Doric Greek, but for most others interpreters were needed for communication between the two related languages. In any case, there does not seem to have been a written Macedonian language, at least a literary one, that was wholly unique. While many Greeks and Macedonians emphasized their regional proximity and shared religion and customs, Macedonians emphasized a common Hellenism more often than were Greeks willing to concede that claim.

4 On the ancient sources for Alexander in Bactria and the subsequent Macedonian occupation—Arrian's *Anabasis,* Curtius Rufus, Diodorus, and Plutarch's *Alexander*— see A. B. Bosworth, *Conquest and Empire: The Reign of Alexander the Great* (Cambridge, UK: Cambridge University Press, 1988), 94–113, and especially F. Holt, *Into the Land of Bones: Alexander the Great in Afghanistan* (Berkeley:

University of California Press, 2005), 165–72. Alexander recovered 50,000 silver talents at Susa alone (Arrian, *Anabasis* 3.16.6; cf. Diodorus 17.66).

5 On the soldiers' reaction following the death of Darius, see Diodorus 17.74.3. On Alexander's murdering, especially in ancient Afghanistan, see V. Hanson, "Alexander the Killer," *Military History Quarterly* 10.3 (Spring 1998): 8–19. See also D. J. Lonsdale, *Alexander the Great, Killer of Men: History's Greatest Conqueror and the Macedonian Art of War* (New York: Carroll and Graf Publishers, 2004), 150–66. And for a review of current scholarship that assesses Alexander's spate of violence between 331 and 327 BC and the morality of his reign, see V. Hanson, "Alexander the Greatest," *Times Literary Supplement* (October 7, 2004).

6 Initially, Alexander seems to have told his followers that they were simply pursuing Bessus without any intention of permanently settling and colonizing the region; cf. P. Green, *Alexander of Macedon* (Berkeley: University of California Press, 1991), 330–31, on the rumors that the Macedonians would soon all return home on news of the death of Darius III.

7 On Alexander's strategy of pacification, cf. Diodorus 76–77.

8 For a narrative of these events, see H. Sidky, *The Greek Kingdom of Bactria: From Alexander to Eucratides the Great* (Lanham, MD: University Press of America, 2000), 38–82. Of this constant tribal and insurgency fighting, cf. Green, *Alexander of Macedon*, 338: "Bessus, and his successor Spitamenes, were fighting a nationalist war, with strong religious overtones: between them they gave Alexander more continuous trouble than all the embattled hosts of Darius."

9 On the nature of the Greek and Macedonian military "colonies" and "cities" in Bactria, see W. W. Tarn, *The Greeks in Bactria and India* (Cambridge, UK: Cambridge University Press, 1966), 6–10. Initially, new colonists were given a *klêros,* or land allotment, in exchange for required military service in the phalanx; eventually, such farmer-soldiers were expected to raise families on their land and help transform the colony into a westernized polis. For the antipathy of Alexander to the Greeks in the service in the east, and vice versa, cf. P. M. Fraser, *Cities of Alexander the Great* (Oxford, UK: Clarendon Press, 1996), 192–96.

10 See Plutarch, *Alexander*, 45, for Alexander's adoption of Eastern dress; some contemporaries believed that Alexander sincerely wished to fuse the two cultures; others less charitably believed that he wished to appear as an absolute Eastern potentate to his own Macedonians. Ancient sources suggest that Alexander gradually assumed more elaborate Persian fashion until he was soon dressed no differently than the Persian kings themselves (Diodorus 77.13). For descriptions of the toll of Alexander's soldiers in the harsh climate of the region, cf. Curtius 7.5.13–20.

11 Plutarch, *Moralia*, 183F 1. For details of the insurrections of 329, see the review in Bosworth, *Conquest and Empire*, 110–12.

12 On the exterminations, cf. Curtius 7.5.31–6.

13 For Alexander's general swath of destruction, see Curtius 7.5.33–6; 7.6.15; 7.9.13–19; Arrian 4.1.3–5; 4.2.3–4; 4.4.7–8.

14 The thirty thousand: Plutarch, *Alexander*, 47.3–4; 72. For a review of Alexander's counterinsurgency methods of alternating between savage violence and cultural outreach to local tribes, see Bosworth, *Conquest and Empire*, 99–101. It is hard to determine from where the thousands of Greek- and Macedonian-speaking colonists came after the death of Alexander. Population growth in the new Greek cities of the east explains some of the increased migrations, but more likely the influx included many tribes in the southern Balkans, such as the Thracians, once considered barbarians, who in Hellenistic times began to be seen from the distant vantage of Greeks in Asia as more Hellenic than not. Cf. Tarn, *Greeks in Bactria*, 68–70.

15 In 2004, Frank Holt, a classical historian of ancient Bactria, gave a series of lectures on the similarities between Alexander's checkered experience in ancient Afghanistan and the American four-year efforts up to that date in supplanting the Taliban with a constitutional government. He concluded with the bleak assessment that any apparent Western success would likely not last, or have much enduring influence, cf. Holt, *Land of Bones*, 149–64.

16 Cf. e.g., Curtius 7.5–7.6.

17 On Alexander's methods of controlling Bactria, see F. Holt, *Alexander the Great and Bactria: The Formation of a Greek Frontier* (Leiden: E. J. Brill, 1988), 52–70.

18 For a description of Alexander's new cities founded in ancient Afghanistan, see Fraser, *Cities of Alexander the Great*, 31–46.

19 For the destruction of Alexander's inner circle, cf. Plutarch, *Alexander*, 47–57.

20 Curtius 7.4.26–30. On the size of Bactrian cavalry forces, Curtius 7.4.31.

21 On the birth of the Seleucid Empire (constituting modern-day Afghanistan, Kuwait, Iran, Iraq, Lebanon, Syria, and Turkey), see F. W. Walbank et al., *The Cambridge Ancient History, Volume VIII. Part I. The Hellenistic World*, 2nd ed. (Cambridge, UK: Cambridge University Press, 1984), 175–84; cf. 214–16.

22 For the routes of Bactria trade, see Tarn, *Greeks in Bactria*, 362–63, who thought most of the trans-continental commerce from the east was routed through Bactria, sent south to Seleucia in modern-day Iraq, and finally transported overland to the Phoenician ports on the Mediterranean. For the "thousand cities," see Justin, *Epitome of Pompeius Trogus*, 41.4.1.11; Strabo 15.1.3.

23 Accounts of post-Alexandrian Bactria are sketchy, given the lack of a continuous extant ancient narrative. For the array of problems, see the scholarly review in Walbank et al., *Cambridge Ancient History*, 219–20.

24 Revolt of Euthydemus: Strabo 11.9.2. For details of Antiochus's invasion, see Sidky, *Greek Kingdom of Bactria*, 166–77. Only a few fragments remain of Polybius's near-contemporary account.

25 For bits and pieces about the settlement, see Polybius 10.49.15.

26 On the career of Euthydemus, cf. Holt, *Thundering Zeus*, 126–37.

27 For the end of Bactria under the successors of Eucratides, see Tarn, *Ancient Bactria*, 270, 311. Strabo 11.511 has a list of the tribes that invaded Bactria.

28 Curtius (7.3.12). For the practices of dogs eating the dead among the Hyrcanians, and the use of birds to do the same in Bactria, cf. Plutarch, *Moralia* 821D. The gruesome pets were known as the "entombers." Alexander the Great tried to end the custom. Cf. Strabo 11.11.3. Diodorus notes that the Macedonians were surprised that even dormant vines and fruit trees had to be covered to survive the harsh winters (e.g., Diodorus 17.82; cf. Curtius 7.3.5–7).

29 Strabo 11.11.1; on the farming potential of Bactria, see Curtius 7.4.24–30.

30 Polybius, 10.49, has the details of the invasion of Antiochus and the numbers of troops. On Bactrians and nomads, cf. Strabo 11.11.3. For an introduction to how Macedonian-Persian fusion worked out on a practical level, cf. Romm, *Arrian*, 380–87. In general, scholars are divided over the degree to which Alexander's plans for Asian-European unity were idealistic or utilitarian, and the degree to which his successors rejected, followed, or did not think consciously about his efforts at joining east and west into a hybrid culture. For Bactrian aristocratic allegiance to Greek speakers, cf. Tarn, *Ancient Bactria*, 124–26.

31 Cf. Holt, *Thundering Zeus*, 19–20. Cf. 137: "the Hellenistic Greeks never faced a greater danger than themselves." "Feeble": Sidky, *Greek Kingdom of Bactria*, 226–27.

32 For the steady arrival of western Greeks into Bactria, see Tarn, *Greeks in Bactria*, 118–19.

33 Fraser, *Cities of Alexander*, 198–99.

34 Holt, *Land of Bones*, 164.

CHAPTER 3

Afghan Paradoxes

Thomas Barfield

Afghanistan has a long history that is too often characterized by misinformation and myth. Analysts and reporters constantly assert that Afghanistan is a place that no one has ever conquered and whose people have never been successfully governed. It is the graveyard of empires and a land of endemic insurgencies. In reality, all such generalizations are false. Until 1840, Afghanistan was better described as a highway of conquest that was regularly ruled by outsiders. That list of imperial rulers is long and distinguished: the Persian Empire (6th to 4th centuries BC), Alexander the Great and the Greco-Bactrian Kingdoms (4th to 1st centuries BC), the Kushans (1st to 3rd centuries AD), Sassanians (3rd to 7th centuries), Arabs (7th to 9th centuries), Ghaznavids (10th to 12th centuries), Genghis Khan and the Mongols (12th to 14th centuries), the Timurids (14th to 15th centuries), Mughal India and Safavid Iran (16th to mid-18th centuries). The Afghan Empire only came into being in 1747 and this was the first time Pashtuns established a ruling dynasty.[1] The Afghans may have forced the British to withdraw from the country twice in the nineteenth century, but the British maintained indirect control over its rulers afterward, and such defeats never weakened their control over India.[2] Similarly, the problems in Afghanistan may have exposed weaknesses in the Soviet Union, but neither the casualties nor the cost of that occupation led to its demise.[3] Nor were insurgencies endemic: Those against the British lasted less than eighteen months and rebellions against Afghan governments until 1978 were equally brief. More to the point, after each war or insurgency the Afghan state always successfully reemerged to restore order. The relatively weak Musahiban dynasty, for example, kept the country at peace from 1929 to 1978 and never faced an insurgency.[4]

Separating Afghan legends from Afghan realities would only be an academic exercise were it not for the influence such beliefs continue to have on those who set policy. For example, in 2009, Canadian prime minister Stephen Harper declared, in a television interview, that "We're not going to ever defeat the insurgency. Afghanistan has probably had—my reading of Afghanistan history, it's probably had an insurgency forever, of some kind."[5] That there were no insurgencies before 1840, and that Afghanistan has had longer periods of peace than war, implies that Harper's understanding of Afghanistan's history likely begins no earlier than its current troubles in 1978. Still, that would put him ahead of those for whom Afghan history begins only in 2001. Coming to grips with Afghanistan's problems today demands a much broader perspective that asks why a country that has restored political order so many times in the past finds it so difficult to do so today. To answer this question we need to examine the historic nature of the Afghan state, how its rulers gained and lost legitimacy, and why state power has always been so fragile. These lessons from the past suggest pathways that could lead to stability there again. The first step is to examine what Afghans historically expected from the state, and what the state expected from them.

The modern Western view of a state is monolithic. Lines on a map indicate precise boundaries and a state's authority is presumed to be universal and absolute within its territory, with its inhabitants bound under a single rule of law that is the same whether they live in the capital city or in some distant rural district. Deviations too far from this ideal constitute "failed states" like the one in Afghanistan today that should be improved by buttressing state power until it takes on a healthier glow.[6] In past centuries, however, Afghanistan had a very different history and conception of the state. It was based on a model of state power and sovereignty in which rulers sought direct control of urban centers and productive irrigated agricultural lands, together with the lines of communication that linked them. Inhabitants in poor or geographically marginal areas were left to fend for themselves as long as they did not challenge state authority. If they did, the state resorted to tactics well short of direct rule to bring them back into line. These included denying uncooperative districts access to vital urban markets, encouraging internal rivalries to divide the opposition, and punitive military campaigns designed to emphasize the cost of resistance. The goal was to intimidate a population and its leaders into acquiescence without changing the existing political structure. Although it was a messy strategy that required constant maintenance, because changes in policy or local mismanagement could turn formerly cooperative groups into enemies, rulers effectively controlled Afghanistan for many centuries with this model of government.

More recent leaders of Afghanistan, beginning with Amir Abdur Rahman in the late nineteenth century, abandoned this traditional model of governance for a more exclusive and centralized state.[7] They believed that modern weapons gave the state such a decisive advantage over geographically marginal regions that they and their people could be administered like all others in the country. Governments in Kabul, therefore, attempted to impose policies that reinforced state sovereignty, but the Afghan people, particularly in rural areas, never fully reconciled themselves to this change. They saw state interference in their affairs as illegitimate if it transgressed established boundaries of autonomy.

These opposed views on the limits of national sovereignty were never reconciled, but caused only periodic difficulties when governments in Kabul limited themselves to preserving order in rural areas and let local communities live life as they saw fit. However, when Kabul governments attempted to use state power to make radical changes in Afghan society, it provoked violent opposition that proved difficult to suppress.[8] This led to state collapse in Afghanistan twice in the twentieth century in response to modernizing governments: once in 1929 in a short civil war that led to the ouster of the reformist King Amanullah, and during the decade of resistance against the Soviet-backed government in the 1980s.[9]

The rapid collapse of the Taliban in 2001 after the American invasion can also be interpreted as a tacit reaction against a government intent on pursuing its radical Islamist policies by force. Disputes over the legitimacy of state sovereignty, the structure of national government, and attempts to change Afghan society remain a source of instability today. It is important to understand and appreciate how the traditional system worked and why it remained viable in Afghanistan long after it disappeared from neighboring countries. This chapter explores that history, which still holds lessons for policymakers in today's Afghanistan.

Long-Lasting Social and Economic Structures: Ibn Khaldun and Afghanistan

In Afghanistan the marginal peoples of the mountainous borderlands have always maintained their autonomy from state institutions. The independence of such marginal peoples and their distinctive social organization has a long history in the Islamic world. It was first identified and analyzed in depth by Ibn Khaldun, a fourteenth-century Arab social historian whose examples came primarily from North Africa and Arabia, although it still has relevance for understanding the political dynamics in Afghanistan today. Based on his own observations and a study of history, ibn Khaldun distinguished between two different types of societies in the Islamic world of his day: "desert civilizations" and "sedentary civilizations."[10]

Desert civilizations encompassed communities with low population densities located in marginal deserts, steppelands, or mountains—areas that proved difficult for outsiders to dominate militarily or that did not repay the cost of doing so. Their social organizations were primarily kinship based and their economies were dependent on subsistence agriculture or pastoralism. In contrast, sedentary civilizations were defined by their high population densities and complex economies that produced substantial agricultural surpluses and manufactured goods. People were organized on the basis of residency but divided by class and occupational structures with considerable division of labor. They supported centers of learning and high culture as well as markets for regional trade and international commerce.

Desert Civilizations

The resilience of desert civilization people and their ability to resist outside authorities was rooted in the simplicity of their subsistence economies and the solidarity of their social organizations. (While ibn Khaldun used the Bedouin as his prime example of desert civilization, in Afghanistan it was the inhabitants of the mountains and marginal foothills that played this role, particularly Pashtuns and Tajiks.) Their subsistence economies produced little in the way of surplus and, because everyone produced the same things, there was little internal trade. Wealth was measured in terms of property (land and livestock, particularly) rather than money. Economic divisions were few because surpluses funded hospitality, communal feasts, gift giving, and other forms of redistribution that raised the social status of the givers but made personal accumulation of wealth difficult. Although status differences existed, they were minimal. Leaders had no strategic assets (land, money, trade goods) that would give them or their families any permanent economic or political control over their poorer neighbors. Instead, leaders gained and retained power by demonstrating personal characteristics of leadership displayed in resolving disputes, serving as effective military commanders, or representing their community's interests in dealings with outside political powers.

Desert civilization communities were characterized by strong group solidarity. Based on kinship, descent, or personal clientage, they had an *asabiya* (group feeling) that bound all members of a social group together when facing the outside world. Group interest superseded individual interest to such an extent that people were willing to sacrifice themselves if necessary. It was an honor-based culture in which reputation was a critical element. Positive acts by any member of the group redounded to the group's benefit, but any shameful acts or insults against its members damaged the reputation of the group as a whole. Attacks or slights against an individual were therefore met with a collective community response.[11]

In the absence (or rejection) of government policing institutions, crime victims mobilized their own kin group to seek retribution or compensation. If one man murdered another, the murdered man's kin were collectively obligated to seek blood revenge. Similarly, the murderer's kin were collectively responsible for his act (and might even be targets in revenge killings), even though they had no direct role in it. If compensation was agreed on to end the threat of revenge, the whole group was liable for its payment. Not only did overt acts such as assault, murder, or theft demand a collective response, so did threats to a group's honor and reputation.[12]

The military advantage of this solidarity was particularly evident in times of conflict. Such groups were renowned as fierce fighters because individuals would rather die than shame themselves in front of their kin by running away. Of course, the group itself could decide to retreat collectively (and usually did) if the odds turned against them.

This strong group solidarity was undermined by a number of structural political weaknesses, however, that made them vulnerable to stronger outside powers. Their local descent or locality groups were necessarily of small size and, because they had a strong cultural predisposition toward equality, it was difficult for a leader either to consolidate power or combine subgroupings into larger units. Anyone in a leadership position was undercut by rivals looking to replace him, or at the very least throw obstacles in his way. This pattern was so ubiquitous among close relatives in Afghanistan that it acquired a specific term in Pashto: *tarburwali,* the rivalry of agnatic cousins.[13] Even if a leader succeeded in surmounting this rivalry, his political position was structurally weak, lacking the right to command and so dependent on his ability to persuade others to follow. For this reason, ibn Khaldun noted, religious leaders were often more successful than tribal ones in uniting large groups.

Coming from outside the system and calling on God's authority, they could better circumvent tribal rivalries.

Sedentary Civilizations

Sedentary civilizations had surplus and luxury as their defining characteristics, products of a complex division of labor that created an urban cash economy in which money trumped kinship. City markets provided a wide range of local and imported goods as well as services that ranged from the utilitarian to the extravagant. Many of these products were vital to the survival of even distant rural communities and created a dependency relationship between city markets and subsistence mountain villagers or nomads. As ibn Khaldun explained, "While (the Bedouins) need the cities for their necessities of life, the urban population needs (the Bedouins) for conveniences and luxuries.... They must be active on the behalf of their interests and obey them whenever (the cities) ask and demand obedience from them."[14] This complex economy produced a surplus of production beyond the imagination of those living in a subsistence economy, but at the cost of inverting the relationships found in the margins. In subsistence economies people had deep social bonds but few necessary economic ties. In the city people had few strong social bonds beyond their own families but were economically dependent on one another in all aspects of daily life. Social and economic distinctions among hierarchically ranked classes were large and obvious; people identified themselves by residence (not kinship), and individual interests trumped group interests.

The political strengths of a sedentary civilization lay in its higher degree of centralization, wealth, and population density. Its rulers had "royal authority": the ability to issue commands with the expectation that they would be obeyed. Unlike desert chieftains, rulers here were not consensus builders or redistributors of wealth but rather acquisitive autocrats. They secured their power by accumulating wealth for themselves and the state on a grand scale through various forms of taxation, control of trade or markets, and the large-scale ownership of productive land. Such wealth was the foundation of a centralized government. It paid for a bureaucracy composed of appointed subordinates who carried out the ruler's commands with a military force behind them. Such military forces in the medieval Islamic world consisted of paid mercenaries or slave soldiers, not a citizen soldiery. Warfare was thus in the hands of military professionals who were paid servants of the state, not the ordinary inhabitants of any class.[15]

This complexity, hierarchy, and wealth created political weaknesses as well as strengths. Urban and peasant populations had little political autonomy. They expected to be ruled by others as part of a highly centralized polity in which officials often abused their authority and accumulated personal wealth through corruption. This weakened the state by siphoning off its revenue and alienating its population. A state's subjects were so uninvolved with government that it mattered little to them who the ruler was. Hence regimes could fall very quickly and their new rulers did not fear opposition by the population at large.

Although the two systems were very different, they had intense interactions. Remote communities that might maintain their political autonomy were nevertheless economically dependent on trade with cities to obtain manufactured products and sell their own surplus goods. There was also considerable population flow from the rural hinterland to cities that offered a higher standard of living or economic opportunities to new migrants. More surprising was that desert civilization people provided most of the ruling dynasties for their sedentary civilization counterparts because they had stronger social solidarity. This solidarity took on significance when sedentary states weakened because of economic and bureaucratic mismanagement. Such weakness attracted attacks by poor but aggressive military leaders from the margins who then established themselves as new ruling elites in regions in which they conquered and then settled. Ibn Khaldun remarked that most of the ruling dynasties in the medieval Islamic world had their origins within such groups of desert-dwelling Bedouin or nomads from the steppes of Central Asia.

Those who made themselves masters of societies far more complex than those in which they were born soon separated themselves from their rural origins. Although nominally the members of the same ethnic groups, their diverging interests soon divided them. Thus in Afghanistan an urbanized Pashtun in Qandahar or a Tajik in Kabul had little in common with fellow Pashtuns or Tajiks inhabiting poor, remote, and mountainous Uruzghan or Badakhshan provinces.

Over the past 150 years, ibn Khaldun's distinction between desert civilizations and sedentary civilizations became less relevant to understanding the politics in most of North Africa and the Near East. During this time new modes of transportation, communications, and military technology reduced or eliminated the ability of people there to avoid political domination by national governments. Economic development and better integration into national economies also reduced the group solidarity as individuals were no longer as dependent on the communities they were born into. But this was not the case in Afghanistan or parts of neighboring Pakistan, where marginal geographic territories and peoples have still maintained their autonomy.

Moreover, despite advances in weapons technology, mountainous terrain proved much harder to dominate militarily than did the flat steppelands or deserts, whose people had far less protection against motorized military vehicles or aircraft. As a result the dynamic described by ibn Khaldun still typifies Afghanistan and it remains a place that he would easily recognize. Its rural economy remains largely subsistence based, and its road and communication infrastructure are only minimally developed.

Far from participating in a single political sphere, Afghanistan remains two worlds, interacting but not integrated. These contrasting patterns of subsistence, social organization, and regional political structures underlie the country's long-standing ethnic and tribal divisions. Many rural communities are still beyond the direct control of a weak Afghan central government in Kabul. (What power that state had gained in the century prior to the communist coup of 1978 was then lost in the quarter century of war that followed.) Ibn Khaldun would also be familiar with the cultural tensions still alive in Afghanistan between the people of the plains and cities and those who inhabited the country's mountains, deserts, and steppes. To city people, those in the hinterlands are more barbarian than civilized. And people in the countryside had little good to say about the political elite in the capital, regardless of their ethnic origin.

Traditional Patterns of Governance and Political Legitimacy

The distinction between core and periphery that underlay ibn Khaldun's models of social organization was a foundation of a dual governance strategy in which states controlled the most productive or strategic parts themselves and allowed territories that were deemed either unprofitable to rule or of little strategic value to fend for themselves. As a result, states asserted nominal sovereignty over people in marginal areas within the boundaries of the state without bothering them much. Rulers recognized that such regions did not need to be ruled directly or subjected to the same style of government as were the peoples of the irrigated plains and valleys. This was particularly true in their dealings with communities inhabiting mountainous valleys. It was always difficult to move invading troops into mountainous terrain, and even harder to fight effectively when they were subject to ambush. The greatest military powers of the day could easily find themselves stymied.[16]

The difficulties that Alexander the Great faced in fighting the mountain tribes in the Kunar Valley in the fourth century BC were not that much different from those faced by the Americans there in the twenty-first century, except that the Afghans in Alexander's day dropped boulders, and today they shoot rockets from their mountain perches. It was easier to come to an accommodation with such people than to continually fight them, and most state powers indigenous to the region eventually chose that policy. This inability of states to assert full state control in mountain areas, as well as large stretches of steppe or desert, also meant that they were more likely to establish flexible frontiers in such regions than precise borders.

Unlike their borders with adjacent states, there was never a single line in these areas that determined absolute inclusion or exclusion. Rather, zones of control ran from direct at the core, through indirect at the margins, to the purely theoretical or symbolic in the outlands. In Afghanistan, such ungoverned spaces were often labeled *yagistan*, which can be translated either as "rebel lands" or just "lawless places."[17] Where to call an end to sovereignty was frequently a vexing question that was answered by weighing the costs against the benefits. In Afghanistan this meant that direct state authority was historically confined to only a small part of the country. Just how concentrated these areas are can be seen by looking at a map of the most significant agricultural regions (see figure 3.1). The compact darker spots indicate the key agricultural districts (mostly irrigated) that a conqueror would be seeking and these constitute less than 5 percent of the country's total land area.[18] If one controls these, one controls the major sources of wealth and the most productive populations.

The problem for states centering on the territory of Afghanistan, however, is that its territory has more margins than cores. Afghanistan's regionally productive areas are also so divided by deserts and mountain ranges that they are hard to integrate into a single state structure and by default maintain considerable autonomy.

If premodern state rulers concluded that the direct administration of the marginal territory was not necessary, or even desirable, it was a lesson constantly relearned by new dynasties that encountered problems when their reach exceeded their grasp. The resistance of the Pashtun tribes against the Mughal dynasty in the sixteenth and seventeenth centuries, for example, flared up when rulers sought to

FIGURE 3.1. Land Use in Afghanistan

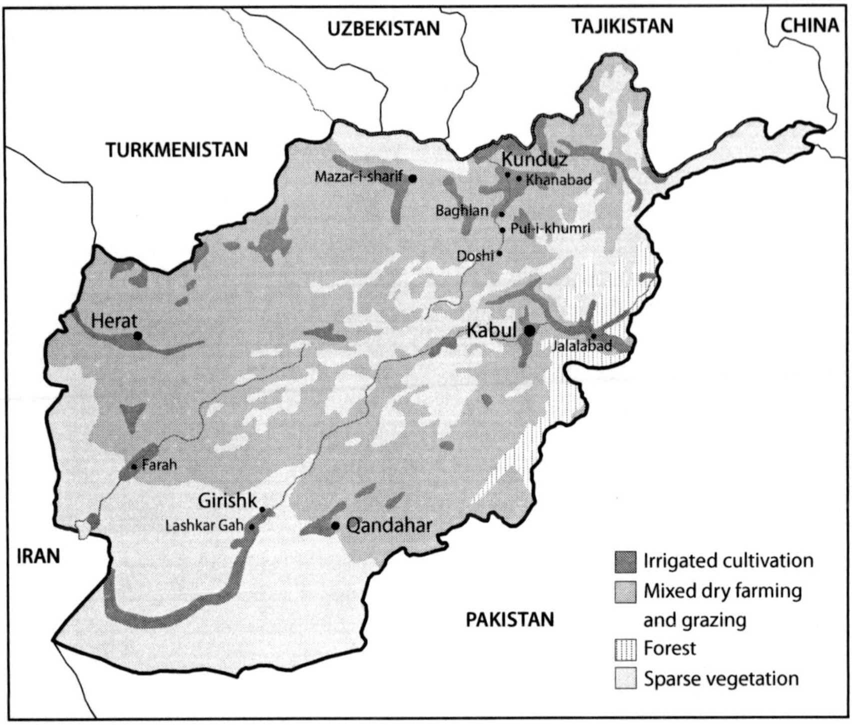

impose direct control in such areas. But since it was access to the trade routes passing through their territories that was really important, it was cheaper to buy them off or negotiate a political accommodation with them. The Pashtuns could therefore rightfully boast that their mountain fastnesses were never conquered, but that was because successive empires chose to bypass them or else imposed only symbolic elements of sovereignty. To extend their claim of autonomy to all of today's Afghanistan involved more than a little exaggeration.

Even among the Pashtuns, those who inhabited the irrigated plains around Qandahar, Peshawar, or Herat experienced foreign rule on a regular basis because their territories constituted the productive hearts of their regions that no ruler would willingly ignore. Yet one might ask, since the productive regions of Afghanistan have not changed significantly in the past five hundred years, why the same strategy did not work for the British in the nineteenth century or the Russians in the twentieth century? The answer has two parts. First, Western powers had a model of the state that was quite expansive and that put them in conflict with the peoples of the periphery. By the time they realized the limits of state power and began to look more favorably on decentralized strategies of governance, their home governments were only interested in leaving Afghanistan. But a more significant development over time was a change in perception of what made Afghan governments legitimate. In this respect premodern conquerors of Afghanistan were more fortunate than their modern counterparts. They worked within a political system where the number of contestants for power was limited and they were only rarely challenged by the people they ruled.

States have historically used wars of conquest as the primary means to incorporate contested territory into their polities. For premodern states in Afghanistan, wars of conquest were largely competitions among rival elites to control a subject population because the state as an institution was viewed as the property of the ruling elite that ran it. For this reason, conquerors were not at war with the people of the territory but rather with their rulers. Since control was the issue, it was common to allow defeated rulers to retain local power after they had acknowledged their submission to a new overlord and agreed to pay tribute, so that wars did not so much wipe the board clean as redistribute the existing pieces. And for most of history despised "foreign" rule was not only legitimate, it was the norm because almost all of Afghanistan's ruling dynasties were foreign in origin. The rise of the indigenous Pashtun Durrani state in the mid-eighteenth century was a break from this long pattern, although outside of ethnically Pashtun regions its rulers were just as foreign as any dynasty that originated in Iran or Central Asia. Because it was relatively easy to turn raw physical coercion into legitimate authority, all that foreign rulers and their successors needed to achieve was the restoration of public order and perhaps put down a rebellion or two. They could then count on Islamic religious institutions, local economic power brokers, and other states to recognize them as legitimate rulers so as to minimize the disruption that would ensue by resisting such claims. The greatest asset for achieving long-term acceptance, however, was sheer inertia, as generations passed and their royal executive power became routinized and traditional. Afghanistan's half century of peace from 1929 to 1978 under the usurping Musahiban dynasty owed far more to this tradition of acquiescence than to its ability to project coercive power.

Acts of violence and physical coercion that first gained possession of a territory were transformed into legitimate authority by drawing on political theories supported by Islamic jurisprudence that put few barriers between de facto conquest and swift de jure recognition, which was justified by the Quranic obligation to "obey the Prophet and those in authority over you."[19] One of the first actions that any new Muslim ruler took was to have the *khutba*, the Friday Islamic sermon at the main mosque, read in his name. Announcing the ruler's name in the *khutba* signified both recognition of his sovereignty and gave public proof of his control. The other step in asserting legitimate sovereignty was to mint coins in the name and title of the new ruler.[20]

Such changes did not always stem from conquest. A regional ruler who decided to declare his independence or compete for supreme power would begin that bid by having the *khutba* read in his own name in his own territory and (if he had enough time) minting new coins. Underlying this normally rapid acceptance of a new regime's legitimacy, whatever its limitations, was the fear of *fitna* (disorder, sedition, or civil war) and the consequences it could bring.[21] In the Islamic legal tradition, rebellion against an established Muslim ruler by his subjects was illegitimate because it created *fitna*. Students of Western political science will note that this line of reasoning closely parallels the conclusions drawn by the seventeenth-century English political philosopher Thomas Hobbes, who argued that any government was superior to lawlessness.[22] He therefore insisted that subjects had a positive duty to obey their rulers, who in turn were obliged to protect their subjects' lives from the predation of other people within the state and invaders from without. Subjects should therefore accept as legitimate any ruler who was capable of protecting them, even if that ruler was defective or abusive in other ways. Rulers were not accountable to their subjects, but subjects had no obligation to remain loyal to leaders who could not fulfill their roles as protectors.

In Hobbes's view, civil war or rebellion was the worst of all political conditions. Given the choice between that and accepting a rule imposed by foreign invaders, he freely recommended the latter. Civil war could destroy society itself. Conquest (even foreign conquest) only threatened to change a society's leaders.

Afghanistan's Change from Highway of Conquest to Homeland of Insurgencies

Until the nineteenth century, the traditional passive model of state sovereignty and governance characterized Afghanistan's response to foreign invasion. This position was summed up by a famous eleventh-century ruler, Mahmud of Ghanzi, when he berated his subjects in Balkh for taking up resistance against a rival who had taken the city: "If any king (at a given moment) proves himself the stronger, and requires taxes of you and protects you, you must pay taxes and thereby save yourselves."[23] It was up to the ruler to defend or retake his territory and ordinary subjects had no role in such affairs. One reason that ordinary people saw themselves as playing no role in politics was that foreign conquerors of Afghanistan were content to maintain the status quo as long as they could be in charge.

Dynastic changes resembled corporate mergers and acquisitions—albeit by the sword rather than proxy votes—in that the business of government and ordinary life proceeded as usual in the aftermath. In areas at the margins this was even more true. As long as their communities were permitted to run their own affairs with minimal interference, who ruled Kabul was unimportant. By contrast, the British were the first in a series of Western powers arriving in Afghanistan with a more ambitious agenda. They could not resist the temptation to do more than just conquer Afghanistan, but sought to change the structure of its government and society as well.

The British planned to remake Afghanistan in a way that would produce a modern state capable of controlling all of its people. In doing so they provoked a conflict with the people of Afghanistan, not just the small elite that ran the country. This not only produced Afghanistan's first insurgency but it changed the criteria for political legitimacy to include the defense of Islam and Afghan national identity. Neither had been an issue previously. Afghanistan's regions had had strong identities, but there was no conception of it as a nation-state. Nor had Islam played a large role in political mobilization since (with the exception of the Mongols) new conquerors had all been Muslim for the previous thousand years. But what was unique, and was to become a long-lasting legacy of Western intervention, was the military mobilization of people at the margins as the main forces in the insurgency against the British.[24]

The British invaded Afghanistan in 1839 with every reason to expect a good outcome. They had already incorporated and reformed many more powerful and better-organized states in India under similar circumstances. As in India, the British found it advantageous to work through a proxy ruler who had local political legitimacy. In the Afghan case they turned to Shah Shuja, an elderly Afghan ruler who had previously been driven into exile in India by his rivals. He had been plotting for years to return to power in Kabul and fully expected that with British support he could achieve this goal. Neither he nor the British expected they would have any trouble after they ousted the existing amir, Dost Muhammad.[25]

This assessment proved correct. Kandahar fell with little fighting, and after winning a fierce battle in Ghazni, the British marched almost unopposed into Kabul and Shuja was restored to the throne. Unable to convince his subjects to rise up against the British, Dost Muhammad initially fled to Bukhara, and his attempt to raise an armed opposition to Shuja and the British the next year failed so badly that he surrendered and accepted a well-paid exile in India. The Durrani Pashtun elite accepted the legitimacy of Shuja (he had a better claim to it than Dost Muhammad) and proved keen to cooperate with the new regime. The Ghilzai Pashtuns who inhabited the margins of the state in the east were bought off with stipends to their chieftains, who saw no reason to weigh in one way or another over which Durrani king ruled Kabul. The Muslim clerics who complained that the British were infidels made little headway. The British had paid off a large number of mullahs in Kabul to win their acquiescence and Shuja was a Muslim ruler who had the right to demand their obedience regardless of who his allies might be. The non-Muslim Sikhs had taken the Afghan winter capital of Peshawar years earlier and had no trouble getting the population there to accept the legitimacy of their rule.

The British viewed the whole Afghan system of government they encountered in Kabul as thoroughly corrupt, inefficient, and in need of reform. Most of its revenue was devoted to funding an elaborate patronage network that attracted support for its ruler. They therefore immediately set about restructuring the Afghan government, increasing its tax revenues, reorganizing its military, and ending the power of the country's existing feudal aristocracy. This was a deliberate act, for as Malcolm Yapp explained, "British policy was aimed ultimately at the destruction of these forces and constant efforts were made to abridge their privileges."[26]

The reforms were intended to create greater stability in the long run, but the process of change produced the very opposite condition in the short run. The old Durrani elite that had supported Shuja's reinstallation as shah felt betrayed when they realized that the British intended to dissolve the irregular forces they were paid to command and replace them by a new model army. Shuja himself proved to be an obstacle to reform. Once he was back in Kabul he resisted all changes the British hoped to implement. He opposed the creation of new army units because it meant that the distribution of patronage would pass from his hands to those of the British. He feared alienating Afghanistan's old elites because he identified with them. To a man whose entire experience revolved around trading favors and buying support, the corruption the British constantly condemned was the very glue that held his political world together.

The frustrated British soon began to work around Shuja and put their own people in charge of running the Afghan government. This led to greater effectiveness but at the cost of making the reforms seem less Afghan and more British. At the same time, the economic impact of the British occupation of Kabul had even wider ripples. So much outside money was pouring into the local economy to pay for the occupation that prices rose sharply. The Afghans accused the British of enriching the grain merchants, starving the poor, and reducing the chiefs to poverty. The old social hierarchy was also upended as money and influence flowed to those who profited from the British presence and away from those who were victims of their reorganization. The infamous complaint that the British fostered immorality and prostitution among the women of Kabul was hardly surprising in a city awash in cash and beyond the control of traditional authorities.[27]

Still, the country was at peace and the British remained confident it would stay that way since the opposition to their changes was divided and unorganized. Conservative calls to preserve the old against the new resonated powerfully with those who had seen their privileges and authority diminish at the hands of a foreign power, but the modernization of the Afghan government would probably have proceeded successfully despite their opposition.

The southern Durrani aristocrats were not in a good position to resist because their power came from access to the very state patronage that was being stripped from them. The independent eastern Ghilzai tribal chieftains appeared satisfied with the subsidies the British provided them, and payments to the mullahs in Kabul undercut the unity of the clergy. Other parts of the country, such as Herat, Mazar-i-sherif, the Hazarajat, and even Kandahar, took little interest in Kabul politics of any sort, since people there barely thought of their regions as part of Afghanistan.

What tipped the balance against the British in Kabul was a demand to cut costs there: In London the euphoria that greeted British successes in Afghanistan soured when the price tag became clear. Although its own occupation of the country consumed the bulk of the money the British were spending in Afghanistan, the planned savings targeted the much smaller sums paid directly to the Afghans. Payments to the Ghilzai tribal chiefs were sharply reduced in the summer of 1841. They reacted in fury by cutting off the roads to the east, and their hostility was shared by the grape-growing Tajik villages north of Kabul, who were the primary targets of the more efficient tax system. When the stipends for mullahs were eliminated in Kabul, they joined in the attacks on the government as a tool of the infidels. A murderous riot in Kabul exploded into an insurgency that laid siege to the British cantonment.

Bad leadership and poor grasp of the deteriorating situation led to the destruction of the entire expeditionary force in Kabul in January 1842. Although Shuja had been criticized as a puppet ruler, the belief in his traditional right to rule was so strong that he survived the destruction of his British backers. While his alliance with the British may have been unpopular, it did not affect his political legitimacy since a king cannot be a traitor to himself. For the next few months Shuja played a double game of publicly supporting the jihad while privately urging the British to return to Kabul as soon as possible. His fatal misstep was in agreeing to leave the safety of the palace in April to meet with the insurgents who had promised to support him. Within hours he was dead, a victim of assassination. Murder of an Afghan ruler was not unusual, but killing him for being out of step with popular opinion was. From that time forward, Afghan rulers would have to take nationalist and religious sentiments into account when making policy.

The insurgency against the British was the first in Afghanistan's history. Whole sections of the Afghan population that had previously been excluded from politics now fought against the British in a national cause, even if they had not conceived of it as such. One reason they were able to do this was that there was a revolution in the technology and economics of warfare. The easy availability of cheap muskets, and later rifles, allowed the people in the margins to participate in war in a far more effective and dangerous manner than in the past.[28] As Rudyard Kipling observed in an often-quoted line from "Arithmetic on the Frontier":

> A scrimmage in a Border station
> A canter down a dark defile
> Two thousand pounds of education
> Drops to a ten-rupee *jezail*.[29]

Such tactics were hallmarks of a classic guerrilla war strategy in which the aim was to make it more costly for the invader to continue the occupation than to leave. The British were driven from Afghanistan by the setbacks suffered at the hands of such irregulars, not because they lost pitched battles with regular armies. To prove this point the British returned to Kabul in fall 1842 to take revenge and they easily defeated every Afghan force that resisted them.

The political consequences of the First Anglo-Afghan War were profound and long-lasting, but the lessons that the British, the Durrani elite, and the Afghan people drew from it were quite different. It made the British wary of considering future direct occupations of Afghanistan, even with the cooperation of client rulers. At the very least, it would demand a military commitment far out of proportion to the perceived value of the country. This strengthened those factions who favored a more indirect approach, in which British India would control Afghanistan's external affairs without actually occupying it, through the support of compliant Durrani amirs. The failure of a Second Anglo-Afghan War (1878–80) seemed to prove their point. It also had an impact in their thinking about how to organize India's Northwest Frontier Province. While the cities and plains fell under direct British rule, the tribes in the hinterland were left to rule themselves, although their territories remained under British sovereignty.[30]

This was a style of rule, continued by Pakistan after 1947, that would have been familiar to the Mughals or even ibn Khaldun. While no one ever accused British India of being a failed state, even at the height of its imperial power, the raj understood that in some cases the cost of extending direct state power did not repay the trouble of doing so.

The Durrani dynasty that ruled Afghanistan drew a different set of lessons. The success of the rural insurgency meant that its ruler needed to redefine his own political legitimacy in the eyes of his own people in a way that would command more popular support; otherwise he too might fall victim to the same types of uprisings that had driven the British from the country. As a result, rulers began to portray themselves to the Afghan people as the necessary preservers of the nation's independence and Islamic religious identity against potential aggression by both the British raj and czarist Russia. The second lesson they drew was that the Afghan state and military needed to be much stronger to maintain their grip on power. They moved away from the traditional "live and let live" policy of noninterference in local affairs and began relying much more on military force.[31]

This policy culminated in the state-building policies of Amir Abdur Rahman (1880–1901), who used military force to subjugate all parts of the country to his direct rule for the first time in Afghanistan's history.[32] Future rulers would use his level of control as a benchmark for their own policies. Afghan rulers achieved this state-building success by getting international powers to fund and equip their armies. This began after the First Anglo-Afghan War, when rulers in Kabul convinced the British that they needed to provide such assistance to make their states stronger. Otherwise, they would be unable to prevent the supposedly rebellious Afghan people from constituting a serious frontier problem for India.

The brilliance of this strategy was that the amirs would receive payments to keep themselves in power while keeping the British out of the country. In the absence of foreign forces to unite against, Afghan governments had little trouble suppressing or co-opting nascent insurgencies. Afghan rulers used a similar strategy to maintain the country's independence. It was British fear of the czarist Russians that preserved Afghanistan's independence as a buffer state between the two rival empires in the nineteenth century. But Afghan rulers were quick to change with the times and take advantage of new international big-power rivalries. In the twentieth century they would play off rivalries between the Germans and British from 1914 to 1945 and then the Soviets and Americans in the post-1945 era.[33]

For the Afghan people, the First Anglo-Afghan War was a demonstration of their new political power. Ordinary Afghans had taken a decisive role in national politics and proved, for the first time, their ability to remove a government. Because they could not see themselves as potential rulers of the country, however, leaders of insurgencies never attempted to replace the old Durrani elite, or even force it into a power-sharing relationship. Instead, they continued to see themselves as mere allies of existing Durrani factions whose members they appointed as the leaders of their struggle. The fact that the clergy had framed their opposition to the British in terms of a religious jihad against non-Muslims reinforced this attitude but the clerics did not seek to change the structure of the Afghan government.

Afghanistan's dynastic rulers therefore valorized the legitimacy of popular revolts against outsiders in religious and national terms, while condemning as treasonous and illegitimate any revolts against their own governments. A 1929 insurgency against the reforming King Amanullah drove him from his throne, but the rebels could not overcome the belief that rulers should be chosen only from the established set of Durrani royal clans. Therefore, a collateral line restored the Durrani grip on power a year later. It was not until 1978 that a communist coup ended 230 years of that dynasty's control of Afghanistan.

In late 1979, when the Soviet invasion sparked Afghanistan's largest and most long-lasting insurgency, it mobilized so many groups that had previously been excluded from power that the old system collapsed in its wake. This destroyed the traditional structure of government, and in the aftermath of that regime's collapse in 1992, Afghanistan entered a period of civil war in which there was no agreement about what type of government Afghanistan should have or who had the right to rule it.

When the United States entered Afghanistan in 2001 after the defeat of the Taliban, it and the international community gave priority to establishing a stable government in Kabul. Its Afghan interlocutors used the opportunity to lobby for a highly centralized government. They argued that without firm control from the center, Afghanistan would split apart because of ethnic and regional differences. In fact, no faction had ever proposed dividing the country on ethnic or regional lines, although during the civil war they had effectively become autonomous.

With strong international backing, however, the regime led by Hamid Karzai pushed through a highly centralized constitution that vested almost all power in the president and offered little or nothing in the way of local autonomy. This was hardly surprising since the 2004 constitution was based on the one created by King Zahir Shah in 1964. The enthusiasm for restoring a highly centralized government was confined to the international community and the Kabul elite that ran it. Other Afghans saw such governments as the source of the country's past problems. Critics contended that decentralization better suited Afghanistan because such governments had so badly neglected the rest of the country. The nondemocratic regimes that had ruled Afghanistan previously saw this as an acceptable price for the greater political control it gave them, particularly by preventing the reemergence of powerful regional elites, which had characterized Afghan politics before 1880. But the impact of twenty-five years of warfare changed this situation.[34]

Regions wanted a direct choice in how they were to be governed at the local level. The international community saw assertions of such regional autonomy as signs of disorder that needed to be curbed. They dismissed decentralization proponents as supporters of warlords who would bring the country to ruin. In fact, establishing governmental order and services by region, rather than centrally from Kabul, had considerable merit. It would have proven more effective and given people more of a stake in local administration. In addition, it avoided the risk that if a highly centralized government faltered, the consequences would be nationwide.

Although a flawed structure might succeed if run by a talented leader, a fragile state could not easily survive with a badly designed government in the hands of a poor leader. This is unfortunately what the Afghans experienced under Karzai's presidency. Since Afghans judged the legitimacy of a state by its actions rather than the process that created it, his government's failures have had significant consequences.

Lessons from the Past

Looking back at Afghanistan's history, two lessons can be drawn that remain applicable to the country's current difficulties. First, Afghan society is still sharply divided by level of economic development and cultural values between what ibn Khaldun identified as sedentary civilizations and desert civilizations, and the low level of Afghanistan's economic development and the weaknesses of its governments have preserved that distinction. The values, social structures, and attitudes toward governmental authority between the two have remained quite distinct. During the twentieth century this division became sharper when modernizing governments in Kabul attempted to use state authority to transform Afghan society.

The desire to establish strong state institutions, by foreign armies coming into Afghanistan and Afghan regimes in Kabul, should be evaluated in light of a second lesson from Afghan history: Strong centralization of power in Kabul creates a backlash against any government there because it ignores the historic ability of people to govern themselves. By the time governments in Kabul recognize the need for a more nuanced approach to governance, the political situation is often too dire to retrieve. To the extent that Kabul governments made themselves the champions of a secular state that had the power to enforce its will nationwide, they generated an opposition that seized upon the banner of Islam and the defense of rural values as their platform. The first Afghan insurgency against the British, in 1841, was provoked by fears of such changes and set the template for future wars, at first only against foreigners but later against activist Afghan regimes as well. These were wars in which neither side seemed capable of winning a decisive victory. Those who sought to transform Afghanistan were never able to displace their opponents permanently, but those who resisted change found they could not keep Afghanistan frozen in time either. With particular intensity during the twentieth century, Afghan regimes with opposed ideologies replaced one another in an ever more violent manner. Each began with the confident illusion that its new policies would finally break the old cycle, only to have its world collapse when it fatally underestimated the strength of the opposition. Foreign armies in Afghanistan followed a similar trajectory. All entered Afghanistan intoxicated by high expectations of quick transformations of the country in their own image. All left Afghanistan more sober, far less idealistic, and content to let the Afghans handle their problems in their own way.

The basic mistake of state-builders was to ignore the distinction between government and governance. Government is the action of ruling, the continuous exercise of state authority over the population it governs. Governance is the manner in which communities regulate themselves to preserve social order and maintain their security, and this can be done in the absence of state authority. While governments in the developed world are the unquestioned suppliers of governance to their local communities, this has not been the case historically in Afghanistan. Here, adequate local governance in the absence of formal government institutions was the norm rather than the exception. Local populations expected, where possible, to solve their own problems through mediation and arbitration conducted by people of their own choosing.

Successful regimes in Afghanistan recognized this reality by devolving considerable informal decision-making power to local communities, letting them solve their own problems so that the state did not have to intervene. In return, local communities recognized the sovereignty of the Afghan national state and did not challenge its legitimacy. This compromise approach worked because communities in rural areas that resisted the Kabul government's attempts to interfere in their affairs never rejected the need for governance. They just believed that their own informal institutions better maintained long-term local order than any distant government could.

As significantly, all communities in Afghanistan, even those most insistent on preserving their own autonomy, accepted the need for an Afghan government in Kabul that could take on the higher-level responsibilities that require a state structure. These include preserving internal security, protecting the country from hostile neighbors, and negotiating on the nation's behalf for benefits from the larger international community. Those governments that understood this worked best, those that ignored it fared badly.[35]

This question will be reopened in 2014 when, according to the Afghan constitution, President Karzai must relinquish his office. While Karzai has always opposed such decentralization, his view might change significantly when he considers the implications of having someone else wield the same strong executive power that is currently his alone. Of course, if Karzai attempts to maintain the status quo by refusing to relinquish his office, then Afghan politics may take a different turn. While all previous Afghan rulers have assumed the office was theirs for an unlimited period, political reality has proved otherwise. Since the peaceful death of Amir Abdur Rahman in 1901, every succeeding Afghan head of state has either been assassinated or driven into exile.

Notes

1 For a detailed description and more complete timeline, see Louis Dupree, *Afghanistan* (Princeton, NJ: Princeton University Press, 1980).

2 Rose L. Greaves, "Themes in British Policy towards Afghanistan in Its Relation to Indian Frontier Defence, 1798–1947," *Asian Affairs* 24, no. 1 (1992): 30–46.

3 Artemy Kalinovsky, *A Long Goodbye: The Soviet Withdrawal from Afghanistan* (Cambridge, MA: Harvard University Press, 2011).

4 Vartan Gregorian, *The Emergence of Modern Afghanistan: Politics of Reform and Modernization, 1880–1946* (Stanford, CA: Stanford University Press, 1969).

5 Stephen Harper, Canadian Prime Minister, interviewed by CNN, March 2, 2009, http://edition.cnn.com/TRANSCRIPTS/0903/01/fzgps.01.html.

6 Asraf Ghani and Clare Lockhart, *Fixing Failed States: A Framework for Rebuilding a Fractured World* (Oxford, UK: Oxford University Press, 2008).

7 Hasan Kakar, *Afghanistan: A Study in Internal Political Developments, 1880–1896* (Kabul, Afghanistan: Punjab University Press, 1971); Kakar, *A Political and Diplomatic History of Afghanistan, 1863–1901* (Leiden: Brill, 2006).

8 Leon B. Poullada, *Reform and Rebellion in Afghanistan, 1919–1929* (Ithaca, NY: Cornell University Press, 1973); Senzil K. Nawid, *Religious Response to Social Change in Afghanistan, 1919–29: King Aman-Allah and the Afghan Ulama* (Costa Mesa, CA: Mazda Publishers, 1999).

9 Martin Ewans, *Conflict in Afghanistan: Studies in Asymmetric Warfare* (London: Routledge, 2005), 79–219; Ali Jalali, *The Other Side of the Mountain: Mujahideen Tactics in the Soviet-Afghan War* (Quantico, VA: US Marine Corps, 1999).

10 Ibn Khaldun, *The Muqaddimah: An Introduction to History*, ed. N. J. Dawood, trans. Franz Rosenthal (Princeton, NJ: Princeton University Press, 1969).

11 Khaldun, *Muqaddimah*, 91–123.

12 This remains true in rural Afghanistan today. Thomas Barfield, "Culture and Custom in Nation-Building: Law in Afghanistan," *University of Maine Law Review* 60, no. 2 (2008): 348–73.

13 David Edwards, *Heroes of the Age: Moral Fault Lines on the Afghan Frontier* (Berkeley: University of California Press, 1996), 63–64.

14 Khaldun, *Muqaddimah*, 122.

15 Khaldun, *Muqaddimah*, 108–9, 263–66.

16 Ewans, *Conflict in Afghanistan*; Stephen Tanner, *Afghanistan: A Military History from Alexander the Great to the Fall of the Taliban* (New York: Da Capo Press, 2002).

17 Bernt Glatzer, "War and Boundaries in Afghanistan: Significance and Relativity of Local and Social Boundaries," *Weld des Islams* 41, no. 30 (2001): 379–99.

18 Johannes Humlum, *La géographie de l'Afghanistan; tude d'un pays aride* (Copenhagen: Gyldendal, 1959), 166, 203–4.

19 Anne Lambton, *State and Government in Medieval Islam: An Introduction to the Study of Islamic Political Theory* (Oxford, UK: Oxford University Press, 1981), 19–20, 249–50.

20 Aziz Al-Azmeh, *Muslim Kingship* (London: I. B. Taurus, 2001), 136, 150.

21 Gilles Kepel, *Fitna: Guerre au Coeur de L'Islam* (Paris: Gallimard, 2004).

22 Thomas Hobbes, *The Leviathan*, ed. Michael Oakeshott (New York: Touchstone, 1651/2008).

23 Vasili V. Barthold, *Turkistan Down to the Mongol Invasion* (London: Gibb Memorial Series, 1968), 291.

24 The classic work (from a British perspective) remains John William Kaye, *History of the War in Afghanistan*, 3 vols. (London: Bentley, 1857), although the war has been taken up in scores of others.

25 On Dost Muhammad and the details of intra-Afghan struggles for power, see Christine Noelle, *State and Tribe in Nineteenth-Century Afghanistan: The Reign of Amir Dost Muhammad Khan (1826–1863)* (Richmond: Curzon, 1997).

26 Malcolm Yapp, "The Revolutions of 1841–42 in Afghanistan," *Bulletin of the School of Oriental and African Studies* 27(2): 339.

27 Yapp, *Bulletin*, 341; Shah Mahmoud Hanifi, *Connecting Histories in Afghanistan* (Stanford. CA: Stanford University Press, 2008), 77–94.

28 Compare to Rudi Matthee, *Unwalled Cities and Restless Nomads: Firearms and Artillery in Safavid Iran, in Safavid Persia: The History and Politics of an Islamic Society*, ed. Charles Melville (London: I. B. Tauris, 1996), 389–416.

29 Rudyard Kipling, *Departmental Ditties, Barrack-room Ballads, and Other Verses* (New York: United States Book Company, 1890), 212. A *jezail* was a locally produced Afghan musket.

30 Charles Miller, *Khyber, British India's Northwest Frontier: The Story of an Imperial Migraine* (New York: Macmillan, 1977).

31 Thomas Barfield, "Problems in Establishing Legitimacy in Afghanistan," *Iranian Studies* 37, no. 3 (2004): 263–93.

32 Hasan Kakar, *Government and Society in Afghanistan* (Austin: University of Texas Press, 1979).

33 Thomas Barfield, *Afghanistan: A Cultural and Political History* (Princeton, NJ: Princeton University Press, 2010), 64–225.

34 Thomas Barfield, "The Roots of Failure in Afghanistan," *Current History* 107 (December 2008): 410–17.

35 Thomas Barfield and Neamatollah Nojumi, "Bringing More Effective Governance to Afghanistan: 10 Pathways to Stability," *Middle East Policy* 17, no. 4 (2010): 40–52.

CHAPTER 4

America's Longest War

Hy Rothstein

"When you are in a hole and want to get out, stop digging," the saying goes. The history of US strategy in Afghanistan, after the fall of the Taliban, is largely one of digging a deeper hole. The brilliant initial success that resulted in the collapse of the Taliban regime and pushed al-Qaeda into hiding was followed by eight years of inept policy and strategy. As a result, operations on the ground could not produce lasting improvements commensurate with the investment of American blood and treasure.

Remarkably, the "digging" stopped sometime in late summer 2010 and the climb out of the hole began. The turnabout has been dramatic and swift. Why did it take so long to get on the right track? This chapter hypothesizes that the appropriate mix of persuasion and coercion ("carrots and sticks") necessary to succeed in counterinsurgency warfare eluded the United States until the summer of 2010. The civilian and military leaders directing the war effort grossly misunderstood the nature of this special kind of warfare. Finally, things that seem too good to be true require a sober examination, not unquestioning acceptance, especially when so much is at stake. These are the issues upon which this chapter is based.

In the Beginning—Unorthodox Warfare

The events surrounding September 11, 2001, resulted in the president of the United States asking his secretary of defense what could immediately be done to respond forcefully to al-Qaeda's attacks on America. President Bush made it clear that he wanted to inflict pain and destruction upon those responsible for the attacks, nothing more. Al-Qaeda was the target. And since the Taliban-led government of Afghanistan harbored the terrorists and refused to turn Osama bin Laden and the al-Qaeda leadership over to the United States, they would also have to pay the price.[1]

While it was necessary to go after the Taliban, our invasion of Afghanistan unintentionally and inextricably linked the Taliban to al-Qaeda for the duration. To a large extent, the United States lost sight of the fact that the Taliban was not actively involved in 9/11. This quandary was somewhat simplified by noting the relationship between the Taliban-led Afghan government and the al-Qaeda terrorist organization: The Taliban openly supported al-Qaeda and it was impossible (at least in 2001) to clearly separate Taliban military forces from al-Qaeda fighters. But still, it was al-Qaeda that was responsible for attacking the United States. The Taliban was never a direct threat to US interests. And now, with al-Qaeda essentially gone from Afghanistan, the fight there continues almost solely against the Taliban.[2]

On October 7, 2001, President Bush ordered military strikes against the Taliban and al-Qaeda. After fourteen days of "strategic" bombing, the Taliban still hung on to power. Only after US Special Forces teams assisted the anti-Taliban Northern Alliance by delivering food, ammunition, medical supplies, and winter gear—as well as by fighting at their side—did the momentum shift in favor of the United States. For the first time, air strikes were directed by Special Forces teams against Taliban military and al-Qaeda forces on the ground in support of a Northern Alliance ground offensive. The results were impressive. This unorthodox campaign that linked US Special Forces and the Afghan Northern Alliance on the ground with US air power resulted in every major city falling by early December 2001. The Taliban and al-Qaeda had been crushed by an effective display of power.[3]

This striking result was not the product of a blueprint put together by military leaders; it was the brainchild of the CIA's counterterrorism chief, Cofer Black.[4] While some people may find it odd that the military didn't develop the concept for the invasion of Afghanistan, those who are more familiar with the dissimilar cultures in the various agencies of the US government are not surprised. Gen. Tommy Franks, the commander of US Central Command (USCENTCOM), told the secretary of defense that it would take months to draw up plans and deploy enough forces for an invasion of Afghanistan. For the president and the secretary of defense, this would not do. The CIA's culture is more conducive to moving fast with limited forces and accepting greater risk.[5] Still, all during the swift-moving campaign that decimated the Taliban and al-Qaeda, the Pentagon was developing contingency plans to Americanize ground operations by putting fifty thousand troops into Afghanistan. As the Taliban and al-Qaeda dispersed and began to organize an insurgency, the US military quickly responded as if the emerging threat were conventional. The US response was exactly the opposite of what it should have been.[6]

The US Military Gets Traction

US military leaders wanted to "recover" from the unorthodox nature of the initial and successful phase of the war and get on with the business of waging the type of war that was more comfortable and familiar to them. Large combined and joint headquarters were formed and a campaign plan was created to help rid Afghanistan of Taliban, al-Qaeda, and other threats.

While conventional forces mounted a rolling series of security operations that temporarily suppressed the enemy, there was a growing awareness of the need to shift from an enemy-centric strategy to a population-centric strategy.[7] Accordingly, the *written* campaign plan was gradually transitioned away from recognizable combat operations.[8] Secretary of Defense Donald Rumsfeld reinforced this idea during a visit to Kabul in May 2003, when he said: "We have concluded we're at a point where we clearly have moved from major combat activity to a period of stability and stabilization and reconstruction activities. The bulk of the country today is permissive, it's secure."[9]

Rumsfeld's comment is instructive. His first sentence reveals the direction that coalition operations should have taken but didn't (in spite of the updated campaign plan), while his second sentence accurately describes a level of security that was going to dramatically change for the worse. The failure to adequately attend to stabilization and reconstruction issues caused the gradual and significant deterioration of security. The only logical conclusion is that those in charge underappreciated the requirement to secure the villages in order to preclude the Taliban from having the option to return.

The official US Army history of the war describes the evolving recognition of the requirement to develop Afghan security forces and to deliver services to the population in rural areas as key to legitimizing the fledgling Afghan central government.[10] The official history acknowledges the difficult problems in creating a modern, professional army. However, it neglects to mention the US military's revealed preference for sustaining combat operations designed to root out Taliban and al-Qaeda fighters over developing local capacity, a key component of any exit strategy.

Organizing to Build Afghan Security Forces

The organization that emerged to create the Afghan National Army (ANA) can best be described as a conglomeration of "pick-up" teams. The US Headquarters (OMC-A), which was understaffed itself, was ultimately asked for assistance from coalition allies to train an Afghan army. The British were asked to train noncommissioned officers (NCOs). The French army began to conduct officer training. Contingents from the Romanian, Bulgarian, and Mongolian armies provided instruction on how to operate and maintain Soviet-designed weapons and equipment.[11] Initially, US National Guard and Reserve units provided individuals for mobile teams that would be responsible for advanced training, advising, and employing Afghan units. US Special Forces, whose comparative advantage for training foreign forces is well recognized, steered clear of this important training mission for the most part. The US military simply did not seriously attend to the business of training the ANA. This important job was essentially "contracted out."

The Afghans also contributed to this inefficient and ineffective effort to create an ANA. Provincial strongmen would not send qualified men to Kabul for training; doing so would undermine their own power. The result was that the first battalions of the ANA completed training at about half strength. Worse was the attrition inside the initial battalions: desertion rates further rendered the ANA incapable of mounting combat operations.[12]

The Return of the Taliban

The US military's preference for combat operations over what Secretary Rumsfeld called stabilization and reconstruction activities, coupled with a weak Afghan effort to create a competent ANA, facilitated the Taliban's return. The Taliban, which was defeated and in disarray in 2002, began to regroup by 2003 and would undo much of what US troops and their coalition partners had accomplished during the initial phase of the war.[13] Some analysts suggest that the war in Iraq and the associated shift in priority led to the return of the Taliban. This explanation is convenient, but the Taliban was in such a state of panic and confusion in 2002 that securing the countryside would have been met with little, if any, opposition. Simply stated, much of Afghanistan was ripe for reestablishing traditional governance and security structures once the Taliban was out of the way. A modest amount of US assistance could have facilitated this and inoculated the population, politically and physically, from future Taliban encroachment. However, this was no longer the case when the Obama administration conducted its assessment of the war in March 2009. Obama's surge of additional troops to secure Afghanistan would not have been necessary during the first several years of the war.

War in Afghanistan: 2009

Between 2003 and 2009, the focus of US foreign and military policy was in Iraq. Accordingly, Afghanistan was a secondary theater in terms of both physical resources furnished and high-level attention from Washington. Lack of resources and attention were not the proximate causes of the return of the Taliban, but the deteriorating situation was masked by the scale of the fighting in Iraq.

In March 2009, the Obama administration announced a new strategy to disrupt, dismantle, and defeat al-Qaeda and deny terrorists the use of safe havens in either Afghanistan or Pakistan. The strategy called for properly resourcing the war and refocusing civilian and military efforts to make them mutually reinforcing. The priorities for the overall counterinsurgency (COIN) campaign would be security, governance, and reconstruction and development. The focus of US forces would be first, to provide security for the Afghan people, and second, to train Afghan security forces to ultimately take responsibility for security. This "clear, hold, and build" framework would have unambiguously stated "measures of effectiveness" to periodically evaluate progress.[14]

By April 2009, the security situation continued to deteriorate to a point that threatened the existence of the Karzai government. Insurgent attacks on coalition forces were increasing. Equally important was the fact that the Taliban's efforts to control the population through influence and intimidation were succeeding. Insurgent-initiated attacks were up 57 percent and US personnel killed in action increased by 24 percent from the previous year.[15] The Brookings Institute Afghan Index estimates that the number of Taliban in Afghanistan increased from less than three thousand in 2004 to roughly thirty thousand in 2010.[16]

In early May 2009, at a hastily convened Pentagon news conference, Secretary of Defense Robert Gates announced: "We have a new strategy, a new mission and a new ambassador. I believe that new military leadership is also needed." Gates had requested the resignation of the top American general in Afghanistan, Gen. David D. McKiernan, making a rare decision to remove a wartime commander. McKiernan was viewed as too cautious and conventionally minded. This act was partly in response to the Obama administration's increasing alarm about the country's downward spiral. Gates also concluded that "fresh thinking" and "fresh eyes" on Afghanistan were needed. The secretary recommended that President Obama replace McKiernan with a veteran Special Operations commander, Lt. Gen. Stanley A. McChrystal. His selection was welcomed by many, since it was felt that McChrystal was well-versed in the art of COIN warfare and that nontraditional leadership was required to win in Afghanistan.[17]

New Thinking and Old Realities

A lesson that seems to have been learned in both Iraq and Afghanistan is that overwhelming military force—shock and awe—fails to win the peace. This lesson is evident and reinforced in the new strategies, doctrines, policies, and countless official statements by military and civilian leaders. In fact, writing about population-centric warfare has become a cottage industry and has created a corps of self-proclaimed "COINISTAS." This implied self-criticism reveals an honest recognition that the US military was not adequately prepared to fight and win in Afghanistan and Iraq in 2001 and 2003. This new thinking also reveals a profound misunderstanding of COIN warfare that can result in defeat.[18]

Looking for Love in All the Wrong Places

Although the realization that the United States was losing the tenuous peace in Afghanistan culminated with the relief of General McKiernan, the military knew for some time that things were not going well. It reached out to civilian agencies and academics (and in particular anthropologists) to help decode the "human terrain." Human Terrain Teams became embedded with combat forces in an attempt to help field units understand local culture. Provincial Reconstruction Teams consisting of military, diplomatic, and development personnel worked together to improve life in Afghanistan for its people. The "softer side of COIN" became internalized doctrine for US troops. At some level the goal was to create renaissance men and women with cultural knowledge and language skills sufficient to interact with and influence the people of Afghanistan. While these efforts are commendable, it is not clear that they made any difference toward achieving desired outcomes.[19]

Three Cups of Tea Is Not Enough

A key theme in the new "COINISTA" thinking is that genuine compassion and empathy for the people are effective weapons against insurgents. Many refer to this as the "hearts and minds" concept of counterinsurgency. The idea is that the act of engaging and developing amiable relationships with local populations will result in getting them to help coalition forces fight a war we assume they feel is theirs.

It is one thing to sit with local elders or children to try to gain a sense of what is important to them and what repels them. It is quite another matter to believe that sharing their tea, no matter how many cups, will result in a trusting relationship that is sufficient to lead an Afghan to tell any outsider about his son or uncle who meets at night with the Taliban.[20]

Drinking tea, playing soccer with children, showing family photos, or having friendly conversations about politics and religion can become almost intoxicating. It can also create a feeling of cultural savvy and professional accomplishment. No doubt, many American troops feel that they have created a bond with local leaders and as a result have developed insights and understanding about the motivations of Afghans. But who is gaining more insight and who is manipulating whom?

Education and intelligence often go hand in hand, but it would be wrong to conclude that the average, uneducated Afghan can be manipulated by the infinitely better educated American. In fact, Afghans increasingly have the advantage. Afghans are a permanent fixture on their landscape. Americans may spend a year in a particular area trying to build sufficient rapport to change how an Afghan behaves. The reality is that the Afghan sees many Americans and learns how to get what he wants. He is not the one who needs to build rapport. Therefore, the Afghans have the advantage. There is nothing inherently nefarious about this. It is a natural element of human interaction. What are the possible costs associated with this reality?

Major Jim Gant, US Army Special Forces, wrote an influential paper called "One Tribe at a Time." The paper describes how a small, culturally attuned military unit could unite with an Afghan tribe to become a trusted and respected band of brothers to make a difference in the war against the Taliban. Gant describes the genesis of this relationship when a local tribal leader invited him and his Special Forces team to sit, eat, drink some tea, and talk. Gant and his team ultimately befriended the tribal leader and one tribal faction. He took sides without ever meeting the leader of the other tribe. Gant and his men succeeded in resolving the conflict in favor of their new friends. Perhaps the outcome was just; perhaps Gant was manipulated by a savvy local leader into upsetting the local balance that had evolved over generations.[21]

The point is not to discredit the efforts of Gant or others like him; Afghans are extremely pragmatic. It is important for Americans to remember that Afghans may not like the Taliban but they have more in common with them than with Americans. Just as important, Afghans know that long after the United States departs, some form of the Taliban will still exist. They understand conflict and the delicate power relationships that pervade their country. They will calibrate their options almost exclusively based on an accurate assessment of their interests. Coalition cordiality does not alter their interests or long-term behavior. Afghans know that coalition warmth is mostly instrumental, and though they may try to disguise it, coalition forces can't effectively hide this fact. The war in Afghanistan is not about persuasion or tea. It is, like all wars, about power, resources, and influence.[22]

The McChrystal Era

A gross misunderstanding of the essence of counterinsurgency reached its height under General McChrystal. To be fair, McChrystal inherited a very bad situation that resulted from many years of misdiagnoses and inappropriate remedies. Accordingly, his initial assessment of the situation was bleak. The general told President Obama that Afghanistan was on the brink of collapse and the United States was at the edge of defeat. McChrystal presented the president with a momentous policy decision that called for an extensive American commitment to include a permanent surge of as many as forty thousand additional troops. The goal seemed to be building a reasonably modern Afghan state where one never existed. The general essentially got the resources he asked for to fight the war.[23]

McChrystal not only wanted to change Afghanistan but he also aimed to radically change the way the coalition was waging war. His strategy had three fundamental principles: protect the Afghan people; build an Afghan state; and make friends with whomever you can, including insurgents. Finding, fixing, and killing Taliban became one of the least important tasks expected of coalition troops. A series of directives were issued to codify his strategy. For example, one directive instructed coalition troops about how to behave when they interacted with Afghans ("Think of how you would expect a foreign army to operate in your neighborhood, among your family and your children, and act accordingly"); another instructed on how to fight ("Think of counterinsurgency as an argument to win the support of the people"); and one even showed how to drive ("in ways that respect the safety and well-being of the Afghan people"). To reinforce his concept of counterinsurgency, McChrystal drastically restricted the circumstances under which air strikes would be permitted. When civilians might be in danger, coalition troops had to be at risk of being overrun before bombs could be dropped. Backing away from a firefight with the Taliban was preferable to potentially putting civilians in harm's way.[24]

The central epiphany of the "new" McChrystal COIN strategy was the importance of the population. This message comes through clearly in General McChrystal's initial assessment of the situation and his counterinsurgency guidance. The following quotes are taken from these documents:[25]

- "Protecting the Afghan people is the mission."
- "We need to understand the people and see things through their eyes."
- "While a conventional approach is instinctive, that behavior is self-defeating."
- "Think of counterinsurgency as an argument to earn the support of the people."
- "Our strategy cannot be focused on seizing terrain or destroying insurgent forces; our objective must be the population."
- "Pre-occupied with protecting our own forces, we have operated in a manner that distances us—physically and psychologically—from the people we seek to protect."

General McChrystal also emphasized the key role that coalition forces have in supporting the Afghan central government. The above quotes are symptomatic of the misunderstanding that exists in the US military about counterinsurgency warfare.

Karzai's Dozen

In 2009, President Karzai also weighed in to influence how the coalition would engage the enemy. While this is to be expected of a president of a sovereign nation, Karzai's motivation seemed questionable. He was justifiably concerned about the coalition causing unnecessary civilian casualties. The Taliban exploited civilian deaths through their own information and propaganda channels. However, the Taliban was killing far more civilians—in addition to beating and threatening others—but Karzai (and coalition information specialists) didn't exploit this fact. Some may argue that Karzai was more concerned about upsetting the Taliban than he was about enabling security forces to both protect the population and capture and kill the enemy.

"Karzai's Dozen" refers to Hamid Karzai and a list of rules put in place by General McChrystal to try to keep Afghan civilian casualties to a minimum. The troops describe the rules as a method to ensure cultural sensitivity in planning and executing operations. It has become part of the published rules of engagement (ROE), but these rules sometimes make a perilous mission even more difficult and dangerous. Many times insurgents have escaped because US forces are observing the rules. Most disturbing, the toll of US dead and injured increased. A partial list of these rules includes:

- No night or surprise searches.
- Villagers have to be warned prior to searches.
- Afghan army or police must accompany US units on searches.
- US soldiers may not fire at the enemy unless the enemy is preparing to fire first.
- US forces cannot engage the enemy if civilians are present.
- Only women can search women.
- Troops can fire at an insurgent if they catch him placing an improvised explosive device (IED), but not if insurgents are walking away from an area where explosives have been laid.

There is little doubt that many of these rules deprived coalition troops of significant tactical advantages.[26]

In his August 30, 2009, assessment of the situation in Afghanistan, General McChrystal partially justified these measures, saying that "the legitimacy of the NATO-led International Security Assistance Force (ISAF) had been severely damaged ... in the eyes of the Afghan people because of an over-reliance on firepower and force protection." There is some logic in the notion that counterinsurgency requires accepting some risk in the short term in order to ultimately prevail. However, one must remember that the people will calculate whom to side with based on which side is more likely to prevail. Unfortunately, these rules severely limited the coalition's ability and willingness to pursue the Taliban.[27]

Although General McChrystal was clear that nothing would ever prevent people from defending themselves, the rules as interpreted in the field had a pernicious effect on operations. It became increasingly difficult, if not impossible, for combat units to justify missions aimed at killing Taliban. Any operation that violated one of "Karzai's Dozen" underwent additional scrutiny. This resulted in a significant decrease in operations that were specifically designed to kill or capture the enemy. More disturbing was the fact that the well-understood ROE resulted in increased freedom of movement for the Taliban and a corresponding increase in the effectiveness of their operations. The initial surge simply provided the Taliban with more targets without increasing their risk of being engaged by coalition forces.[28]

One battalion commander attempted to mitigate the harmful effects of these policies. He wrote a commander's guidance that suggested the appropriate language to use in order to get a mission request approved. Combat patrols to find, fix, and destroy the enemy were referred to as "find, feel, influence, and understand" or "projecting and protecting patrols." Cordon and search operations were called "secure and engage the population."[29]

This extremely capable battalion commander was doing everything he could to support the policies of his headquarters and conduct the types of operations necessary to thwart the enemy. When elements of his battalion, engaged in a firefight, called for air support to destroy an approaching convoy of Taliban, unfortunately, the civilians accompanying the Taliban were also killed. The investigation of the event apparently focused more on the civilian casualties than on the circumstances surrounding the entire event. The incident ruined the careers of several highly competent people and sent a clear message to every US military commander that engagements with the enemy that result in civilian casualties are "career enders."[30]

One senior officer described this new way of war as "random acts of touching."[31] One coalition general officer actually recommended creating a combat medal for "courageous restraint." An International Security Assistance Force (ISAF) headquarters spokesman said that the idea of such a medal "is consistent with our approach."[32] The idea of such a medal reinforces the troubling rules of engagement.

In a society that understands and respects power, "random acts of touching" as a method to separate the population from the insurgents on one hand, and unite the people with their government on the other, only emboldened the Taliban. As a result, Taliban control of the Pashtun areas expanded and was strengthened in areas where it already existed. Coalition presence in an area actually resulted in increased Taliban repression against the population and more IEDs placed on and off the roads. In early 2010, on one relatively short section of "secured" road near Kandahar, fifteen IED strikes against coalition targets were recorded within forty-eight hours.[33]

All of this "restraint" resulted in mild-to-severe frustration on the part of many coalition leaders and troops. Everyone understood that the trust and support of the population was key. But Afghans knew the rules that the coalition was forced to play by and consequently thought the coalition was weak and the Karzai government weaker. Therefore, the genuine trust and support of the population that ISAF was counting on was not to be had.

The Myth of a Kinder, Gentler War

The humanistic value of the new American way of war—population-centric counterinsurgency—offers a seductive ideal for future warfare. On the surface it appears to adhere to a higher ethical standard. Some suggest that embracing the people in order to win their hearts and minds is the key to establishing the legitimacy of government. Others are more likely to embrace counterinsurgency as an instrument of statecraft, believing that national interests can be secured "on the cheap." Unfortunately, the history of counterinsurgency is not a story of war waged by benevolent soldiers providing for an enhanced quality of life to grateful natives. Counterinsurgency is a recurring tale of coercion and violence that inevitably reaches out and touches unarmed civilians. Civilians are ultimately the engine fuel of war (and peace). COIN experts correctly claim that controlling the population, by whatever means, is the key to success. However, counterinsurgency is, at its core, war, and attempts to portray COIN as benevolent and less violent than other modes of conflict are dangerously misleading.[34]

Counterinsurgency Truth

Historically, the degree of importance placed on the control of the population by the counterinsurgent cannot be overstated. As a result, defeating insurgents has been characterized more by exercising "authoritative control" than by winning "hearts and minds." The US military's first overseas venture into counterinsurgency was in the Philippines from 1898–1902. Initially the US military focused on legitimizing the Filipino government by restoring order through civic projects such as building schools and roads and providing health care and proper sanitation. But this policy of persuasion was not enough to overcome guerrilla resistance and the insurgency persisted and grew more cruel and bloody.[35] The United States dramatically shifted its approach, realizing that it could not offer adequate incentives to win the population's "hearts and minds," nor could it effectively protect the people from guerrilla retaliation. An aggressive coercive program ranging from the destruction of crops and property to resettling civilians by force into "protected zones" was implemented to separate the average Filipino from the insurgents. This program was successful, but costly, and resulted in an estimated three hundred thousand Filipino civilian deaths. As Kipling predicted, the Philippine War proved to be a "savage war of peace."[36]

The British counterinsurgency experience in Malaya is studied by defense professionals as a model of enlightened, population-centric war fighting. Sir Gerald Templer is credited with the successful outcome; and modern COIN advocates conclude that the conciliatory approach adopted by Templer after his arrival in 1952 proved decisive.[37] A closer look reveals that the British success necessitated the use of coercion against the civilian population together with civil action and amnesty programs. By the time Templer arrived in Malaya, the Chinese population had been separated from the insurgents by a draconian program consisting of mass arrests, the death penalty for carrying a weapon, food control, curfews, fines against communities as a form of collective punishment for individual infractions, detention without trial, deportations, and burning down the homes of communist sympathizers. Sir Harold Briggs, Templer's predecessor, instituted the forced resettlement of more than half a million ethnic Chinese. The stage for Templer's "hearts and minds" approach was preceded by a coercive trail of tears.[38]

The coercive policies enacted in the Philippines and Malaya were replicated on a grander scale by the French in Algeria. French excesses resulted in short-term military success, but ultimately proved politically disastrous and resulted in France's humiliating withdrawal. During the height of the Algerian insurrection the French military systematically tortured and executed insurgents. During the battle of Algiers, the decisive campaign of the war, an estimated 35 percent of the male population in the Casbah was arrested at some point and more than a million citizens were sent to "regroupment" camps.[39]

Violence and coercion in Vietnam never reached the same level as in the Philippines, Malaya, or Algeria. Still, the United States followed the edict about the necessity of separating the population from the insurgent. Early in the war, the US strategic hamlet initiative forcibly relocated rural civilians into "secure" villages. This relocation devastated local communities and sowed the seeds of deep-seated hatred toward American forces and the South Vietnamese government.[40]

Both Algeria and Vietnam provide similar lessons, and some that differ from the Philippine and Malayan cases. Vietnam reminds us of how difficult it is, especially for a democracy, to maintain public support for a protracted war. Another important lesson from Algeria and Vietnam is that the cause of the insurgent is simply more appealing than anything being offered by the counterinsurgents. Without a credible and compelling countercause that is embraced by the population, the effort is destined to fail.[41] Finally, these two conflicts highlight the constraints that liberal democracies must adhere to in such wars. American counterinsurgents simply cannot wallow in the same muck as the insurgent and expect a favorable political outcome.

Persuasion and Coercion in Counterinsurgency Warfare

The purpose of these examples is not to advocate for increased coercive policies or to suggest a future path for US COIN strategy. However, they do suggest the limitations of COIN strategies that cannot successfully separate civilians from insurgents.[42] To be clear, highly coercive practices today are not only unrealistic for the United States; they are also wrong. Nevertheless, all of the above cases show, to varying degrees, that both coercive and persuasive measures were equally necessary and were required to be synchronized to have positive effect. Until security forces are able to protect people who want protection from insurgent intimidation and control, little can be expected from programs designed to persuade via "carrots." Government forces must gain the upper hand militarily before acts of benevolence can sway civilians to openly side with the apparent victors. Persuading insurgents to surrender also calls for a clear understanding about the bleak future of the insurgent cause. Public support tends to follow rather than lead control, authoritive or otherwise.[43]

Climbing Out of the Hole

On June 23, 2010, President Obama relieved General McChrystal from his position as the top US commander in Afghanistan because of his connection to remarks belittling administration officials. Obama replaced him with General David Petraeus, who was the commander of United States Central Command. General McChrystal's tenure had lasted one year. The president also spoke to President Karzai to inform him of the decision. Interestingly, and despite the anger in the White House over McChrystal's comments, Karzai threw his full support behind McChrystal and warned that his departure could disrupt the US–Afghanistan partnership.[44]

News of McChrystal's dismissal and Petraeus's selection was met with surprise in Afghanistan, but also with a sense of relief that an experienced commander would take the helm. Petraeus was widely credited with turning around the Iraq war in 2007. Lawmakers were also uniformly happy with the president's choice to replace McChrystal. General Petraeus is not only a tested field commander but a skilled diplomat who understands the psychological and political elements of counterinsurgency. Such understanding is at the very heart of a military strategy that hinges on progress in governance and the real security needed to sustain military gains. Petraeus's confirmation on Capitol Hill was swift. More importantly, it refocused attention on aspects of counterinsurgency that had been absent from the fight for many years. General McChrystal's departure marked the first step in climbing out of the hole.

The urgency of the crisis for the Obama administration, brought about by the Taliban's progress and exacerbated by the relief of a wartime commander, afforded General Petraeus new opportunities that were unavailable to any of his predecessors. Petraeus would certainly benefit from the surge of troops requested by General McChrystal, but it is not clear whether the old blueprint for employing forces would have delivered a satisfactory return on investment had McChrystal remained in command.

In an article by General Petraeus titled "Counterinsurgency Concepts: What We Learned in Iraq," he reminds us that the emphasis on new ideas and programs designed to deliver better quality of life to Afghans and improve local governance cannot marginalize the very real need to relentlessly pursue the enemy, take away his safe havens, degrade his ability to plan, and ultimately cause him to run or reconcile.[45] This article recognizes that counterinsurgency requires properly integrating coercion and persuasion (or carrots and sticks) to achieve effects.

The New Strategy Up Close—Slow and Bloody Nation-Building

The testing of the new, highly aggressive approach would take place in Afghanistan's southern provinces of Kandahar, Kunar, and Helmand, which together account for over 60 percent of the violence that plagues the country.[46] The Arghandab Valley had been a staging area for insurgent attacks into Kandahar for a long time. This region gave birth to the Taliban and housed its most ardent supporters. As a result, the Taliban controlled the valley until late in 2010.[47]

The heaviest fighting since 2001 took place in this valley throughout the summer and fall of 2010. Security forces in the area increased dramatically: US forces were increased by twenty thousand; Afghan brigades were tripled from two to six; and Afghan police were increased by 30 percent.[48] The relentless pursuit of the enemy by the coalition paid off. By December it was not only possible, but relatively safe, to drive through the valley. The valley is now swarming with security forces who occupy a chain of outposts along the valley. Checkpoints are manned by alert, sharp-looking police officers.[49]

The result was remarkably low insurgent activity in southern Afghanistan, though commanders conceded this may have been partially due to the end of the fighting season and the onset of winter.[50] The success also did a great deal to alleviate the frustration that existed throughout the coalition, when engaging the enemy was hampered by both real and perceived constraints based on the ROE.

But something else was different that was part of this reversal of fortune. Perhaps it was a happy coincidence, but for the first time since 2002, the chain of command, from top to bottom, was intent upon pursuing the same goals. Priorities and purpose were synchronized and the necessary resources were in place to reverse the downward security spiral. Years of experience on the part of troops serving their third and fourth tours of duty came together with a senior commander who understood the coercive and persuasive dimensions of counterinsurgency. The effects achieved on the ground, though limited, were impressive considering the failures of the previous eight years. More importantly, the insurgents were now reacting to coalition actions for the first time. As a result, there was discord and uncertainty within the Quetta Shura, the Taliban's senior leadership body.[51]

The COIN Manpower Dilemma, the Limits of Coercion, and the Need for Local Defense

The new approach seemed to work in the Arghandab, but Afghanistan is a big place. Not all residents of the valley, and possibly only a small number, support the coalition. For the initial success of the new approach to have lasting effects, control over the population must be sufficient to prohibit the insurgents from remaining ensconced in the local communities. And if the success in the Arghandab is to be replicated elsewhere, more boots on the ground, beyond the US surge and projected growth of Afghan security forces, will be required. However, some of these "boots," perhaps most of them, could come from friendly Afghans, including "turned" insurgents, much as the war in Iraq benefited from tens of thousands of young soldiers who left the insurgency in favor of fighting on the side of government.

Force ratios for counterinsurgency warfare have been traditionally looked at in one of two ways: counterinsurgent-to-insurgent or counterinsurgent-to-population. Bernard Fall felt that a counterinsurgent-to-insurgent force ratio of 20:1 was reasonable to isolate and destroy insurgents. If the goal was simply stabilizing the threat, a 10:1 force ratio would be adequate. Fall's ratios pertain only to combat troops and do not account for the massive support structure the US military seems to require. Accordingly, if ten thousand insurgents are operating in Afghanistan, two hundred thousand combat troops would be required to isolate and destroy them. If combat forces comprise about 20 percent of the total force (a conservative figure in Afghanistan), then the total number of counterinsurgency forces comes to one million.[52]

Using the counterinsurgent-to-population ratio does not solve this manpower dilemma. The new US Army/Marine Corps counterinsurgency manual suggests twenty to twenty-five counterinsurgents for every one thousand residents. For Afghanistan's population of thirty million, 750,000 counterinsurgents would be required. When considering the standard tooth-to-tail ratio, the number is overwhelming and impractical.[53]

The difference between what the force ratios suggest and the total number of security forces now operating on the ground is significant. In the cases cited previously, the British, French, and Americans were able to mitigate the requirement for more boots on the ground through extremely harsh population-control measures that amounted to coercion. Today, using similar measures would be impossible and wrong. One logical way to solve the dilemma is to develop well-regulated local defense forces.

Local Defense in Afghanistan

Civil defense is not a new concept, even for the US military. The Marines' Combined Action Program (CAP) in Vietnam embedded marines in Vietnamese villages to live alongside villagers and security forces to provide them with training, equipment, and security. The program was one of the most successful of the war, enabling villages to establish control of their critical surrounding terrain. In El Salvador, US advisors pushed a civil defense program that became a "game changer." Local defense forces were trained, equipped, and certified by US Special Forces advisors in cooperation with regional military commanders. Attacks by insurgents on villages were pushed back by local forces and, when necessary, were reinforced by regular Salvadoran military units. Such successes alienated the insurgents and legitimized the central government. Fortunately, Afghanistan has a long history of grassroots, tribal-based community policing grounded in volunteerism.

The challenges of restoring a reasonable level of security to large parts of Afghanistan forced the coalition to turn to local armed groups. For a long time the coalition was reluctant to entertain such an approach because it looked too much like the independent militias that had challenged the state in the past. President Karzai, in particular, had vivid memories of the fighting by rival militias for control of Kabul after the Soviet withdrawal. The carnage inflicted by the militias was still fresh in the minds of Afghanistan's new leaders who took office in the wake of the American invasion at the end of 2001.[54] As a result, early initiatives to create local defense forces had mixed results.

The first official attempt to develop local forces after the Taliban's collapse was the Afghanistan National Auxiliary Police (ANAP), which was launched in

2006 by the Ministry of the Interior (MOI) and supported by the international community. Recruits were selected, trained, equipped, and deployed mostly in the southern provinces. Problems quickly emerged. Logistical support was almost nonexistent, the vetting of recruits was based on nepotism, command and control was troublesome, and the loyalty of the force was questionable. Contrary to the intent, this program was ill-suited for community policing and was shut down in 2008. Unfortunately, there was no serious effort made to learn from this experience before launching an "improved" version.[55]

The second program, also launched by the MOI and working almost exclusively with US Special Forces, was the Afghan Public Protection Program (AP3). This program was designed to extend the reach of the central government to the communities to provide stability and development through grassroots security forces. The test location for the program was in Wardak. Roughly eleven hundred men were recruited, mainly through direct patronage by elders, local power brokers, and well-known jihadi commanders, bypassing the intended shura system. The same shortcomings of ANAP plagued AP3. Not surprisingly, AP3 was not considered successful enough to replicate in other provinces.[56]

The next program was known as the Local Defense Initiative (LDI) and started discreetly in mid-2009. The LDIs were nonstandard and tailored to the particular circumstances of the different villages. Each village became a unique experiment in civil defense. The differences were so great that it is difficult to evaluate the program as a single initiative. The goal of LDIs was to secure local communities by giving responsibility and employment to village members to preclude them from providing support to the insurgents. The LDI was also charged with not allowing insurgents to live within their village. Working with US Special Forces, a few LDIs had some success in the Arghandab district; the results in other areas were less positive.[57]

There were problems with all these "local" initiatives. To begin with, they were top driven mostly by the US military. General McKiernan felt that a top-down approach to local defense was more appropriate to alleviate President Karzai's concerns. Even the US Embassy withheld cooperation and funding, sensing that the Afghan government was not genuinely behind developing local armed groups. But Karzai always had an effective mechanism to manage any US initiative for local defense. The Afghan president picks his police chiefs and provincial governors, who in turn handpick the district subgovernors. In effect, interference "from the top" disrupted and destroyed most of the program's intent.[58]

Village Stability Operations (VSO)—A Potential Game Changer

Hamid Karzai was able to interfere with the implementation of local defense programs, but his government and the coalition continued to have scant control in the rural towns where the Taliban insurgents ruled. Because the implementation of extreme population-control measures was not an option, local defense was still needed to reclaim the rural areas from the insurgents or secure the areas after conventional forces cleared them. In a welcomed step for the Obama administration, Karzai approved a new, US-backed plan in mid-July 2010, to create local defense forces across the country. Winning Karzai's approval was the top initial goal for General Petraeus, who had by then been in command for little more than a week.[59]

The latest incarnation of local security is Village Stability Operations (VSO). Following Afghan approval and support for the program, the Pentagon requested congressional approval to divert $35 million from the budget for Afghan security forces to form the new local groups. This plan differs from earlier ones in that local tribal leaders are expected to play a major role in shaping their force. More importantly, the US Special Forces teams responsible for implementing VSO understand the importance of ensuring that local tribal leaders are, in fact, local and recognized by the local population as the legitimate representatives of their communities. In previous efforts to revitalize local governance, shuras were "made up" of greedy power brokers whose sole aim was to receive the development benefits connected to local defense for their personal use. These "made up" shuras selected security forces based on patronage rather than competence or ties to the local community. This further undermined any bond between the people and their government.[60]

The purpose of VSO is that of previous efforts. It is supposed to be a grassroots counterbalance to the insurgents and fill a security vacuum in rural villages that the overstretched US and Afghan regular forces cannot reach. Development aid comes with security. Coalition leaders also hope that the program will incite rebellions against the Taliban. Some people also suggest that creating genuine local defense forces will force Kabul to pay more attention to what goes on in rural areas.[61]

This new program will use as many as ten thousand local policemen organized to defend their respective villages. They are trained by US Special Forces teams and paid approximately 60 percent of what official Afghan National Police earn. VSO has limited authorities. They are purely defensive and will not have any expeditionary capabilities. They have the authority to detain people temporarily but would then turn them over to established law enforcement or security forces.[62]

VSO is more refined than previous large-scale efforts. This true bottom-up approach is being counted on to make a significant contribution to securing the countryside against unwanted insurgent advances. Still, care must be taken not to inadvertently prop up warlords that are hated by the local population. The blueprint for VSO limits this possibility. Unfortunately, it also limits its potential long-term positive impact. Specifically, VSO is only a stopgap measure, intended to last about two years. Then, the most effective members of the local force would have the option of entering one of the permanent security forces and receiving additional training. Essentially, local defense by locals may have a very short life span.[63]

Even with these shortcomings, VSO has the potential to change the security dynamics in rural communities more than any previous program. VSO returns authority and accountability to actual local leaders whose legitimacy is based on what Afghans recognize—dynastic and religious roots. Additionally, resources are provided to enable communities to defend themselves and thereby determine their own futures. Taliban attacks on VSO communities have a high probability of backfiring and ultimately strengthening communities and motivating other villages to adopt VSO. The United States must be prepared to expand and sustain VSOs with or without consent or support from Kabul.

A Tale of Three Wars: The Good, the Bad, and the Ugly

VSO is the number-one priority for theater-level US Special Operations Forces. One senior commander said that the program is expected to play an essential role in achieving US strategic objectives. While expectations are high, others recognize the limitations of any individual initiative. There are no silver bullets. This reality becomes clear when you visit current and potential VSO locations and spend time listening and learning about whether a particular village wants the same thing that the US military is trying to sell. The three situations described below are located in southern Afghanistan.[1]

The Good

The good district governor is unequivocally pro-coalition and staunchly anti-Taliban. He is closely tied to Kabul but is a lifelong resident of his district. He fights and directs security forces to protect the population. Not surprisingly, he is well-respected. He also embraces VSO and as a result his district benefits from the development aid linked to self-defense. The governor counts on the material support provided by the US military.[64]

The Bad

When asked by a US Special Forces captain to adopt local defense during a shura, the village elder responded sharply. The elder wanted to know what the US military had against the Taliban. The elder informed the captain that "we are all Taliban" and taking up arms against his brothers was out of the question. He further stated that his area was quiet and safe before the US military established its outpost near his home; now IEDs could be found on the roads and firefights were frequent. The elder then urged the American officer to take his men and go away if he really wanted to bring peace to the area. It was clear that VSO would not be established in this area in the near future, nor would it likely ever.[65]

The Ugly

The US commander and his men operating in this location have perhaps the toughest assignment in the war. The police chief in this area seems to possess all the proper attributes of a close partner. He is aggressive, pro-coalition, anti-Taliban, and respected by the majority of the residents. He is also favorably disposed toward supporting VSO. However, a closer look at this individual reveals a darker truth. His relationship with and support for the coalition has made him extremely wealthy. He is connected in some way to all development projects in his area, taking a percentage of all contracts. He provides security for coalition forces in the area, also for a price. There are indications that he places IEDs in front of coalition convoys only to later identify the IEDs in order to demonstrate his worth. His anti-Taliban stand is limited to Taliban who are not members of his tribe. In other words, his politics are tribal, not anti-Taliban. Still, this police chief has earned the respect of most of his region's population because he does deliver law and order. He is also closely connected to President Karzai.[66]

These three different situations represent the somber challenges faced by the coalition. They also illustrate the limitations of VSO—ostensibly a key component in achieving US strategic objectives.

Conclusions

It is important to differentiate between *effects* and *outcomes*. The military has liberally used the word "effects" for decades. In fact, "effects-based operations" briefly formed a large part of strategic discussions—until the concept lost its cachet. Effects are generally short term and are brought about by concentrating resources in a specific location for a specific purpose. For example, the increased tempo of recent operations around the Taliban's stronghold of Kandahar has produced favorable effects. It is not clear that these positive effects persist when security forces depart.

"Outcomes" constitute a higher order of concern related to the above question. "Outcomes" are long lasting, durable, permanent effects that are self-sustaining. It is difficult to determine whether the recent significant progress is a case of the glass being half empty or half full. Almost everyone counsels that more time is needed for the current strategy to work. After all, it took until the middle of 2010 to come up with the proper resources and a coherent plan that blended persuasion and coercion appropriately. It is not clear that the current upbeat mood about the positive effects achieved in recent months is warranted or if they will produce the outcomes the United States seeks.

Lessons about Persuasion and Coercion

History reveals that states that strive to counter an insurgency tend to overestimate the impact of moderate, persuasive policies. Initial optimism eventually moves toward a more sober calculus of the need to go after the enemy ruthlessly. Unfortunately, the historical myopia of modern counterinsurgency doctrine almost resulted in disaster in Afghanistan. The seductive appeal of winning "hearts and minds" through a strategy that uses predominantly carrots rather than sticks is grossly misleading and dangerous.[67]

The "attack" on the village of Marjah in early 2010 was the high-water mark of this policy. Military leaders went to great lengths to make it clear that protecting civilian lives was more important than targeting the enemy. The military gave up the element of surprise by actually broadcasting plans to take the town. The results were best described by General McChrystal when he called Marjah "a bleeding ulcer." The Taliban controlled Marjah even during its occupation by US marines. But, as counterinsurgency expert David Galula once aptly pointed out, fear—not hope—is a greater motivator for a civilian population caught in the crossfire of war. And so the more humane approach tried by General McChrystal may simply have been too limited in its ability to instill the proper amount of fear. It was also inconsistent with the timeline for US military engagement in Afghanistan—which will likely see very limited numbers of American forces on the ground after 2014.[68]

Counterinsurgency requires a combination of positive and negative measures to suppress insurgents. There is no simple formula for fusing these two essential ingredients. Coercion alone is incompatible with American values, but without force there can be no lasting pacification. Recent attempts by new "COINISTAS" to reduce counterinsurgency's complexities to slogans such as "hearts and minds," "nation-building," "there is no military solution," and so on, is grossly misleading and makes counterinsurgency sound like a popularity contest. The reality is that persuasion and coercion are inextricably intertwined. Persuasion may ultimately prevail, but only when backed by adequate strength to enforce. It took nine years to come to this conclusion.[69]

The Limits of Village Stability Operations

VSO may be the last best hope for stabilizing Afghanistan. It has been referred to as "the second Afghan front." It recognizes that the Taliban's greatest advantage is their closeness to the population. VSO attempts to step in between the people and the Taliban. Its importance is highlighted by the amount of attention and resources diverted to the program. Great returns are expected from this investment.

Nevertheless, the tale of the "good, bad, and ugly" discussed above demonstrates the limitations of even the VSO approach. VSO is not viable everywhere and may never be. Furthermore, there are a limited number of US Special Forces teams available to ensure that VSO develops as a true local defense force. Additionally, VSO is perhaps a bit too hopeful about the impact of the development aid tied to local defense. Economic capitalism and political democracy are not sure remedies for embattled populations, especially in Afghanistan. Money and development projects are not likely to be decisive. Even benevolence represents a form of intervention. Furthermore, the push in the Pashtun south against the Taliban cannot lose sight of the fact that the Taliban are Pashtuns, mostly from the south. The idea that US troops can develop a counter-cause that prevails over Pashtun solidarity is far-fetched.

Finally, VSO has a built-in life span of only a few years—hardly enough to bridge the gap between current government capabilities to provide security in rural villages and what is actually needed. The United States must be willing to underwrite VSO (thus effectively undermining the central government in Kabul) for the program to be a game changer. In Afghanistan, perhaps more than any place else, all politics is local.

Overbuilding

Implied throughout this discussion is the extraordinary level of resources and effort being expended to prop up the Afghan government and security forces. We are building massive security structures in our own image with all the attendant equipment and administrative accoutrements. The fact that Afghanistan lacks a competent and respected central government and is therefore a poor setting for a successful counterinsurgency campaign is either underappreciated or deliberately ignored by those who are charged with developing state capabilities. The fact that the Taliban lacks sophisticated military capabilities also seems to have limited impact on the structures the United States is committed to build.

Creating Dependency and Counterinsurgency Effectiveness

A recent RAND Corporation study about how insurgencies end reveals something that seems counterintuitive—governments that receive no external support at all do better against insurgents. Once support is given it almost always creates a dependency on the external sponsor. Intervention can often bolster the insurgents' cause and undermine the government's credibility. Karzai himself has said that American dollars are the biggest source of corruption in Afghanistan, not the Afghan government. He may be half right.[70]

The list of positive contributions to the war effort by the Karzai government is short. Some people argue, quite convincingly, that Karzai is an impediment to progress. What is clear is that all the positive effects created in recent months are the direct product of US and allied efforts. Even the building, resourcing, payment for, and tactical employment of Afghan security forces is the result of outside intervention. While the capabilities of Afghan security forces slowly grow, there is no indication that the Afghan government is willing (even if it becomes capable) to sustain such massive infrastructure. We have created an Afghan security apparatus whose existence and employment is connected to a US life-support line. Senior Afghan officials themselves benefit materially from this lifeline. Stepping away from the current level of commitment will likely result in the collapse of this massive, yet fragile structure.

The current positive effects created by recent combat operations in southern Afghanistan have tended to reinforce the idea that US strategy is succeeding and that the Afghans will be ready to take over the responsibility for their own security in 2014. This success has ironically lessened the pressure on the Obama administration to bring the troops home prematurely. After all, for the first time in the war a coherent strategy, properly resourced and competently executed, is in place. Insurgents are being hunted and killed, significant progress in training Afghan security forces and police is evident, and the recruiting, training- and equipping of military and police units is ahead of schedule. But on almost every other front progress is harder to identify. Vast sums of money spent on development have produced modest effects. Government corruption fuels the insurgency and undermines the potential for an Afghan government ever to take competent charge of what is being built by the United States and its allies. In other words, for all the good that has been done, it may not matter in the long run. Leaders in Washington and military commanders in Kabul must remain wary of confusing short-term effects with the long-term outcomes that really matter.[71]

Notes

Andrew Bacevich suggested that the main title of this book be *America's Longest War*. I like it so much that I use it for the title of this chapter.

1 See Bob Woodword, *Bush at War* (New York: Simon & Schuster, 2002), 25, 43, 79–84, 139–43, and Hy Rothstein, *Afghanistan and the Troubled Future of Unconventional Warfare* (Annapolis, MD: Naval Institute Press, 2006), 4–10.

2 Leon Panetta, interviewed by Jake Tapper, *This Week*, June 27, 2010.

3 See Woodward, *Bush at War,* 202–10, and Rothstein, *Afghanistan and the Troubled Future,* 10–13.

4 See Woodward, *Bush at War,* 43–44.

5 It is important to note that although the CIA developed the initial plan to topple the Taliban, US military forces were used to carry out the plan.

6 Rothstein, *Afghanistan and the Troubled Future,* 4–7, 12–14.

7 Donald P. Wright et al., *A Different Kind of War* (Ft. Leavenworth, KS: Combat Studies Institute, 2010), 237.

8 There was no appreciable change to operations on the ground despite a changing campaign strategy.

9 Wright et al., *A Different Kind of War,* 237.

10 Ibid.

11 Ibid., 232.

12 Ibid., 230.

13 Ibid., 233.

14 US Department of Defense, *Report to Congress in accordance with the 2008 National Defense Authorization Act* (Section 1230, Public Law 110–181):*Progress Towards Security and Stability in Afghanistan* (Washington, DC: Government Printing Office, June 2009), 5.

15 Ibid.

16 The Brookings Institute, "Afghan Index, 29 March 2011," www.brookings.edu/~/media/Files/Programs/FP/afghanistan%20index/index20110329.pdf, accessed April 19, 2011.

17 Ann Scott Tyson, "Top U.S. Commander in Afghanistan Is Fired," *Washington Post,* May 12, 2009.

18 Michael Miklaucic, "The Tea Fallacy," *Small Wars Journal,* http://smallwarsjournal.com/blog/2010/03/the-tea-fallacy/, accessed January 15, 2011.

19 Ibid.

20 Ibid.

21 See Major Jim Gant, *One Tribe at a Time* (Los Angeles: Nine Sisters Imports, Inc., 2009); and Miklaucic, "The Tea Fallacy."

22 Miklaucic, "The Tea Fallacy."

23 Dexter Filkins, "His Long War," *New York Times Magazine,* October 18, 2009, 38.

24 Ibid., 42.

25 See Headquarters International Security Assistance Force Kabul Afghanistan, *ISAF Commander's Counterinsurgency Guidance Letter,* and Commander, NATO International Security Assistance Force, Afghanistan, US Forces Afghanistan, *Commander's Initial Assessment*, 30 August 2009.

26 See "U.S. Troops Battle both Taliban and Their Own Rules," *The Washington Times*, November 16, 2009, www.washingtontimes.com/news/2009/nov/16/us-troops-battle-taliban-afghan-rules/?page=1, accessed January 14, 2011; and troops interviewed by author, Afghanistan and Ft. Lewis, March and September 2010.

27 Commander NATO International Security Assistance Force, Afghanistan and US Forces Afghanistan, *Commander's Initial Assessment,* 30 August 2009, 2–10.

28 March and September interviews by author.

29 See SOTF-South Commander's Guidance Letter #2, 23 March 2010; and March interviews by author.

30 March interviews by author.

31 Ibid.

32 J. P. Freire, "NATO Rewarding 'courageous restraint' Awards," *Washington Examiner. Com,* May 9, 2010 http://washingtonexaminer.com/blogs/beltway-confidential/nato-rewarding-quotcourageous-restraintquot-awards, accessed May 13, 2011.

33 March interviews by author.

34 Michael A. Cohen, "The Myth of a Kinder, Gentler War," *World Policy Journal* (Spring 2010): 75.

35 Ibid., 78.

36 See Cohen, "The Myth of a Kinder," 78; and Brian McAllister Linn, *The Philippine War: 1899–1902* (Kansas: University Press of Kansas, 2000), 322–28.

37 See Cohen, "The Myth of a Kinder," 78–79; and Richard Stubbs, *Hearts and Minds in Guerrilla Warfare* (Singapore: Oxford University Press, 1989), 1–3, 5.

38 Stubbs, *Hearts and Minds,* 98–107.

39 See Cohen, "The Myth of a Kinder," 80; and Gen. Paul Aussaresses, *Battle of the Casbah* (New York: Enigma Books, 2002), 92–93.

40 See Cohen, "The Myth of a Kinder," 81; and Larry Cable, *Conflict of Myths* (New York: New York University Press, 1986), 196–99.

41 Cohen, "The Myth of a Kinder," 82.

42 For our purposes, reconciliation is considered a form of separating insurgents from civilians.

43 Andrew Birtle, "Persuasion and Coercion in Counterinsurgency Warfare," *Military Review* (July–August 2008): 50.

44 Jonathan Weisman, "Obama Turns to Petraeus," *Wall Street Journal*, June 24, 2010.

45 David Petraeus, "Counterinsurgency Concepts: What We Learned in Iraq," *Global Policy* 1, no. 1 (January 2010): 116.

46 Matthew Kaminski, "The Second Afghan Front," *Wall Street Journal,* December 24, 2010.

47 "The Petraeus Strategy Up Close," *The Economist*, October 9–15, 2010: 58–60.

48 Nick Carter, "800 Words on the Last Year in Afghanistan," *Small Wars Journal,* December 13, 2010, http://smallwarsjournal.com/blog/2010/12/800-words-on-the-last-year-in/, accessed January 20, 2011.

49 See "The Petraeus Strategy Up Close"; and interviews by author, Afghanistan, December 2010.

50 "The Petraeus Strategy Up Close."

51 Headquarters International Security Assistance Force/US Forces-Afghanistan, Kabul, Afghanistan, COMISAF assessment letter to the troops, January 25, 2011.

52 See Raymond Millen, "Time for a Strategic and Intellectual Pause in Afghanistan," *Parameters* (Summer 2010): 37, 45; and James T. Quinlivan, "Force Requirements in Stability Operations," *Parameters* (Winter 1995): 59–69.

53 Millen, "Time for a Strategic," 38.

54 Karen DeYoung and Rajiv Chandrasekaran, "Afghan President Karzai Approves Plan for Local Defense Forces," *Washington Post*, July 15, 2010.

55 See Mathieu Lefevre, "Local Defence in Afghanistan—A Review of Government-backed Initiatives," AAN Thematic Report, www.aan-afghanistan.org/uploads/20100525MLefevre-LDIpaper.pdf, accessed March 15, 2011; and interviews by author, March 2010.

56 Ibid.

57 Ibid.

58 Eric Furey, "A Comprehensive Approach to Local Engagement in Afghanistan," *Small Wars Journal,* October 24, 2010, http://smallwarsjournal.com/blog/journal/docs-temp/585-furey.pdf, accessed January 6, 2011.

59 "Afghan President Karzai Approves Plan for Local Defense Forces," *Washington Post*, July 15, 2010.

60 Interviews by author, March, September, and December 2010.

61 Julian Barnes and Adam Entous, "US, NATO Look to Use Local Police in Afghanistan," *Wall Street Journal,* September 16, 2010.

62 Ibid.

63 Yaroslav Trofimov, "U.S. Enlists New Afghan Village Forces," *Wall Street Journal*, July 1, 2010.

64 Interviews by author, December 2010.

65 Ibid.

66 Ibid.

67 See Cohen, "The Myth of a Kinder," 84; and Birtle, "Persuasion and Coercion," 52.

68 Cohen, 84.

69 Birtle, 51–53.

70 Ben Connable and Martin Libicki, *How Insurgencies End* (Santa Monica, CA: Rand Corp, 2010), 49–50.

71 "The War in Afghanistan—Still Pouring," *The Economist*, December 18–31, 2010: 49.

PART II

Strategic Alternatives

CHAPTER 5

A Case for Withdrawal

Andrew J. Bacevich

If Barack Obama's ascent to the presidency signified anything for American soldiers, it was this: There would be no rest for the weary. As a candidate, Obama had vowed to wind down the Iraq War. Once installed in the Oval Office he endeavored to make good on that promise. Yet hard on the heels of Iraq came Afghanistan—again.

As President Obama ratcheted down US involvement in the Iraq War, he simultaneously ratcheted up the US military effort in Afghanistan, or AfPak, to use the term coined by his administration. In short order, George W. Bush's forgotten war became Obama's war and, to a considerable degree, his albatross. In national security circles, "whither Afghanistan" established itself as topic number one. In nonstop succession, study groups, think tanks, and self-proclaimed experts of varying persuasions began to vie with one another in offering views on what was at stake, how to proceed, and when, how, and if ever to call it quits.

Yet the ongoing debate concealed this crucial fact: Whatever course the war in Afghanistan might take, the verdict that counts is already in. By the end of 2009, when President Obama officially unveiled his Afghan "surge," America's post–9/11 effort to impose its will on the Greater Middle East had failed. That failure is conclusive and irreversible. To the extent that the so-called global war on terror had formed the centerpiece of US national security strategy during the younger Bush's presidency, Obama inherited a situation in which strategy— defined here as the principled application of power to advance the nation's vital interests—had long since ceased to exist.

In Washington, clichés continue to abound, almost always starting with some putative American "obligation" to "lead," but frequently including references to freedom, democracy, and the rights of women. Both President Obama and Secretary of State Hillary Clinton demonstrate a commendable aptitude in reciting them. Missing for some time has been this: a sober assessment of where the world is headed, a realistic appraisal of US accounts, a vision of the role the United States can expect to play in the emerging order, and a road map for getting there.

Rather than arguing over tactics in Helmand Province, filling the void left by the collapse of President Bush's Freedom Agenda (the Big Idea that for a time lent a semblance of coherence to US actions after 9/11) ought to top Washington's policy agenda. In other words, "whither Afghanistan" is fundamentally the wrong question. It is wrong in the sense that it assigns undeserved importance to the fate of a country that qualifies at best as a third-tier issue. (For the United States, the fate of Mexico is a matter of vastly greater importance; yet Washington treats Mexico like an afterthought.) "Whither Afghanistan" is also the wrong question in the sense that US exertions there, resulting in the misuse of scarce resources on a stupendous scale, actually make the restoration of strategic common sense far more difficult, and indeed unlikely. The farther you go down the wrong road, the harder it becomes to get back on track.

The frustrations and disappointments resulting from President Bush's mismanaged wars, dramatically compounded by the impact of the Great Recession of 2008, have provoked a nervous debate about whether the United States—its dominant position seemingly beyond challenge just a decade ago—has today begun irreversibly to "decline." The issue is impossible to resolve one way or the other and is probably beside the point.

What we *can* say with reasonable assurance is this:

- With the end of the Cold War, the international order entered a period of enormous flux, with rising *powers* (China, India) jockeying for admission to the front rank, new *forms* of power (cyber warfare, asymmetric conflict) reducing the significance of more established forms, and a new *agenda* (disease, demography, and climate change) vying for attention alongside more traditional considerations of power politics. An end to this period of change is nowhere in sight.
- The collapse of the Soviet empire corrected the misperception, widely held in Washington, that Soviet machinations had constituted the principal source of global instability. It now became apparent that the nexus of instability lay in the Islamic world, a product of underdevelopment, abysmal governance, distorted religiosity, and the lingering effects of Western imperialism and of the Cold War itself. If doubts on that score persisted, the events of 9/11 ended them.
- In formulating a response to this tidal wave of new challenges, the military and economic resources available to the United States are finite and fall well short of estimates that were widely held just a decade ago. The unipolar moment, if it ever existed, has ended.
- As a consequence, US global preeminence—the basis of the privileged place in the global order that Americans have for long taken for granted—is no longer a given. The need for creative statesmanship to preserve those privileges, guaranteeing the safety and prosperity that Americans consider their birthright, is great.

To solve a problem you need to first identify it correctly. Granting that historical comparisons necessarily lack precision, history can nevertheless provide some insight into the predicament in which the United States has landed. Consider these three examples.

Roughly speaking, the United States today faces a situation similar to that which Great Britain confronted at the dawn of the twentieth century. Still the world's dominant commercial and maritime power, Britain found itself in a position of *relative* decline in that the economies of Germany and the United States were growing at a considerably higher rate. Although cognizant of the implications of this shift (which found concrete expression in the battle fleets that Berlin and Washington were building), British statesmen allowed imperial flights of fancy to take precedence over long-term, strategic calculation. South African gold and diamonds, along with visions of a Cape-to-Cairo railroad linking all of Great Britain's African possessions, persuaded the likes of Joseph Chamberlain, Cecil Rhodes, and Alfred Milner that Boer independence represented an unacceptable affront. So the British government provoked a war with the two Boer republics, the Transvaal and the Orange Free State, cynically citing Boer abuse of native black Africans to create a tissue of moral justification for what was little more than a naked land grab.

Far and away superior by any conventional measure of power, British forces expected an easy win. The Boers did not cooperate, however, and demonstrated an aptitude for guerrilla warfare that gave a stodgy and complacent British army fits. It eventually took three years of bitter fighting for a force of five hundred thousand troops, recruited from throughout the empire, to subdue the Boers. Among the British innovations devised along the way was the "concentration camp," in effect an outdoor prison in which British authorities interned noncombatants. Twenty-six thousand Boers, mostly women and children, died in these camps.

Britain's hard-won and costly victory proved to be pyrrhic. The Boers may have lost the war, but in short order they won the peace, gaining and enjoying very considerable autonomy as one of the "white dominions" occupying a privileged tier within the British Empire. (Not surprisingly, black Africans ended up the Boer War's real losers, an outcome that ostensibly high-minded British statesmen accepted without any evident qualms of conscience.)

Still worse was the fact that the effort to pacify the Boers proved utterly irrelevant to the looming threats the British actually faced. Apart from helping to midwife some long-overdue military reforms, bringing all of South Africa under British control contributed not a whit to the problem posed by the rise of German and American power. Greed and careerism had produced a distorted understanding of British interests. In circumstances that called for consolidation, British leaders instead had fecklessly frittered away resources on their strategic periphery. Rather than demonstrating British strength, the campaign to pacify the Boers, even if ending in victory, served to expose the limits of British power.

In the Obama era, Afghanistan has become America's Boer War, a costly distraction and a sideshow misconstrued as the main event.

Or consider next the case of France in Algeria, another instructive example of a nation recklessly squandering limited resources on a subordinate issue while neglecting more pressing concerns.

By the time of World War II, French citizens had long since become accustomed to considering Algeria an integral part of metropolitan France. Many among the Arab Muslim majority thought otherwise. Seeking independence, they took up arms to achieve their ambitions.

For the French government, the Algerian challenge had both substantive and psychological dimensions. The drubbing France had suffered at the hands of the

Wehrmacht during the opening rounds of World War II left raw psychic wounds that Nazi Germany's eventual defeat at the hands of Soviet and Anglo-American forces had not healed. Eager to reclaim its place in the front rank of world powers, France began by seeking to regain control of its Far Eastern empire. By 1954 at Dien Bien Phu, that effort ended in abject failure. The once indomitable French army had succumbed to a determined force of Asian insurgents.

For French soldiers and civilians alike, permitting Algerians to go their own way would be one humiliation too many. So the French government declared its intention to use all means necessary to crush the Jabhat al-Tahrīr al-Waţanī or *Front de Libération Nationale* (FLN) and restore unquestioned French authority in Algeria. In Paris, authorities cited their concern for the fate of Algeria's European minority (the *pieds noirs*), thereby creating a tissue of moral justification for what was in fact an attempt to prevent a colonized and oppressed people from exercising their right to self-determination.

A brutal six-year struggle ensued. France (like Great Britain in southern Africa a half century earlier) committed an army of five hundred thousand soldiers in hopes of pacifying a recalcitrant population that demonstrated a surprising aptitude for protracted armed struggle. For France, the war produced tactical successes without a favorable political outcome. Among the innovations devised along the way (or imported from the failed war in Indochina) were various interrogation techniques amounting to torture and employed systematically to gain intelligence about the FLN.

As the war dragged on, popular support waned and war weariness afflicted the home front. Fearing abandonment, the French officer corps became alarmed. A profound crisis in civil-military relations ensued. In 1958, an attempted military *putsch* led to the collapse of the Fourth Republic, with Charles de Gaulle—the living symbol of French greatness—summoned to power. The army in particular backed de Gaulle, expecting him to support without reservation the cause of keeping Algeria French.

The army miscalculated. Once he was firmly established as president of a new Fifth Republic (its constitution written to his specifications), de Gaulle decided to liquidate the Algerian commitment. Pouring money into the effort to keep Algeria French was undermining rather than enhancing prospects for a restoration of France's greatness. As de Gaulle saw it, French strategic priorities were all mixed up. Colonialism, however disguised, had become a losing proposition. Europe, not North Africa, was the venue in which *La France* would achieve its destiny. In that regard, the overriding imperative was to end once and for all France's historic rivalry with Germany, paving the way for a Franco-German condominium that would steer Europe on a course independent of the Anglo-Saxons and the Soviets. Rather than conducting *ratonnades* throughout the vast Algerian *bled*, France needed to focus its military efforts on other priorities—on joining the exclusive ranks of the world's nuclear club, for example.

So in 1961, de Gaulle decided to cut Algeria loose. Among the *pieds noirs*, and with certain elements of the officer corps, the decision evoked intense resistance. In hopes of subverting a diplomatic resolution resulting in Algerian independence, the *organisation de l'armée secrète* (OAS) launched a campaign of terrorism, which included attempts to assassinate de Gaulle.

Ultimately, the OAS failed to shake de Gaulle's resolve or his command of events. On July 5, 1962, Algerians gained their independence and France turned to more important things. What had once seemed unthinkable was now a fact, with subsequent events vindicating de Gaulle's appreciation of the situation. The costs of accepting failure in Algeria proved to be far less than the costs of "staying the course." The *pieds noirs* paid most of those costs and ended up the Algerian war's real losers. Dispossessed from the land they considered their home, they received a chilly welcome when they arrived in France as refugees. Moralistic French elites accommodated themselves to this outcome without apparent difficulty.

De Gaulle understood that, for France, Algeria had proven to be the wrong war in the wrong place at the wrong time. Manifesting both strategic insight and political courage, he showed that a nation need not be imprisoned by previous errors of judgment. Sovereignty confers freedom of choice. To deny the existence of strategic choice—the view, for example, of those who insist that the United States has no alternative but to fight on in Afghanistan—is to forfeit control of a nation's destiny. To do so is the height of both irresponsibility and cowardice, as de Gaulle would have been the first to understand.

Finally, and most disconcertingly, consider the case of the USSR, which suffered through its own fateful Afghan quagmire during the 1980s. When the Red Army entered Afghanistan in December 1979, many Western observers interpreted Soviet actions as an indication that a confident Kremlin leadership was exploiting the perceived weakness of the United States after Vietnam to flex its muscles and expand the Soviet Empire. That perception was incorrect. The Soviet Union intervened in Afghanistan not to expand its empire but to prevent its dissolution. As it turned out, of course, the decade of war that ensued produced precisely the outcome that Soviet military actions were intended to avert.

Over the course of the 1970s, Islamist militants had sought to overthrow the pro-Soviet regime in Kabul. Unable to quash the insurgency, the Afghan government petitioned the Kremlin for assistance. Soviet authorities, reluctantly at first, acceded to this request, resulting in an incremental intervention that eventually culminated in a full-fledged invasion that began on December 27, 1979.

What apparently persuaded the Soviet leadership to take such drastic action was fear that Islamist success in seizing control of Afghanistan could inspire similar Islamist insurgencies throughout the USSR's Central Asian republics, each of which contained large and potentially restive Muslim populations. Whatever the Soviets may have intended, what they actually got was a debilitating and unwinnable war; their problems were made all the more difficult by the fact that the United States, the United Kingdom, Saudi Arabia, Pakistan, and the People's Republic of China all generously supported the Afghan resistance.

Although President Ronald Reagan described them as "Freedom Fighters," members of the Afghan resistance or *mujahideen* were not fighting for the sort of freedom delineated by the Declaration of Independence and the US Constitution. Their purpose was simply to purge Afghanistan of godless infidels.

Of course, the locus of the real threat to the Soviet Empire lay not in its near abroad, but within. By the 1980s, the Soviet economy, never robust, was approaching collapse. So too was Soviet morale; the people of the Soviet Union had largely ceased to believe in the promises of Marxism-Leninism. The Soviet leadership was old, hidebound, unimaginative, and corrupt. There was no chance that waging a war to pacify Afghanistan, even if that war were to conclude successfully, would fix what was broken in the Soviet system.

Mikhail Gorbachev knew this. Ascending to the top spot of the Communist Party of the Soviet Union in 1985, he initiated a program of radical domestic reform, intending to open up Soviet politics (*glasnost*) and to rejuvenate the Soviet economy by restructuring it (*perestroika*). Gorbachev's efforts proved to be too much, too late—like performing open-heart surgery and CPR simultaneously on the same failing patient. Part of the reason for Gorbachev's failure was the ongoing war in Afghanistan, where the Soviet Union continued throughout the decade to hemorrhage blood, money, and legitimacy that were already in short supply. Although in February 1989, the last Soviet soldier finally left Afghanistan, by then it was too late. The Soviet Empire had already begun to unravel. The following year the Soviet Union itself began a slow process of dissolution. In August 1991, Gorbachev survived an attempted coup, but found his own credibility shattered. On December 31, 1991, the once-great Soviet Union ceased to exist.

To say that the Afghan War caused the collapse of the Soviet Union would be going too far. To say that the Kremlin's unwillingness or inability to terminate that ill-advised war exacerbated the problems confronting the Soviet Union would be both fair and accurate.

The United States is unlikely to share the fate of its erstwhile Cold War rival. When measured against the Soviet Union in its dotage, American institutions remain comparatively robust and enjoy deep-seated legitimacy. Yet the Soviet experience in the 1980s is not without relevance to the United States three decades later. Indeed, it should serve as a warning.

In terms of its political economy, the United States finds itself in considerable disarray. The facts speak for themselves: persistently high unemployment; trillion dollar federal deficits; a national debt that will soon exceed in size the annual gross domestic product; unaffordable entitlement programs; a political system seemingly unable to deal effectively with the most basic problems. The rise of the Tea Party movement offers but one signal of an increasingly restive, angry electorate. Disappointment with Barack Obama for failing to deliver on his promise to "change the way Washington works" offers another.

At present, America needs its own version of *glasnost* and *perestroika*. (Arguably, it needs its own de Gaulle as well.) Solutions to what ails the country—a failing educational system; crumbling and outdated infrastructure; the absence of a sound energy policy—won't be found in Afghanistan; they must come from within. If anything, the perpetuation of the Afghan War serves to impede the search for those solutions. By exaggerating the threat posed by violent, anti-Western Islamism, the United States has repeated the cardinal error that led the Soviet Union into Afghanistan in the first place. To a degree that should make Americans very uncomfortable, the United States finds itself replicating much of the Soviet experience there.

In Afghanistan, the United States should do today what it should have done in South Vietnam by the summer of 1967 at the latest: get out, deal with the consequences, and move on. Ironically, the arguments insisting upon the imperative of the current course in Afghanistan today echo those made forty-some years ago for staying the course in Vietnam. Americans have lost sight of the fact that failing to prevail in that earlier, misguided war did not lead to the predicted disastrous consequences for American safety and well-being. Although defeat in Vietnam exacted costs, they fell far short of those predicted by the war's most ardent proponents. The Red hordes did not turn up in San Francisco; key American allies did not lose heart and throw in with the Soviet camp; in the aftermath of this painful failure, the United States did not slide ineluctably toward retreat, withdrawal, passivity, and isolationism. Just the reverse occurred: Shedding its commitment to Vietnam allowed the United States to rebound from the adverse effects of that war. Indeed, fourteen years after lamenting the fall of Saigon, Americans were celebrating the fall of the Berlin Wall and the collapse of communism (while mistakenly claiming primary credit for both).

Of course, proponents of the Afghan War insist that this time, in contrast to Vietnam, the stakes *really are* of first-order importance. The arguments they advance come in three variations, two emphasizing strategic consequences and the third, moral obligations.

- First, if the United States withdraws from Afghanistan, the Taliban will inevitably regain control of that country, once again allowing it to become a haven for al-Qaeda, with another terrorist event like 9/11 (if not something much worse) necessarily following.
- Second, the acceptance of failure in Afghanistan will energize Islamists everywhere, offering proof that the United States is indeed a "weak horse" and thereby paving the way for the rise of a new caliphate, uniting an angry and hostile Islamic world implacably committed to waging jihad against the West.
- Third, pulling out of Afghanistan will abandon to the clutches of brutally vengeful fanatics the "good" Afghans, those who have aided the United States and its allies, secularists opposed to the imposition of *shari'a* law, and above all, Afghan women, who will be subjected to violent abuse and oppression.

All three arguments resuscitate rationales offered in the late 1960s and early 1970s for prolonging the Vietnam War. The first two were bogus then and remain so today. The third was disingenuous then and remains so today.

The argument that pulling out of Afghanistan will lead to another event like 9/11 is problematic on several counts. It assumes that (1) Afghans will be unable to prevent the Taliban from returning to power; (2) once in power, the Taliban will welcome al-Qaeda back to Afghanistan; (3) neither the United States nor any other interested power will be able to influence the policy choices that Taliban leaders would thereafter make. Each one of these assumptions is highly suspect. Even if (1) and (2) were to come to pass, for example, the United States could still retain the option of conducting periodic "spoiling attacks" aimed at disrupting al-Qaeda activities in Afghanistan and demonstrating to Taliban authorities the price to be paid for providing sanctuary to anti-Western terrorist organizations.

More importantly, however, the argument for prolonging the Afghan War overlooks the fact that preparations for the 9/11 attack occurred not in Afghanistan but within the West itself, notably in Germany and the United States. Violent anti-Western jihadism is not centered in Afghanistan and does not require Afghanistan as a base of operations. Indeed, if the United States and its allies were able to transform Afghanistan into a liberal democracy tomorrow, the Islamist threat would persist. Indeed, such a putative success would not appreciably reduce that threat. Trying to pacify Afghanistan with expectations that doing so will prevent further terrorist attacks on the United States makes about as much sense as outlawing booze to prevent drunkenness. The approach both misconstrues and even inadvertently serves to exacerbate the problem it aims to fix.

The argument that US failure in Afghanistan will energize the Islamists and lead to the fulfillment of Osama bin Laden's dream of creating a new caliphate is equally flawed. It likewise rests on several dubious assumptions: (1) that the Islamist program, amounting essentially to a full-fledged retreat from modernity, enjoys broad appeal among the Muslim masses, who presumably yearn to live not in the twenty-first century but in the fifteenth; (2) that the regimes currently wielding authority in Muslim-majority nation-states—whether those regimes are secular or religious, authoritarian or reformist—lack the will or the resources to resist radical Islamists in order to retain their hold on power; that they will supinely cave in to all demands, or simply fall from power; (3) that the new, victorious caliph will possess the skill, shrewdness, and ruthlessness to govern and hold together a vast region so sharply divided along tribal, ethnic, nationalistic, and sectarian lines as to call into question the very formulation of an "Islamic world."

The seriousness with which some Americans take the prospect of a new caliphate emerging in the wake of a US withdrawal contrasts with the confidence expressed by almost all Americans that American values—freedom, democracy, individual rights—have universal appeal and applicability, and that they express the most fundamental aspirations of all humankind. If that proposition is true, then the much-feared Islamist triumph seems unlikely.

Indeed, where Islamists have gained actual power, as in Iran after the overthrow of the Shah in 1979, their efforts to export their credo and even to impress it upon their own people have achieved little success. If the Iranian uprising of 2009—the Green Revolution—demonstrated one thing, it was this: Very large numbers of Iranians, especially those who are young and educated, have long since decided that they have no interest in buying what the mullahs are selling. The failure of the Iranian Revolution of the 1970s demonstrates the fact that Islamism has exceedingly transitory and limited appeal. Its triumph is no more likely than the triumph of Marxism-Leninism; it's a value system that doesn't work.

Then there is the Arab Spring that began in late 2010, with no end in sight. Although prudence cautions against making firm predictions about what the ongoing upheaval will ultimately produce in terms of political change (or change deferred), few of the demands voiced by protesters in Tunisia or Egypt, Bahrain or Yemen, Syria or (yes) Iraq suggest an affinity for al-Qaeda and its vision for the Muslim world. In many respects, events had rendered Osama bin Laden largely irrelevant even before American commandos eliminated him in May 2011. (The contrast between the massive resources that Washington funnels into Afghanistan and the relatively trivial sums it devotes to helping Arab reformers further illustrates the American inability to distinguish the important from the unimportant.) Finally, there is the moral argument for prolonging the Afghan War—that once having overturned the preexisting order the United States has an obligation to put in place something better, no matter how long it takes or how much it costs to do so.

Let us note, before pursuing this matter further, that the issue is almost entirely a theoretical one. There exists precious little evidence to suggest that moral considerations *in practice* figure substantially in the making of foreign policy. Americans readily accept that statement as true when applied to Beijing or Moscow or especially Paris. It is long past time that they accept it with reference to Washington as well. Perhaps moral issues *should* influence the formulation of American statecraft; yet they don't, except perhaps as an afterthought. To imagine that Barack Obama and his lieutenants sit around the Oval Office anguishing over "doing the right thing" serves only to impede our understanding of how power actually gets exercised. (To imagine that members of the previous administration did so is risible.)

The notion that moral considerations affect *public perceptions* of policy (even in France) is undoubtedly true, hence the efforts of policymakers to justify their actions by citing some higher purpose. In the case of, say, a Franklin Roosevelt or Richard Nixon, this is almost entirely cynical. Yet there are also cases—Woodrow Wilson is one example, George W. Bush is another—where individual statesmen beguile themselves with their own rhetoric and genuinely come to believe what they initially found simply convenient to believe.

The problem is that what passes for moral discourse is almost invariably superficial. While pretending to probe deeply, it actually serves to trivialize, notably so when it comes to Afghanistan. To illustrate the point, consider the following four questions:

- To the extent that US officials should take moral considerations into account, which comes first: the government's obligation to provide for the well-being of the American people or the government's obligation to provide for the well-being of people who are not Americans?
- To the extent that the US government has a moral obligation to people who are not Americans, why should the US moral obligation to the people of Afghanistan qualify as a particular priority?
- To the extent that the US government has a specific and pressing moral obligation to Afghanistan, why does open-ended war qualify as the preferred way to meet that obligation?
- To the extent that fulfilling America's moral obligation to the Afghan people requires the prolongation of war, what should we make of the fact that responsibility for fulfilling that obligation falls on the backs of a small segment of our fellow citizens while the rest carry on as if there were no war?

On the first question, my own view is that US officials have a moral obligation to the American people that takes precedence over all others. Those officials take an oath to the Constitution. That document does not commit the United States to saving or policing the world. It declares that the purpose of our union is to "secure the Blessings of Liberty to Ourselves and our Posterity." Although it is not necessarily evident to those who make their living in well-heeled Washington think tanks, that obligation remains unfulfilled. (Were foreign policy analysts to set up shop in downtown Detroit or Cleveland, they might have greater sympathy for the challenges facing many of their fellow citizens.) Indeed, with military adventurism helping to swell annual US federal deficits, posterity is in for a rude awakening: By the time young Americans of today get around to filing for Social Security and Medicare, there won't be any. When the coffers are bare, that failure will be moral as well as fiscal.

On the second question, if the United States does have an obligation to others, it is not at all clear why the Afghans should come first. Does anyone think that America's moral debt to the Iraqi people, accrued during years of chaotic occupation, has been paid in full? How about the Vietnamese? Iranians? Filipinos? Nicaraguans? Guatemalans? Cubans? The list goes on.

On this score, Mexico might well claim a place near the front of the line. Americans stole Texas. The United States launched a war of naked aggression to seize California and the Southwest. From the nineteenth century until well into the twentieth, American corporations pillaged Mexico's resources. We meddled in their revolution. We have a long track record of siding with kleptocratic elites against the Mexican people. Today the American demand for illicit drugs and lax US gun laws are helping to transform Mexico into a violence-riddled narco-state. To be sure, Mexican institutions (like Afghan institutions) are weak, inept, and thoroughly corrupt. But does that provide a moral justification for treating Mexico like a footnote? If the US Treasury has extra billions available for nation-building, simple justice demands that the United States ship the money south of the border before attending to Central Asia.

And even if Afghanistan deserves to be first in line, why does it follow that war provides the best means of doing right by the Afghan people? The truth is that few of the resources that Washington expends in Afghanistan actually benefit the people. Instead, most dollars go to arms merchants and private security contractors, a.k.a., mercenaries, who could care less about the people's well-being. Meanwhile, US operations regularly kill and maim innocent civilians. US commanders may regret that fact, but regret hasn't ended the practice. If the United States were serious about actually doing something for Afghans, it would spend less on munitions and more on economic assistance and social development. Better still, US officials could offer interested Afghans the chance to get out of Afghanistan altogether and pursue the American dream, welcoming any and all to settle in the Land of Liberty. A permissive immigration program would demonstrate that expressions of solidarity with suffering Afghans go beyond mere rhetoric. The very absurdity of the suggestion that the United States admit large numbers of Afghan refugees exposes how thin American moral concerns actually are. Americans may want to ease their consciences, but not if it results in any personal discomfort or inconvenience.

And finally, even if prolonging a war that is already a decade old really does provide the best way to meet some overriding, collective US obligation toward Afghanistan, it would seem to follow that the burden of service and sacrifice should be equitably distributed among Americans. Rather than passing the bill to future generations, the present generation of Americans should pay for the war through higher taxes or by reducing domestic spending. They might also consider changing the socioeconomic composition of the American military, ensuring that the US forces sent off to Afghanistan "look like" America itself. Surely it cannot be moral to pursue a policy of endless war when the burden of service and sacrifice falls on the shoulders of .5 percent of the population, drawn disproportionately from a narrow portion of the socioeconomic spectrum.

Here is the bottom line: How the United States extricates itself from Afghanistan is less important than that it do so promptly. To continue a costly war that makes no sense strategically is not only stupid but deeply wrong, and it is an insult to the soldiers sent to fight in order to camouflage the intellectual bankruptcy and lack of political courage to which Washington has succumbed.

How then should the United States make its exit? That question falls within the realm of operations rather than strategy. Tell the commander that the mission has changed. Let him work out the details. Give him six weeks to draft a withdrawal plan. Give him six months to implement it. This is a task that the senior leadership of the United States military can manage on its own.

Meanwhile, senior officials in Washington who are responsible for the formulation of basic policy should focus on the urgent task of devising a realistic and sustainable national security strategy, free of cant and respectful of the lives of the soldiers whom they purport to revere—a strategy that gives up on the notion that Islamism represents an existential threat to the United States and that invading and occupying countries provides a plausible way of dealing with that threat.

Policymakers should undertake this task with a spirit of humility and with modest expectations, taking into account a bipartisan record of malfeasance compiled over the past decade and characterized by the following:

- *an inability to anticipate*, whether the events of 9/11, the consequences of invading Iraq, or revolutionary upheavals in Egypt, Libya or Syria;
- *an inability to control*, with wars begun in Iraq and Afghanistan, along with various and sundry financial scandals, economic crises, and natural disasters, exposing the limits of American influence, power, and perspicacity;
- *an inability to afford*, as manifested by a badly overstretched military, massive deficits, increasingly unaffordable entitlement programs, and rapidly escalating foreign debt;
- *an inability to respond*, demonstrated by the dysfunction pervading the American political system, especially at the national level, whether in the Congress, at senior levels of the executive branch, or in the bureaucracy; and,
- *an inability to comprehend* what God intends or the human heart desires, with little to indicate that the wonders of the Information Age, however dazzling; the impact of globalization, however far-reaching; or the forces of corporate capitalism, however relentless, will provide answers to such elusive questions.

In light of this record, Americans today would do well to temper any claims or expectations of fixing Afghanistan, much less of completing the world's redemption. Like every other country that confronts circumstances of vast complexity and pervasive uncertainty, the United States is merely attempting to cope. Prudence should oblige Americans to admit as much. What we need from Washington is not the next Big Idea, but pragmatism, common sense, and a modicum of competence.

A US battalion commander assigned to Afghanistan got it right. Speaking to a newspaper reporter in late 2010, he put it this way: "The best thing we can do is to pull back and let the Afghans figure this place out." Pull back and then pull out: We've got far bigger fish to fry.

CHAPTER 6

A Case for Staying the Course

Frederick W. Kagan

America has enduring, vital national interests in South Asia that can only be secured in current circumstances by the implementation of a successful comprehensive counterinsurgency strategy in Afghanistan. The failure or abandonment of that strategy would do serious harm to American security interests globally. The strategies and approaches that are proposed as alternatives, or as mitigations, offer little hope of even limiting the damage. It may be impossible to succeed in Afghanistan, or the United States and its allies may choose to give up trying, but the consequences of the failure or abandonment of the current effort will be dire and must be factored into any such decisions.

Today, America has three primary strategic interests in Afghanistan: preventing the reestablishment of terrorist safe havens, affecting the Pakistani strategic calculus regarding Islamist groups that threaten the stability of the Pakistani state and the subcontinent, and not losing a war. Preventing the defeat of NATO in its first out-of-area operation is a fourth interest that has gained new urgency. A few months ago it seemed highly unlikely that the Alliance would undertake another out-of-area operation. But NATO forces have now operated in Libya as well as Afghanistan, and the effectiveness and cohesiveness of the Alliance remains important. It is definitely not in the interest of the United States or the West for NATO to be humiliated in Afghanistan.

The Consequences of Defeat

It has been common for decades to dismiss the third interest—not losing a war—as an invalid reason to continue fighting. America lost the war in Vietnam, after all, and nevertheless won the Cold War. This reasoning is specious. America's defeat in Vietnam was followed by a very bad decade. The Soviet Union surpassed the US nuclear arsenal. America's principal ally in the Middle East, the Shah of Iran, fell in 1979, giving way to the current, virulent Islamist regime in Tehran that began its tenure in power with an act of war against the United States (seizing the American embassy) and by holding American hostages. In Central America, Anastasio Somoza, another important ally, fell in 1979 as well, to a diverse collection of revolutionary groups from which the Soviet-aligned Sandinista regime emerged as the ruling clique. The Soviet Union invaded Afghanistan in December 1979, following the seizure of power eighteen months earlier by a Soviet-aligned communist revolutionary movement. Nor did Ronald Reagan's accession to power in 1981 immediately transform the situation. A communist faction took Americans hostage again in Grenada in 1983 in the process of seizing control of the tiny island state. That same year, Cold War tensions reached their peak with the deliberate shooting-down of Korean Airlines flight 007 after it strayed into Soviet airspace.

Thus, within a decade of America's defeat in Vietnam, American policies in Latin America, the Middle East, and South Asia were in ruins; the Soviets appeared to be advancing and gaining power; and the threat of nuclear conflict was probably higher than it had been since the Cuban missile crisis. Did these events result from US failure in Southeast Asia? Each certainly had local roots driven by local dynamics not related to that withdrawal, but the general perception that the United States was weak and could be defeated by staunch resistance had turned inward, and helped, at least, to fuel some of these policy disasters.

It does not seem to have occurred to the Soviet Politburo as it invaded Afghanistan that the United States might make any significant response.[1] The Iranian hostage-takers, and the cannier Ayatollah Khomeini (who made the ultimate decisions in that crisis), were confident that the United States would not respond effectively to their provocation.[2] The Sandinistas, and the Cubans and Soviets who backed them, were similarly confident that no meaningful American operations would unhinge their success. It is at least as appropriate to ascribe part of the policy disasters of the decade following the US withdrawal from Vietnam to the perception of American weakness as it is to pretend that those disasters had nothing to do with an American defeat consummated four years earlier.

It is also inaccurate to dismiss those defeats as irrelevant, in light of America's subsequent victory in the Cold War, for there was nothing inevitable about the peaceful end of the Cold War in 1991. Mikhail Gorbachev acceded to power by one vote in 1985. When he launched the policies of *glasnost* and *perestroika,* his aim was to strengthen the communist system in the USSR. His miscalculation led to internal unrest and also unrest among the Soviet Union's Eastern European satellite states. Although Gorbachev showed himself to be far more humanitarian than any of his predecessors, he did attempt crackdowns within the USSR, particularly in Georgia and Lithuania, but he refused to use overwhelming military force to maintain his state's integrity. As the Central and East European satellites fell away, he chose not to fight for them, in stark contrast with the performances of almost every one of his predecessors. Gorbachev's relative gentleness and ultimate willingness to allow the USSR to fall rather than commit the atrocities that would have come easily to other Soviet leaders most probably sparked the coup attempt against him in 1991. The failure of that coup attempt was predictable; the whole sequence of decisions leading up to it was not. Today, counting on a repetition of one of the most implausible events in world history following an American and NATO defeat in Afghanistan would be the strategic equivalent of drawing to an inside straight.

In reality, the downside risks of American defeat in Afghanistan are obvious and predictable. The al-Qaeda movement has always relied on a narrative of being able to attack and ultimately defeat superpowers to maintain a steady flow of recruits and donations. In the 1990s it claimed (falsely) that it had defeated the Soviet Union. In the first decade of this century the narrative revolved around its successful attack on the US homeland and its progress against US forces in Iraq.

Then the tide began to turn against al-Qaeda. The 2007 surge in Iraq began the process of defeating al-Qaeda there. Saudi Arabia turned against the group in 2006 following a series of ill-advised al-Qaeda attacks on Saudi targets, forcing the terrorist leadership to flee. (Many went to Yemen, where they ultimately helped form al-Qaeda in the Arabian Peninsula [AQAP]).[3] Pakistan has steadily increased its efforts against al-Qaeda and has allowed the United States to conduct drone strikes against senior al-Qaeda leadership, activities that have significantly disrupted the group's safe havens and its ability to operate from a traditional stronghold. American operations in Pakistan reached a high point with the killing of Osama bin Laden in May 2011. Al-Qaeda franchises in the Caucasus (the Islamic Emirate of the Caucasus or IEC) and Northwest Africa (al-Qaeda in the Islamic Maghreb, AQIM) have been unable to conduct major attacks against even local, much less global, targets, and AQIM has been unable thus far to benefit much from the overthrow of Moammar Qaddafi in Libya. For the past five years, in other words, things have been going badly for al-Qaeda and there is little in the real world on which the group can base claims of progress or success (which doesn't, of course, mean that al-Qaeda propagandists do not make such claims, but it does temper the reception of those claims in the Muslim community).

If the United States were to withdraw from Afghanistan in a way that looks like Washington has decided to accept the failure of its current efforts, it would provide al-Qaeda with the most powerful propaganda tool it has had since 9/11 and a means of overcoming the blow to the network's morale suffered following bin Laden's death. The al-Qaeda senior leadership would undoubtedly claim credit for the victory, and would likely seek to reestablish bases quickly in Afghanistan to cement such claims and to expand its footprint, now that its Pakistani safe havens appear less safe than they once were. A US withdrawal could well prove to be a catalyst to al-Qaeda attempts to reconstitute its capabilities and regain the global credibility that events of the past five years have seriously eroded.

An American abandonment of the current Afghan government—something that is implicit in any discussion of early withdrawal and transition to a purely counterterrorism mission—would also send a chilling message to allies throughout the Muslim world who are already concerned about America's staying power. The prospect of a full American withdrawal from Iraq has generated fear in the Arab world that the United States is prepared to abandon its Arab friends and partners to the tender mercies of Iran. Moreover, the United States has thus far offered no promise of any long-term commitment to Iraq, whereas negotiations on a long-term relationship with Afghanistan, including a continuing military presence, are now underway. Reneging on that promise will reinforce the already widespread fear that the United States intends to withdraw generally from its commitments, and its interests, in the Muslim world. That fear, in turn, will drive America's current partners and allies to reexamine their own interests and priorities on the assumption that they cannot count on American support. The likely results of that reexamination range from a regional arms race (as Arab states rush to gain the ability to defend themselves without a reliable American partner) to the establishment of Iranian regional hegemony (as the fearful make preemptive accommodations with Tehran in order to get the best possible deal). The burden of proof lies with those who would argue that nothing bad will result from these regional reevaluations, since they are advocating for a positive choice that makes such reevaluations much more likely to occur.

If it became apparent that success with the current strategy in Afghanistan really is impossible, then this line of argument loses some of its force. Failure is failure, and the United States is likely to feel the consequences of losing whether it actually loses in the field or withdraws preemptively for fear of failure. We must be very clear, however, that accepting defeat (or being defeated) in Afghanistan will have serious consequences for American security across a wide region, and those consequences cannot be blithely dismissed with references to previous eras that appear comforting only because we now know what the ultimate results were.

Preventing the Reestablishment of Terrorist Safe Havens in Afghanistan

The easiest case to make for sticking it out in Afghanistan, in principle, should be the high likelihood that failure there will lead to the reestablishment of terrorist bases in Afghanistan. Yet this argument has lost some of its resonance in the public discourse, for reasons that are partly sound and partly wishful thinking. Four arguments, in particular, appear to have gained salience in this regard: (1) the terrorists already have sanctuaries in Pakistan, not Afghanistan, so the prospect of their reestablishment in Afghanistan is moot; (2) the Taliban groups that welcomed al-Qaeda in the 1990s have learned their lessons and will not bring the terrorists back into Afghanistan if they regain power; (3) the United States can handle any ongoing terrorist challenge in Afghanistan using precision strikes, both by drones and by special mission units conducting direct action operations; and (4) terrorists no longer need such territorial sanctuaries, if they ever did, and, in any case, they now have access to such places in Somalia, Yemen, West Africa, and elsewhere. Eliminating sanctuaries in South Asia, according to this line of thought, is thus a fool's errand because it is fundamentally irrelevant.

None of these arguments are foolish. Each accurately portrays a part of the overall situation: There are sanctuaries in Pakistan; some Taliban leaders clearly had buyer's remorse after allowing al-Qaeda into Afghanistan in the 1990s; the United States has done significant damage to some terrorist networks using direct action operations—notably killing bin Laden; and potential sanctuaries do beckon in Somalia and Yemen, at the very least. The flaws in these arguments result from mistaking one aspect of the situation for the whole story.

Pakistani Sanctuaries

Al-Qaeda central (as the core leadership around the late Osama bin Laden and his apparent successor, Ayman al Zawahiri, is generally known) maintains its sanctuaries in Pakistan, primarily in the tribal areas near the Durand Line but—as is apparent from bin Laden's hideout near Islamabad—also in metropolitan Pakistan. It does not appear that this senior leadership spends any significant time in Afghanistan. Pakistan also provides sanctuaries for Afghan insurgent groups linked to al-Qaeda, particularly the Haqqani Network, which maintains its headquarters in Miramshah, North Waziristan. The Lashkar-e-Tayyiba group has extensive sanctuaries and safe havens throughout Pakistan as well, especially in Azad Kashmir (Pakistani Kashmir) near Muzaffarabad and outside Lahore in Punjab. Other Pakistan-based terrorist and insurgent groups include the Quetta Shura Taliban, headed by Mullah Mohammad Omar, and based generally in Quetta, Baluchistan; the Tehrik-e-Taliban Pakistan (TTP), which operates against the Pakistani government in Waziristan and elsewhere in the Federally Administered Tribal Areas (FATA), and al-Qaeda central in and around Waziristan; Jaish-e-Mohammad; Lashkar-e-Jhangvi; Tehrik-e-Nafaz-e-Shariat-e-Mohammadi, now largely subsumed by the Tehrik-i-Taliban Pakistan (TTP); and the Sipah-e-Sahaba Pakistan, among others.[4]

This network of militant Islamist groups is the densest and most tightly interlinked concentration of such organizations anywhere in the world, and, collectively, is by far the most dangerous to American, Indian, and Western interests and security. The component groups do not by any means agree entirely on objectives and strategy. The Quetta Shura Taliban is almost entirely focused on regaining power in Afghanistan and has demonstrated little interest in global jihad. The Haqqani Network in the past had a similar focus. But the transfer of leadership from the old *mujahid* founder of the group, Jalaluddin Haqqani, to his younger and more ambitious son, Sirajuddin, along with the group's close ties to and interactions with al-Qaeda, Lashkar-e-Tayyiba, and other groups with broader visions, may have reshaped the Haqqanis' focus to include a somewhat broader range of final objectives than simply regaining power in its traditional strongholds in Afghanistan.

The Lashkar-e-Tayyiba (LeT) is generally viewed exclusively as a Kashmiri separatist group focused on attacking India. But LeT was formed in the 1980s in close cooperation with bin Laden, and its decision to focus on Kashmir was a conscious choice to take advantage of the most resonant issue of the moment rather than a reflection of anything fundamental to its creation. Its ideology remains very similar to al-Qaeda's, and periodic attempts to attack Western, especially American, targets both in Afghanistan and outside the region indicate that it should be viewed beyond the prism of Kashmir. The TTP was formed as an umbrella organization to coordinate groups operating against Islamabad itself in revenge for President Musharraf's decision to support American counterterrorism efforts after 9/11. Its activities create strains in its relations with groups such as the Haqqani Network, the Quetta Shura, and even LeT because they undermine the generally good relations those groups maintain with Islamabad. Strong ties nevertheless apparently bind TTP to some of the Pakistani-supported (or, at least, tolerated) groups, since they have very rarely undertaken or supported operations against the TTP or tried to force the TTP to move out of their own base areas.

The very density of Islamist groups in Pakistan provides one of the clearest explanations for why al-Qaeda central and other groups have not fled to Somalia, Yemen, or elsewhere, even in the face of Pakistani cooperation with American efforts against them, and why they are unlikely to do so except under extreme duress (an issue we will consider in more detail below). Islamist groups such as LeT, the Quetta Shura, the Haqqani Network, and others face almost no pressure and, in some cases, receive active support from elements within the Pakistani government. Their sanctuaries are extremely secure, and they are willing to share their facilities with al-Qaeda. Al-Qaeda will find no similar dense and secure support network anywhere else in the world.

But this situation does beg the reasonable question: Why are we not then fighting in Pakistan rather than Afghanistan? The answer is simple: Pakistan is a state with 180 million people, nearly 100 nuclear weapons and the means to deliver them, and a large standing army equipped, with American help, with reasonably modern weapons systems. Invading Pakistan, or effectively going to war with Pakistan by conducting unrestricted direct action operations against Islamabad's will, would be an insane policy choice. To be very blunt, the US military does not have the capability to conduct any large-scale intervention in Pakistan against Pakistan's will, and it is almost impossible to imagine the success of any such intervention as long as Islamabad remains committed to supporting the Islamist groups that concern us. Anyone who seriously believes that we should consider or conduct such an operation must also consider, describe, and advocate for the very significant increase in American military capabilities that would be required to undertake it and address the enormous political, diplomatic, logistical, and other challenges that it would face. In reality, this is not an option.

The United States is thus compelled to pursue an indirect approach to Pakistan. Such an approach must include well-developed and carefully calibrated policies toward Pakistan itself, as well as a regional strategy addressing Pakistan's fears about malign activities in India and Afghanistan, its two most important neighbors. Additionally, Pakistan does have some limited areas of contention with Iran, notably the persistent use of its territory to attack Iran by the al-Qaeda-linked terrorist group Jundallah, smuggling, and the joint concerns raised by other Baluchi separatist movements. However, these tensions are trivial compared to those Pakistan feels and faces internally, and in India and Afghanistan and the United States, in any case, has extremely limited leverage to affect them. Since this chapter and this volume are focused on Afghanistan, we cannot delve into the challenges and complexities of building an American strategy toward Pakistan itself or toward the Pakistan-Indian relationship. Our interest here is confined to the role Afghanistan plays, and must play, in any overall Pakistan strategy.

From Islamabad's perspective, Afghanistan is the most important remaining secondary front in the struggle with India (after the loss of Bangladesh in the 1970s).

Pakistani leaders have traditionally had two primary concerns about Afghanistan: first, that uncontrolled Pashtun violence and conflict in Afghanistan could mobilize the larger population of Pashtuns in Pakistan, undermining the Pakistani federal state; and second, that chaos in Afghanistan would allow India to establish bases there from which to threaten Pakistan from the north and west, even as the main Indian forces menace Pakistan's eastern frontier and capital region.[5]

Pakistani leaders have responded to these concerns over the last two decades by working to establish Pashtun leaders and groups responsive to, and dependent on, Islamabad in order to ensure both that no Pashtun nationalist movement would develop that could excite Pakistani Pashtuns and that Pakistan had a reliable buffer against Indian incursion throughout the Pashtun zone in southern Afghanistan.[6] For a variety of reasons, the groups Pakistan has supported since the 1980s have been religious, even Islamist, in orientation rather than secular, and certainly not nationalistic. They have also tended to be much more focused on fighting—since Pakistan's concerns are fundamentally with military threats and actual control of territory—rather than on state-building, economic development, or the interests of improving the lives of Afghans, something about which Islamabad has historically evinced little concern. Pakistani efforts in Afghanistan have thus tended to reinforce militant Islamism, a fractious and ineffective Afghan state, and patterns of violence and communal conflict. This is one reason for the widespread disdain, distrust, and resentment of Pakistan within Afghanistan, even for the Pakistani Pashtun community. It is one of the factors, ironically, that tends to push Afghan elites to look to India for long-term support.

The Pakistani perception of Indian intentions is badly skewed. New Delhi has shown no desire whatsoever to attack Pakistan, let alone reconquer it. India has been extremely circumspect in its involvement in Afghanistan, partly out of deference to American and Western requests made in the hope of reassuring Pakistani leaders. India has nevertheless done just enough in Afghanistan to support Pakistani conspiracy theories. New Delhi funded the construction of a road from Delaram in Farah Province, Western Afghanistan, to Zaranj in Nimruz Province, on the Iranian border. The purpose of that road, now very heavily trafficked, is to facilitate the movement of goods from Central Asia through Afghanistan to the Iranian port of Chabahar, circumventing the age-old route that runs through Pakistan to Karachi. India is also one of three countries to maintain a large consulate in Kandahar City (Pakistan and Iran are the others), fueling Pakistani paranoia. And reports of Indian intelligence operatives in Afghanistan are frequent and credible enough to maintain Pakistani suspicions. Pressing New Delhi to do less in Afghanistan than it is now doing, however, would do nothing to improve the situation. Those in the Pakistani leadership who believe that India is up to no good in Afghanistan will always find "proof" of their paranoia. The fear is irrational, and reality is almost irrelevant in addressing it. We must expect that it will remain part of the Pakistani strategic calculus for some time, probably for as long as Islamabad believes that India is a serious menace.

We are not going to be able to persuade Pakistan's leaders that they are wrong about India and Afghanistan. Harping on the need to "resolve" the Kashmir dispute misses a basic part of the equation. Kashmir is a symptom of Pakistan's failure to develop a self-definition that is not based on the threat posed to the Muslims of the subcontinent by India, as well as its persistent inability to develop a functional civilian government. There is no conceivable "resolution" of the Kashmir problem that would materially affect this basic illness in the Pakistani body politic. Those who call for "realism" in Afghanistan must be equally realistic about Pakistan. American policies and strategies could be better than they are, and should be improved as much as possible. But there is no magic bullet that will solve Pakistan's problems or address our own concerns in that country.

The question, then, is how can American actions in Afghanistan affect what goes on in Pakistan? Objectively, the United States and its allies could accomplish two things in Afghanistan that could have significant positive impacts on Pakistan: We could defeat Pakistan's Islamist proxies in Afghanistan, and we could establish a stable government in Afghanistan for the first time in over thirty years. Leaving aside for the moment the feasibility of these goals, let us evaluate their possible and probable impacts on Pakistan.

Pakistani support for Islamist groups began in the 1970s under President Zulfiqar ali Bhutto, even before the Soviet invasion. The rationale then had to do with Pakistani internal politics after the loss of Bangladesh and the initial retreat of military rule. It has had severe negative consequences for Pakistan itself. Although the Pakistani governments that initially supported these groups saw themselves as upholders of Islam, the steady march of the Islamist movement toward extremism almost inevitably has led elements of that movement to define the Pakistani state itself as apostate and, therefore, a target. President Musharraf's decision (compelled, according to reports, by the "with-us-or-against-us" ultimatum delivered by Secretary of State Colin Powell) to support American operations against al-Qaeda after 9/11 drew Pakistan into an increasingly difficult and contradictory position.

The Pakistani military became involved in counterterror operations in the Federally Administered Tribal Areas (FATA) and found that it had stirred up a hornet's nest, leading to a serious reverse in Waziristan in 2006. By 2009, elements of the militant Islamist network had solidified into the TTP, which assassinated Benazir Bhutto that year. The Tehreek-e-Nafaz-e-Shariat-e-Mohammadi (TNSM), with TTP support, solidified its sanctuaries in the northern FATA (particularly in Bajaur and Mohmand Agencies), then expanded into neighboring Dir Agency in the Northwest Frontier Province (now renamed Khyber-Pakhtunkhwa). It even pushed into Swat District, where Islamism has historically had very little footing, establishing *shari'a* courts and insisting on its right to uphold Muslim law and tradition in a state whose constitution already requires exactly that. By then, Chief of Army Staff (COAS) General Ashfaq Kayani had had enough. He launched clearing operations in Bajaur, Swat, Dir, and subsequently in South Waziristan to drive out the TNSM and the TTP and reassert Islamabad's control. He even redeployed forces from strategic locations on the Indian frontier to this campaign, which ultimately involved elements of at least five Pakistani regular army divisions along with much of the Frontier Corps.[7]

But continued Pakistani support for Afghan insurgent groups has hindered these operations. The Pakistani military has been reluctant, to say the least, to conduct clearing operations in North Waziristan, one of the last remaining bases of the TTP (and al-Qaeda). The excuses it has offered are transparent pretexts concealing what is almost certainly the real reason for its hesitation: North Waziristan is also the principal sanctuary for the Haqqani Network, and the Pakistani military is unwilling to take actions that would seriously undermine that group. Pakistani military operations have also left Quetta untouched for fear of disrupting the base most important to Mullah Omar. It is difficult, perhaps impossible, to evaluate from available information how much of a problem this inactivity in Quetta is for operations against transnational terrorist groups or groups that threaten Pakistan. By all accounts, Quetta has not been a major base for al-Qaeda, LeT, TTP, or other such groups. But the Quetta Shura Taliban remains intimately connected with those groups and it is difficult to imagine that its solid sanctuary in Baluchistan does not, at least indirectly, assist them.

Pakistani policy in Afghanistan since the 1980s has thus been one of the main drivers of Pakistani support for militant Islamist groups (although it is not the only factor). American pressure to operate against those groups after 9/11 generated enormous tension in Pakistan and fueled the redirection of some of that Islamist energy against Islamabad itself. Continued Pakistani support for elements of the violent Islamist network has created hesitancy in Pakistan's efforts to defend itself and revealed an inherent contradiction in Pakistani strategy: Pakistani leaders operate on the assumption that the Afghan insurgent groups and LeT that they protect do not provide material support to the TTP, TNSM, and other groups that they are fighting, even though it is apparent that this assumption is false. Pakistani policy toward its own Islamist militants will therefore continue to be incoherent, and, very likely, unsuccessful, as long as this contradiction remains.

American and international leaders have made enormous efforts to persuade Pakistani leaders to change their approach, thus far to no avail. Billions of dollars in aid, threats, promises, commitments, and cajolery have had no real effect on Pakistani strategy. It is difficult to imagine what could be tried that has not yet been tried, or why efforts that failed a few years ago should succeed today or tomorrow, with one exception. The Pakistani strategy depends on having effective proxies in Afghanistan. In particular, it depends on the effectiveness of the Quetta Shura Taliban and the Haqqani Network. Before 2009, the United States and its allies had no coherent strategy designed to defeat either of those groups, and did not have the resources to accomplish any such strategy, even if there had been an effective concept of operations. With the increase in US and NATO forces over the last eighteen months and the fundamental reorientation of our approach in Afghanistan, we have seen the first serious degradation in the capabilities of the Quetta Shura Taliban since the reemergence of that group after its defeat in 2001–2.[8] If we can maintain and expand these gains in southern Afghanistan and then add gains against the Haqqani Network in the east, we can seriously reduce the ability of both groups to serve as effective proxies for Pakistan, reversing half-a-decade's worth of their progress.

It is impossible to know how Pakistan's leaders would react to such a development. If they were persuaded that we really were going to defeat, or at least neutralize, these key proxies and, furthermore, that the United States intended to remain engaged in Afghanistan in order to ensure that they did not reconsitute, then the rational choice would be to cut their losses and deal with the emerging new order in Afghanistan. Pakistan does not, unfortunately, have a good track record of making sound strategic choices. We can be reasonably certain only that such a situation would force Islamabad to reevaluate its strategy in Afghanistan and take a broader view of the problem than it previously has. Such a reevaluation would present the United States with the best opportunity it has had since 2001 to try to nurture a new vision among Pakistani leaders of how to assure their real interests in Afghanistan without supporting groups that undermine both Afghanistan and, ultimately, Pakistan itself. As long as Pakistan's proxies in Afghanistan remain potent, on the other hand, there is no reason for Islamabad to engage in any such reevaluation and every reason to think that Pakistan's leaders will continue on something like the present destructive course, if only out of sheer inertia.

The door to continued Pakistani meddling in Afghanistan will remain open as long as the Afghan government lacks legitimacy in the eyes of many Pashtuns and proves unable to govern and secure its territory. Helping the Afghans build an effective government and competent security forces, therefore, is essential to changing the conversation in Pakistan permanently. If and when it becomes obvious that Afghanistan is moving toward being a functional sovereign state, something it has not been since 1978, Pakistani leaders will be confronted with another new reality to reinforce the reevaluation required should we neutralize the Afghan Taliban. On the other hand, as long as it seems likely that Afghanistan will degenerate again into chaos and that the United States and its allies will ultimately permit that to happen, those within the Pakistani government who favor the current course will find their arguments strengthened.

Success in Afghanistan will certainly not solve all of our problems with Pakistan. It will not even entirely solve the problem of Pakistani support for Islamist militants, because it does not fundamentally touch the problem of LeT (whose involvement in Afghanistan at the moment is marginal). It is, however, a condition *sine qua non* for persuading Pakistan to abandon its futile attempts to parse the Islamist movement, sheltering some parts and attacking other parts of what is, in fact, an increasingly integrated organism.

Success in Afghanistan, on the other hand, would fundamentally transform the US-Pakistani relationship. America has been dependent on Pakistan since 1979 for access to Afghanistan and for support to our operations there, first against the Soviets, then against the Taliban, and now more generally. The continued flow of US supplies through Pakistani territory gives Islamabad a great deal of leverage over American policy, leverage that the Pakistanis have not been shy about demonstrating through periodic closures of the key Afghan-Pakistan border crossings through which US supplies move. American pressure on Pakistan to operate against al-Qaeda, Afghan Taliban groups, and other terrorist groups has thus always been muted by the fear of Pakistani retaliation against our lines of communication. The long-term strategic partnership with a successful Afghan state increasingly outlined by American leaders would not be remotely as dependent on lines of communication through Pakistan. The US military footprint would be much smaller than it is now and, over time, would see much less intense combat. The continued, perhaps expanded, supply flows through the Northern Distribution Network, the reestablishment of indigenous Afghan capacity to supply US forces, and the ability *in extremis* to rely on aerial resupply of much smaller forces, if necessary, could effectively emancipate the United States from Pakistan. That emancipation, in turn, would open the possibility of new strategic approaches to the US-Pakistani relationship based on a much more equal footing than our current dependence permits. It would also contribute powerfully to the need for Islamabad to reevaluate its strategic priorities, interests, and the costs of various policy options. Again, there is no silver bullet here. We must recognize, however, that the outcome of our operations in Afghanistan—positive or negative—has a very direct and important effect on Pakistan and on our relationship with Pakistan.

Taliban Buyer's Remorse

This section and the two that follow address arguments that focus narrowly on the problem of keeping al-Qaeda from returning to Afghanistan. This question is important, and these arguments merit consideration. It is vital to keep in mind, however, how very compartmentalized this discussion is. It presumes that success or failure in Afghanistan has no meaningful effect on Pakistan or the region, that al-Qaeda is the only Islamist group in the area whose potential movement into Afghanistan poses a concern for the United States, and that combatting the 100-or-so remaining leaders in the al-Qaeda core group is America's only real interest here. As I have argued above, these assumptions are invalid and discussion along these lines is far too narrowly constrained. Defeating al-Qaeda central is, nevertheless, an important American strategic goal, and many of the considerations relating to these three arguments are relevant in regard to other Islamist groups in the area.

The presence of al-Qaeda in Afghanistan has generated tension and disagreement within the Taliban since the 1990s. Mullah Omar's group itself does not appear to have regional or global jihadi aspirations, and some of Omar's principal lieutenants have long seen the dangers in harboring al-Qaeda. In particular, Mullah Baradar, Mullah Omar's key lieutenant until his arrest by Pakistani authorities in 2010, has long appeared concerned about tying the Taliban too closely to al-Qaeda. This fact has been seized upon by some analysts to argue that the Taliban would not invite al-Qaeda to return to Afghanistan even if they regained power there, and might even commit to resisting the terrorists' return if that were a condition for the United States to leave them alone. Therefore, it is not necessary, in the view of these analysts, to defeat the Taliban, and it may not even be desirable. The United States should, instead, aggressively pursue negotiations for the peaceful return of the Taliban to some kind of power in Afghanistan on condition that they actively prevent al-Qaeda from regaining sanctuaries there.

This argument is not persuasive on several levels. First and foremost, it ignores the fact that debates over the relationship between the Taliban and al-Qaeda have been occurring for more than a decade, but that Mullah Omar has always defended maintaining close ties with bin Laden and his minions, and he has won every time.

Unless and until it appears either that Mullah Omar is losing control over the movement or that he himself has altered his position on relations with al-Qaeda, it is very hard to place much confidence in the likelihood that some future round of this debate will end with a different outcome. Will bin Laden's death alter this calculus? It is far too soon to tell. The tie between Mullah Omar and bin Laden was personal and deep—the Taliban leader does not have the same relationship with Zawahiri. There is a world of difference, however, between a weakening of the relationship between Mullah Omar and bin Laden's successor and a decision by Mullah Omar actively to reject bin Laden's movement.

Even if the Quetta Shura Taliban leadership somehow decided to break ties, or even accept conflict with al-Qaeda, it is extremely difficult to see what would motivate the Haqqanis to follow suit. The ties between the Haqqani family and bin Laden are old and broad: Jalaluddin Haqqani invited bin Laden to set up camp in eastern Afghanistan in the mid-1980s during the fight against the Soviets. Unlike Mullah Omar, the Haqqanis have been living and operating near and with a number of al-Qaeda leaders, not just the late bin Laden. The apparent radicalization of the movement under Sirajuddin's leadership, moreover, including limited indications that Siraj might be interested in more than simply regaining power in Greater Paktia, strengthens the ideological tie between the two organizations. Rivalry for influence in eastern Afghanistan between the Haqqanis, the Quetta Shura, and other groups also creates potential rifts and fears that al-Qaeda can exploit by helping or offering to help the losing sides in those rivalries. And the Haqqanis have long demonstrated that they do not regard decisions taken by the Quetta Shura as necessarily binding upon them. Persuading the Haqqani Network to break ties with al-Qaeda would require a second, much more difficult, set of negotiations for which it is hard to see any basis at this point.

Finally, the track record of any Taliban group being able to exclude extremist fellow travelers from territory nominally under its control is extremely poor. Hotheaded young would-be jihadists within the Taliban movement will always be attracted to the al-Qaeda mystique, and some will be willing and even eager to help bin Laden's successor and his team. The Taliban does not exercise sufficient discipline over its cells to prevent such freelancing, and it has never controlled its territory well enough to use effective police powers to enforce a decision excluding al-Qaeda from Afghanistan. It is simply madness to imagine that a loosely organized collection of Taliban groups that are perpetually squabbling would be able to police the country as well as or better than an Afghan government with hundreds of thousands of police and soldiers backed by nearly 150,000 international forces and the panoply of capabilities they bring with them.

There is, thus, no basis for any confidence that the Taliban, if restored to power in Afghanistan, would actually break with al-Qaeda. On the contrary, there is much reason to be confident that it would be unable to keep al-Qaeda out of the country, even if it made the policy decision to do so.

A somewhat more interesting discussion is whether al-Qaeda would seek to reestablish safe havens in Afghanistan, if that were possible. One could argue that the group has moved itself firmly onto the other side of the Durand Line and that it would gain little from relocating to the more desolate and impoverished Afghan lands once again. However, some factual indicators undermine this argument somewhat: Al-Qaeda maintains a small organization within Afghanistan even now and al-Qaeda fighters periodically enter Afghanistan for various purposes.

The strategic view of this question is likely to prove more definitive, however. If America's leaders intend ultimately to destroy al-Qaeda central, then pressure on the group within Pakistan will have to increase significantly. In that case, sanctuaries in Afghanistan would once again become an attractive alternative to destruction. Moreover, even if the Pakistani government ultimately refused to increase pressure on al-Qaeda within its borders, it could well be tempted to press the group to leave Pakistan for sanctuaries in a collapsing or Taliban-controlled Afghanistan in order to alleviate American pressure on Islamabad. The prospect of safe havens in Afghanistan thus offers al-Qaeda (and Pakistan) numerous options that it does not now possess, precisely at the moment when the United States will be trying to deprive the group of any options other than defeat.

The bottom line is that the United States must harden Afghanistan against a return of al-Qaeda leadership if it is ultimately to achieve the goal of eliminating that group. Deals with the Taliban, to say nothing of simply accepting failure and withdrawing, will not support that goal. Success in Afghanistan is thus a necessary but not sufficient condition for success against al-Qaeda.

Targeted Strikes

Another common argument against the need for succeeding in the current comprehensive counterinsurgency strategy in Afghanistan is that the United States can accomplish all that is needed for its security via direct-action operations using special mission units and precision attacks from the air. This argument has already been addressed on many occasions, so we shall consider it only briefly here.

The fundamental flaw in this line of reasoning is its failure to take account of real-world, pragmatic requirements for successful direct-action operations and of their inherent limitations. It also ignores, however, the extremely high tempo at which such operations are being conducted now in Afghanistan and even, by comparison with previous years, in Pakistan. Comprehensive counterinsurgency does not come at the expense of direct-action operations. On the contrary, it is accompanied by an acceleration and expansion of those operations to a level that would be unsupportable without the presence of a large, conventional military footprint.

Killing or capturing a terrorist leader requires knowing where he will be when the bombs hit or the team arrives. Killing him with bombs requires having good enough intelligence on his movements that we can keep electronic eyes on him until the bombs detonate. A team requires somewhat less intelligence, since it can cordon a small area and capture and question individuals to ensure that it has the right person (whereas a bomb can only kill). Even so, special mission units are highly valued and limited strategic assets, and they cannot be risked on missions requiring them to roam around enemy-held areas for a long time knocking on doors—they require precise intelligence with high confidence about the locations of their targets—as was the case with the raid that culminated in the killing of Osama bin Laden.

The process of collecting, analyzing, generating, and disseminating intelligence fast enough to support direct-action operations is enormously challenging and has a number of inherent bottlenecks. Bottlenecks related to gathering intelligence can be significantly reduced by having a larger and more dispersed footprint on the ground. A more dispersed deployment also allows special mission units to be at the ready in many different locations, increasing the likelihood that they will be able to respond rapidly as intelligence identifies local targets. The farther away the unit's base is from the target area, the greater the amount and detail of intelligence required to launch an operation. Put simply, if a unit is close enough to get to a target area within two hours, the intelligence only has to be able to identify where the target will be two hours hence: the length of a meeting, for instance. If it will take a unit four, eight, or more hours to arrive at a location, the intelligence has to be able to identify not only the target's current location, but his next one, two, three, or four planned moves, including, possibly, where he intends to bed down overnight. It is much more difficult to acquire such intelligence—effectively, foreknowledge of the enemy's movements—than it is to know that a target has sat down for a long lunch or a meeting. As a result, the requirement to concentrate special mission units in a smaller number of centralized locations will reduce the frequency and effectiveness of their operations because acquiring such precise intelligence about our enemies' future plans occurs much less often and because it is more likely to prove inaccurate.

Aerial attacks do not necessarily suffer from the same limitations, since aircraft can orbit on station across the country and fast-moving fighter-bombers can fly from one end of Afghanistan to the other in an hour. But the intelligence challenges of supporting such operations are daunting in different ways, since both rules of engagement and common sense require that targets be positively identified (by the aerial platform in this case) before being attacked. Some argue that such rules of engagement are too fastidious and that the United States should be less concerned about killing and wounding innocent civilians. The legal, moral, and ethical basis of that argument is highly questionable (and I, for one, absolutely reject it), but that is beside the point strategically. Effective direct action requires knowing with pretty high confidence whether we have killed the intended target or not. Positive identification is required in order to evaluate every part of the targeting process and begin to understand the effect of the strike on enemy networks. The bottom line is that targeted strikes require good enough aerial coverage to identify targets positively and then accurately assess the damage done to them. The United States has a limited number of systems capable of providing such coverage, and the nature of Afghanistan's terrain poses challenges of its own. The reality, unsurprising to anyone familiar with how intelligence and targeting systems work, is that the real world imposes strict limits on America's ability to kill-and-capture its way to success. Arguments for the reliance on such an approach that do not address these basic limitations are at best naïve and at worst disingenuous.

Other Sanctuaries

One of the last common arguments against the need to pursue comprehensive counterinsurgency in Afghanistan is that the terrorists will simply move to other theaters in the world, such as Somalia or Yemen, where the United States does not have military forces or effective local partners to attack them. Charlie Szrom and Christopher Harnisch have examined this question in detail for The Critical Threats Project (which I direct) at the American Enterprise Institute.[9] In general terms, although it is possible that al-Qaeda central and even other South Asian terrorist leaders might move to Yemen, Somalia, the Maghreb, or elsewhere in the face of American success in Afghanistan, it is unlikely. Further, any such movement by those leaders would likely result in a significant degradation in the capabilities of their groups for some time, because no other region in the world offers as dense and effective a support network for global Islamists as does South Asia.

Long-lived and successful terrorists are not, by nature, trusting people. They do not lightly place their lives and their organizations in the hands of people they do not know well and with whom they do not have long-established and stable relationships. Those who trust tend to be killed or captured easily, creating a Darwinian cycle within Islamist organizations. Consider the time and effort that was required to locate and kill Osama bin Laden. His successors, Ayman al Zawahiri, Abu Yahya al Libi, and their close associates will not rush to move in with people they have met in terrorist chat rooms.

These leaders and many of their close followers have been in South Asia for more than two decades. Bin Laden knew Jalaluddin Haqqani for a quarter of a century and watched Siraj Haqqani grow up. He had not spent much time in Saudi Arabia or Yemen for many years, nor had Zawahiri in Egypt. Neither they nor any other al-Qaeda senior leader has spent much (or any) time in Somalia, the Maghreb, or the Sahel. Moving into any of those areas would require either trusting local networks with which they cannot be very familiar or taking the time to establish their own trust relationships with local Islamist groups, something that does not appear to be possible for them to do from far away.

These practical reasons likely help explain why al-Qaeda central has neither dispersed nor moved under the increasing pressure of Pakistani operations and American drone strikes. It is certainly possible that even greater pressure or determined Pakistani efforts to destroy the network would drive them out of Pakistan. In that case, they would likely look first to Afghanistan, if the United States abandons current efforts, since they have remained in contact with well-known and long-trusted networks there. If that option were foreclosed, they might then consider moving to Yemen, where they have relatively tighter connections and a more comfortable human environment. Only if that option, too, were foreclosed or some other unforeseen development occurred would they be likely to look beyond their traditional areas of operation and homelands to consider places like Somalia or West Africa.

None of this is inconceivable by any means. But the relocation of al-Qaeda senior leadership anywhere outside of South Asia would almost certainly induce a period of consolidation during which their efforts would be concentrated on firmly establishing themselves in their new sanctuary. They would be inherently more vulnerable in this period because of the much more limited circle of trust in which they could operate, which would, in turn, physically limit the number of safe houses in which they could stay and hold meetings. They would have to establish new operational patterns, new means of communication, possibly new training areas. Their effectiveness would very likely be degraded and the likelihood of successful US direct action against them would be increased. It would be very much to America's advantage, in other words, to uproot al-Qaeda central from South Asia and force it to look for new homes elsewhere.

Prospects for Success in Afghanistan

The discussion above is valid whether or not success in Afghanistan is possible. If the United States does not succeed in its current efforts, then it will suffer a significant setback in its struggle against al-Qaeda and affiliated movements. Arguments against the possibility of success in Afghanistan or against the desirability of trying to succeed must straightforwardly and objectively weigh the scale of that setback and articulate meaningful strategies to mitigate or counter it, and the costs of those strategies.

Still, if success is actually not possible along the current approach, then we should begin now to develop and execute an alternative, however much less desirable it might be. American strategy, thus, must still turn on an evaluation of our prospects in Afghanistan.

As this chapter is written in the summer of 2011, there is considerable basis for optimism. Security gains in 2010 were substantial—coalition forces deprived the Quetta Shura Taliban of almost all of its most important safe havens within Afghanistan, some of which had been under uncontested Taliban control for years.[10] The development of meaningful local defense initiatives (the Afghan Local Police program, along with "village stability operations") that are supported by the Afghan central government, by local communities, and by the United States, and that have already spread to a number of provinces throughout Afghanistan, are promising new departures in light of the many false starts that have plagued earlier, similar efforts. The Afghan National Security Force, particularly the Army and the Afghan National Civil Order Police, have been significantly expanded and have also increased their abilities to plan, move, operate, and fight.

Progress in Afghan governance has been much slower and more halting, but that is not surprising. Improvements in governance generally lag far behind improvements in security (we observed that phenomenon in Iraq as well), and there has been some limited progress already. It is too early, however, to determine how meaningful this progress will be or how much, if any, momentum it will develop. The general trajectory of Afghan governance, however, is more positive than negative at this moment, something that has not been true for several years.

But it is summer as of this writing, and the poppy harvest, which traditionally reduces enemy activity in the south, ended some months ago. Fighting has picked up and violence has increased. The Taliban have launched a number of attacks aimed at unhinging coalition success in the south, including the Kandahar prison break, the assassination of the Kandahar provincial chief of police, and spectacular attacks in Kabul, Kandahar, and elsewhere. The insurgents will continue these efforts and attempt to move the fight into other areas. These developments, along with continued international pressure on the Afghan government to reduce corruption and improve transparency, will put increased strain on that government and its relations with the West. Things will likely get worse before they get better.

The real test of the progress and prospects of the current strategy will come in the very near future. If the enemy is able to retake or seriously undermine security in areas that the coalition has cleared and is holding, then the strategy can be judged to be failing. If the Afghan government turns away from efforts to improve transparency, responsiveness, and inclusiveness rather than increasingly embracing them, then the strategy is not succeeding. The stagnation or serious erosion of the Afghan local police program is another potential indicator that things are off course (although there will almost certainly be some erosion as fighters who "reintegrated" to get through the winter rediscover their commitment to the Taliban come spring). Erosion in the size, quality, and competence of the Afghan National Army would be another serious negative indicator.

These are the signs to watch for. If they are pointing generally in the right direction, then the current strategy is showing real prospects of success and, given the stakes, should continue to receive full support and resourcing. If they are pointing in the wrong direction, then the strategy is most likely failing. In that case, the United States will have to select from a menu of painful and costly alternatives, none of which can really secure American interests adequately. It is well worth trying to succeed as long as success remains possible.

Notes

1 The Cold War International History Project has published an extensive collection of translated proceedings of Soviet Politburo meetings and minutes of private meetings of senior Soviet officials. Possible American reactions to the deployment of Soviet forces in Afghanistan are remarkable for their absence. President Jimmy Carter's likely rejection of the communist Afghan government early in 1979 is treated as an afterthought during a mid-March Politburo discussion. Foreign Minister Andrei Gromyko, evaluating the possible negative effects of such an invasion on Soviet foreign policy, noted only that it would jeopardize détente and possibly the START II Treaty and scuttle a planned meeting between Carter and Communist Party General Secretary Leonid Brezhnev. The Soviet reaction in the wake of Carter's responses to the invasion is, in some respects, even more telling. A February 1980 top-secret communiqué of a meeting of Soviet, Bulgarian, Czechoslovakian, Polish, Hungarian, and East German foreign secretaries concluded: "we must see that Carter's 'new' policy has not had the expected result. The United States could not turn Afghanistan into a base of operations for American imperialism, and it is of principal importance that the USA did not consider it possible to announce military confrontation." See "Transcript of CPSU CC Politburo Discussions on Afghanistan," 3/17/1979 (TsKhSD, f. 89, per. 25 dok. 1, II. 1, 12–25), and "Report on the meeting of the foreign secretaries of the closely cooperating socialist countries in Moscow," 2/29/1980, both available at www.wilsoncenter.org/index.cfm?fuseaction5topics.home&topic_id51409, accessed May 24, 2011.

2 In contrast with the first president of the postrevolutionary Iranian government, Abol-Hassan Banisadr, whose fears of American retaliation were stoked by the failed hostage-rescue attempt, Operation Eagle Claw (better known as Desert One). See, e.g., Shaul Bakhash, The Reign of the Ayatollahs: Iran and the Islamic Revolution (New York: Basic Books, 1984, rev. 1990), 116ff.

3 See the work of Katherine Zimmerman and Christopher Harnisch on al-Qaeda in the Arabian Peninsula for the Critical Threats Project at the American Enterprise Institute, at www.criticalthreats.org.

4 See the work of Reza Jan for the Critical Threats Project at the American Enterprise Institute about these groups, at www.criticalthreats.org.

5 This second matter is a modern restatement of the old Pakistani concept of "strategic depth." Earlier in Pakistan's history, some military leaders apparently did consider the possibility of retreating into Afghanistan in the face of an Indian attack. The current leadership recognizes this notion for the folly that it is; "strategic depth" has come to mean denial of Indian operating bases in Pakistan's rear.

6 For excellent studies of the relationships between successive Pakistani governments and Islamist militants from the 1970s onward, see Shuja Nawaz, Crossed Swords: Pakistan, Its Army, and the Wars Within (New York: Oxford University Press, 2008); Husain Haqqani, Pakistan Between Mosque and Military (Washington, DC: Carnegie Endowment for International Peace, 2005); and Hassan Abbas, Pakistan's Drift into Extremism: Allah, the Army, and America's War on Terror (New York: M. E. Sharpe, 2005).

7 Reza Jan has narrated some of these operations extensively, at www.criticalthreats.org.

8 Jeffrey Dressler and Carl Forsberg have narrated key aspects of the military campaign in their work available at the Institute for the Study of War, at www.understandingwar.org. See also Frederick W. Kagan and Kimberly Kagan, Defining Success in Afghanistan, January 2011, available at www.criticalthreats.org and www.understandingwar.org.

9 Charlie Szrom and Christopher Harnisch, Al Qaeda's Operating Environments: A New Approach to the War on Terror (Washington, DC: American Enterprise Institute, 2011), available at www.criticalthreats.org.

10 See Kagan and Kagan, Defining Success in Afghanistan, for an overview of progress in 2010.

CHAPTER 7

Afghanistan: A Third Way

Edward N. Luttwak

Introduction: The Regional Context

What follows is based on the presumption that the attempt to transform Afghanistan into a pluralist democracy (peaceful at home yet strong enough to keep the agents of Pakistan's institutionalized extremism at bay) has been a quixotic venture of very great cost in blood, treasure, and reputation, sustained against daily evidence of its impossibility by the ignorant arrogance of "counterinsurgency" theorists in and out of uniform. It is true that the Taliban would find few supporters in an Afghanistan developed to Swedish standards of education and affluence, but it was always a fallacy to believe that victory could be won by the insignificant ameliorations possible in less than a century or more of very costly endeavors—and without killing a great number of recalcitrant Afghans.

What is offered instead is an organic solution that accepts the heterogeneity of Afghanistan and recognizes that China, the Russian Federation, and India have more pressing reasons than the United States has to prevent a Taliban victory. The former offers the ready possibility of reconstructing a product-improved "Northern Alliance" that with steady external aid can keep the Taliban from Kabul. The latter indicates where the aid comes from, and it is not the United States, which is so greatly separated by distance and constrained by the need to practice its own fiscal frugality.

This is not a formula for perpetual civil war, but rather a reversion to the formula that ensured Afghanistan's tranquility in the past, and which allowed a young traveler to go from end to end of the country without encountering any form of war: a central government, discreetly helped by foreign powers, that tolerates local diversities under the patronage of duly respectful local potentates.

The patient traveler who follows China's interminable highway 314 from Urumqi through Kashgar to the Pakistan border crossing passes within hiking distance of Afghanistan, at the roadless tip of the Wakhan corridor. The Uyghur dissidents who were encountered and captured during the 2001 US invasion would scarcely have inconvenienced themselves to reach Afghanistan that way, given that Tajikistan offers a much easier route to Kabul, while transit from China via Pakistan offers cheaper bus rides by way of the most scenic highways.

But even if it is only cartographic, the adjacence of Afghanistan to Xinjiang, where some nine million perpetually restless Uyghurs live, reminds us that it is China that should be paying the costs of the war against the Taliban, given that it is ten thousand miles closer to the danger. Only the deeply provincial could view this suggestion as outlandish, given the present financial circumstances of the United States and those of China, and the respective Afghan perils faced by each: one is in the al-Qaeda past, the other is China's unsecured political future.

A debate has been under way in the United States between people who fear that Taliban rule would provide a safe haven for global jihadists, and others who insist that the Taliban are an essentially Afghan phenomenon whose leaders paid a very heavy price the last time they harbored foreign terrorists, and who would not do so again. But there can be no debate about what Taliban rule would mean for China: The certainty of sanctuary for Uyghur fugitives (in the first place within the small Uyghur communities in Afghan cities), and the lively possibility of at least discreet bases for dissidents. Sanctuary just across the border from the Uyghurstan of their dreams has a different meaning than sanctuary in Munich, home of the hereditary leader Erkin Alptekin, or Washington, DC, where Rebiya Kadeer, a prominent Uyghur businesswoman and political activist, lives. Distance matters.

Moreover, Taliban rule could shelter a far greater level of dissidence than that of the Uyghur, because China's Hui Muslim minority is many times larger, and when it revolted in the nineteenth century under the influence of a now indeterminate "new teaching" that may well have been Wahhabism, the rebels ravaged a great part of northwest China centered on Shaanxi for years on end, causing the deaths of millions.[1] More recent outbreaks of Hui violence have been quite small, but there is a militant reassertion of Hui identity: Veiled hair is now the norm in Hui quarters and has become a common sight, even among the tourist throngs in Beijing. With educational progress the possibility of renewed ideological contagions has only increased, because it is not traditional and customary Islam that inspires violence but rather the purist creed imported from Arabia.

For China's leadership, the tranquility of the country's Muslim populations is imperative for internal security and regime stability; as such, it takes absolute precedence over all other considerations. If faced with the alternative of supporting the fight against the Taliban or seeing them take power in Kabul, the Chinese government would opt for the former.

But of course, the Chinese must be presented with the choice and not simply allowed a free ride. As it is, the failure of the US government to demand large material contributions from China is an evident case of *pauvresse oblige*, the pathetic keeping up of appearances of decayed gentlefolk. Only that desiccated form of arrogance can explain why the bill has not been presented to China at a time when the US government is borrowing a good part of the 45 percent of every billion that the United States spends in Afghanistan each month from China, to China's great benefit.

The Russian Federation is not lending money to the United States as China is doing, and at its nearest point it is almost a thousand miles from the Afghan border, but it too has its own dissidents and potentially dissident Muslims, and thus it too has a much more compelling motive to keep the Taliban from power than the United States could ever have. That unrest in Chechnya is now mostly under control, except for episodic terrorist attacks, scarcely solves the entire Muslim problem for the Russian Federation because it includes far larger Muslim populations than Chechnya's scant million. Islamist pressure is constant in Daghestan as well as in Ingushetia and across the Caucasus, while strong identity movements are alarmingly manifest in the multiplication of mosques, even in still-peaceful Bashkortostan and Tatarstan. Exotic only in name and not to Russians, Kazan, Tatarstan's capital on the Volga River, has its own Kremlin whose cathedral holds Russia's holiest icon, the supposedly rediscovered Black Virgin; it also contains more than a hundred new mosques. The advent of an actively Islamist government in Kabul would not be conducive to Russia's tranquility, if only because Muslim dissidents would certainly be sheltered there. In theory, Turkey might be expected to provide a far more functional and infinitely wealthier supporting base for Muslim militants from the Russian Federation; but under its present government, Turkey only supports the national rights of the Palestinians, while ignoring those of all other Muslim nationalities.

Moreover, the borders between the Russian Federation and central Asia remain very porous, as do the Tajik and Uzbek borders with Afghanistan. Besides, the Russian government has its own stakes in the secular regimes of Islam Karimov of Uzbekistan and Emomali Rahmon of Tajikistan, both of which would be much less secure if the Taliban ruled across the Amu-Darya.

It is therefore absurd that the United States should be spending several hundred million dollars to equip the embryonic Afghan air force with refurbished or new M-17 helicopters from Russia, which should instead donate not only the M-17s but all the equipment needed by all Afghan military and police forces, since they rely on ex-Soviet weapons systems.[2] Once the Chinese supply the consumables, including ammunition, fuel, and food, the United States could limit its own contribution to planning, command, and control—fortunately, there is no shortage of American general officers.

As it is, the failure to transfer the costs of the Afghan war to the Chinese and Russian treasuries reflects not only the sadly anachronistic notions of American wealth, but also the essential nature of "counterinsurgency" as a disembodied military cult, oblivious to the regional as well as the Afghan political context. As to the former, this includes two countries besides China and Russia who also have a greater need than the United States to prevent a Taliban victory: India and Iran.

The Taliban are other things as well, but first of all they are Muslims of the most extreme sort, and committed jihadis. Yet India's motive in opposing a Taliban victory has nothing to do with religion as such, or even Taliban jihadism. The Indian government has no reason whatever to fear that its 170–180 million Muslims would be infected by Taliban extremism imported from Afghanistan, because that product is actually manufactured in India, and exported *to* Afghanistan, as well as to Pakistan, the United Kingdom, and countries around the world. The ultimate and still very active source of the doctrine adopted by the Taliban and taken up by Muslim extremists everywhere is the Darul Oloom preachers' and teachers' seminary in Deoband, Uttar Pradesh, India, whose graduates have established hundreds of Darul Oloom schools around the world. Urdu is the primary language of instruction, but the teachings are purely Wahhabi in content, and thus puritanical in the extreme, militantly predisposed to armed jihad, and intensely hostile to all religions except Sunni Islam—in the purist Wahhabi interpretation. Among many other things, this condemns the Shi'a as apostates, and prohibits any sort of friendly dealings with Christians or Jews.

While they added their own intense Pashtun misogyny, the Taliban did not distort the Darul Oloom teaching but merely applied it in earnest. Given this, one would have thought that the Indian government would have shut down the school long ago. Instead, it enjoys tax-exempt status as an eleemosynary establishment. This excess of forbearance dates back to the emergence of Muslim separatism in the 1930s under the future founder of Pakistan, Muhammad Ali Jinnah. Dedicated to Muslim supremacy over all of India, it was founded in 1866 in explicit reaction to the British deposition of the last of the Mughal emperors a decade earlier—the Darul Oloom naturally opposed separatism. That was good enough for the Indian government, which studiously ignored the true motive, just as it now ignores the rank duplicity of Darul Oloom's ritual condemnation of terrorism; its chosen examples are "The barbarous bombing of several countries by USA, Israeli aggression against Palestinians, Russian atrocities in Chechnya and Chinese brutalities against Muslims in Sin kiang."[3]

Therefore, it is for an entirely nonreligious reason that India supports the Karzai government against the Taliban. It is acting in opposition to Pakistan's attempt to convert Afghanistan into its own dependency, thereby achieving multiple aims: the neutralization of Azad Pashtunistan separatism, the acquisition of de facto frontiers with Central Asia and the resulting transport links, and the simple increase in strategic depth that goes some way to diminish India's large advantage in the same. Just as all three would strengthen Pakistan, affecting the balance of power in the subcontinent, to deny them is to India's advantage. Accordingly, India has provided large amounts of aid to Afghanistan; it operates an active diplomatic mission in Kabul as well as consulates in Mazar-i-Sharif, Jalalabad, and Kandahar.[4] Pakistan predictably responded in its usual way, by organizing deniable terrorist attacks, notably the suicide car bombing of the Indian Chancery on July 7, 2008, which killed 58 people and wounded 141.[5] The Indians did not give up, of course, and they continue to be very active, thereby encouraging the many Afghans who strive to resist both the Taliban and less blatant expressions of Pakistan's nefarious influence.

It would therefore be inappropriate to peremptorily demand more from India, as should certainly be done in the case of the free-riding Chinese and Russians. But India may still have to make greater efforts if Pakistan reacts to the success of indigenization (as discussed below) by increasing its own support of the Taliban and the other armed groupings it covertly maintains. In the past, thousands of Pakistani soldiers sometimes fought alongside the Taliban; if that were to happen again, as it could once US and allied forces are no longer present in Afghanistan, then India could apply counter pressure by increasing its frontal deployments along the border, or their readiness level, thus supplementing whatever added support it could provide in-country.

It is not a fine irony but a gross one that Afghanistan's only neighbor that actively works day by day to facilitate a Taliban victory and a US defeat is also the only one that receives large amounts of military aid from the United States. The absurdity of large-scale US military aid to the Pakistan government did not come about because absurd decisions were made by fools, but rather because of perfectly reasonable day-to-day decision making, in which pragmatic compromises were made at each remove. Now, however, with the benefit of hindsight and the ability to consider the whole, it is unreasonable to persist in providing aid to the patrons of the Taliban and of multiple jihadi networks—China's very good ally but not America's. Once military aid is stopped, separate arrangements will have to be maintained for Pakistan's nuclear weapons and not-yet-weaponized fissile material—that is to say a permanent state of operational readiness for their forcible neutralization—but there will be no need to replace supply lines through Pakistan once today's high-cost strategy gives way to the "Afghan" alternative proposed below.

Pakistan's systematically duplicitous role in Afghanistan emerges in starkest contrast with the position of a country that none would confuse with a US ally: Iran. Its Afghan activities have sometimes been hostile to the United States and its allies, and in lethal ways, but mostly Iran's leaders have cooperated with US policy, and in important ways, whereas Pakistan is the natural ally of the Taliban.[6]

Iran's experiences during the years of Taliban rule were certainly most unhappy, so much so that the world's two most fervently Islamic regimes almost went to war in September 1998, after the Taliban capture of Mazar-i-Sharif, the massacre of some eight thousand Hazara civilians, and the kidnapping and presumptive murder of nine Iranians with diplomatic credentials attached to the Islamic Republic of Iran (IRI) consulate.[7] That was not a mere incident of wartime violence: According to their Wahhabi doctrine (of which the subcontinental Deobandi version is merely the Urdu rendition), the Shi'a are apostates deserving of death, and of course both the IRI diplomats and the vast majority of the Hazara are Twelver Shi'a, or infidels in Taliban eyes.[8]

For all their religiosity, the rulers of the Islamic Republic of Iran can be quite pragmatic when they want. for years they have sided with Christian Armenia in its deadly quarrel with mostly Shi'a Azerbaijan. But evidently the collision of two fanatical regimes left no room for pragmatism.

In any case, Iran's interests were damaged by Taliban rule in more mundane ways, specifically by the greatly increased inflow of both heroin and refugees from Afghanistan. Both tended to cross the intervening provinces to make their way to Tehran, forming most undesirable conjunctions as far as the ruling clerics were concerned, as parks filled with thousands of drug addicts, tens of thousands of unemployed Afghans roamed the streets, and on Fridays open-air Sunni prayer gatherings remedied the absence of even one Sunni mosque (present in both Washington, DC, and Tel Aviv but not Tehran).

The Islamic Republic's most concrete response to the Islamic Emirate was its support of the *Jabha-yi Muttahid-i Islami-yi Milli bara-yi Nijat-i Afghanistan* of Ahmad Shah Massoud, Haji Abdul Qadir, Hussain Anwari, and others (and Abdul Rashid Dostum, until his defeat and exile in 1998), sanitized as the "Northern Alliance" for Western ears. I have seen no numbers, but since 1995, when the Taliban conquered Herat, which Iran considers its own Afghan outpost, Iran supplied much-needed cash, complementing India's aid and the CIA's lackadaisical, inexpert, and intermittent help.

It is unsurprising therefore that when the United States invaded Afghanistan in 2001, the Islamic Republic entirely set aside its ideological anti-Americanism, and ignored its religious obligation to succor fellow Muslims under infidel attack (for Twelver Shi'a, Sunnis are not heretical) to instead signal approval and then help the United States to achieve its successive political aims in Afghanistan.[9] Indeed, that has remained Iran's stance until now, aside from occasional if egregious deviations: Material evidence shows that the urge to kill American and British troops was sometimes irresistible. More consequentially, Iran has steadily supported the same Karzai regime that the United States created and still keeps in power, not least by inducing its own lieges to participate in its rule[10] (and not unprofitably, given the proclivities of Karzai and company[11]).

The fact that Iran would be very seriously damaged by a Taliban victory in Afghanistan potentially confers corresponding leverage upon the United States, so long as the US government itself pursues the Afghan war as an optional political enterprise intended to serve American interests, rather than as a "COINISTA" experiment meant to transform Afghanistan into an enlightened democracy one cup of tea at a time.

To be sure, as long as it was assumed that anti-US Muslim terrorism thrived in Afghanistan, there was no leverage to be had over Iran or China, or Russia for that matter, because it was thought that Afghanistan could only be abandoned *to* terrorism. But it has long since been established that anti-US Muslim terrorism can emerge wherever jihadist preaching can enroll recruits; that is, anywhere at all, including US military bases on US soil. Hence, anti-US Muslim terrorism would not be physically precluded even if the US presence in Afghanistan amounted to the fullest control of its territory, which is far from being true.

It is true that there is a less material but more powerful linkage between Afghanistan and global anti-US Muslim terrorism, because a Taliban victory would undoubtedly energize jihadism in many places by attracting funds and recruits for its local organizers. But that would only constrain US policy in Afghanistan to remain on its present, very costly path—the Sisyphean task of building a state and an army of the unwilling, if there were no other way of preventing a Taliban victory.[12] That is far from being true.

An Afghan Strategy for Afghanistan

The salient alternative to present policies that now cost the phenomenal amount of some eight billion dollars a month is to leave the building of the future unitary Afghan nation-state, with its future national institutions civil and military, to the peoples of Afghanistan themselves, while limiting the US role to the material support of any and all armed forces in the field that fight *against* rather than *for* the Taliban.[13]

There is strong historical evidence for the contention that this policy would indeed prevent a Taliban victory. Prior to the US invasion of 2001, notwithstanding Pakistan's large-scale support of the Taliban with weapons, transport, ammunition, money, trained soldiers, and officers, they could not conquer the whole of Afghanistan by finally defeating the bedraggled remnant of the "Northern Alliance," which at this point was receiving only meager outside help, and had lost with the assassination of Ahmad Shah Massoud, by far its most capable war leader (as well as the locally effective Abdul Rashid Dostum by exile three years earlier).

The reason for the failure of Pakistan and the Taliban to complete the conquest of Afghanistan was fundamentally political rather than military, or more precisely ethno-political.[14] The fact that there is no Afghan nation except in official rhetoric—excusably in Kabul, much less so in the Pentagon—is the most fundamental truth known to every Afghan, and readily discovered by any visitor not bound by official pieties. There is no nation as a functioning entity that can evoke loyalty for itself, and hence no political foundation on which a conventional nation-state, with its national army and national police, can be successfully built.

Nor can Islam provide an alternative basis of broad solidarity; on the contrary, Islam provokes its own sectarian divisions, even very violent ones. It is only against non-Muslims that Islam can unite Afghans, but that is scarcely of help in fighting the Taliban, who are undoubtedly Muslim through and through, while their enemies are infidel foreigners or the paid and obedient servants of infidel foreigners. That is how the Taliban depict the Afghan government, its army, and its police. As to the "paid" part, the Taliban are of course right in their assessment—but the "obedience" is very limited.

Nothing can stop the United States or any other foreign power from sending money to Afghanistan to recruit men and a few hardy women, buy weapons for them, and dress them up in uniforms. But there is no sense of national loyalty and no conception of public service that will induce them to train in earnest, let alone risk their lives to fight for the abstraction of a state, and one funded by infidel foreigners to boot, or to impartially police their fellow citizens with a bit of venial corruption on the side, in the manner of all police forces. Instead, the opportunity for extortion is the only motivation in the absence of a sense of duty, so that its absence would result in mere passivity and not honest policing. That, after all, is how police behave every day in many countries less backward than Afghanistan, but in this case there is a war under way that cannot be won by good policing alone. But, it can be lost by police bullying and extortion.

Fortunately, there is an effective alternative to the absent Afghan nation in its own constituent elements, which are indeed capable of evoking loyalty and do so every day. Afghanistan is not an Augustinian *magna latrocinia* of roaming bandits and anarchical warriors. It is a vast mosaic of families, clans, language and local groupings, tribes, tribal alliances, lineage confederations, and at least one *sui generis* politico-religious community, each of which has its own identity and its own conception of political legitimacy, without thereby being in perpetual conflict with its neighbors.[15] Afghanistan is not highland New Guinea, and instead of Hobbesian perpetual war, established patterns of accommodation define most intergroup relationships.

As for the relations of each entity with the central government, through all possible variations under all possible regimes, they are usually defined by the relative prevalence of fiscal evasion and rent-seeking. Thanks to the bounty of the United States and its allies, there is at present very little of the former and vast amounts of the latter, ensuring good relations between local potentates and the central government as long as the cash keeps coming. The flow of money can also secure local tranquility insofar as the potentate in question distributes a decent share of the bounty downward to chiefs and patriarchs, preferably without noisome demands that it be spent on the strange schemes invented by foreigners, or for such un-Islamic purposes as the education of females (although there is overwhelming evidence from all parts of Afghanistan that it is the maladministration of justice that gains support for the Taliban rather than female education).

Foreigners are forever trying to simplify Afghanistan's ethno-political mosaic by focusing on the largest and best-known groupings, without first asking if they are politically meaningful identities for any purpose whatever. The Pashtuns (in Pashtu) or Pathans (in Urdu), supposed followers of the grotesquely misrepresented Pashtunwali code, and the second largest supposed nation, the Tajiks, exist only as labels in the minds of others, for they have no political cohesion whatever.[16] To make a distinction between *Durranis* and *Ghilzais* as members of different Pashtun tribal confederations would be meaningful if they were in fact separate entities, with members loyal to each. Nor is it useful to descend one level down to reach supposed tribes such as the *Ahmadzai*, in reality nothing but a surname that connotes no particular geographic location and certainly no coincidence of interests; there may well have been *Ahmadzais* among the Taliban who beat to death the last communist ruler of Afghanistan, Mohammad Najibullah Ahmadzai.

Likewise, any Persian speakers not otherwise identified are apt to be described as a Tajik, but are much more likely to describe themselves as the residents of this or that town or area. Moreover, there are Persian-speaking members of Pashtun lineage, descendants of migrants who were linguistically assimilated. The same happened to the Aimaks of Turco-Altaic origin, some of whom look just as Mongol as many Hazara do, and who also speak Persian dialects but are Twelver Shi'a and were harshly persecuted for it in the past. It might seem that it should be otherwise in a land inflamed by Sunni Islam in its more fanatical versions, but to be a Shi'a is not identity-defining either, because the Kizilbash, descendants of the "red heads" from Turkey who entered Afghanistan after forcibly converting the Persians and Azeris to Shi'ism, are still Twelver Shi'a. But as well-established city dwellers they are not persecuted for it, and were not, even under the Taliban, who murdered Hazaras for not growing beards (as many of their Mongol ancestors, they have no facial hair).

Given their lack of cohesion, the common demographic estimates of the larger ethnic groups (42% Pashtun, 27% Tajiks, 9% Hazara, 9% Uzbeks, 4% Aimaks) are not even accurate. How could estimators know that someone is, say, a Tajik, if he does not know that himself? Even perfect numbers would tell us nothing that would be of any help in determining political identities and alignments. These numbers do not even define potential recruitment pools because there are more Pashtuns in Pakistan than in Afghanistan, and many more Uzbeks in Uzbekistan than in Afghanistan.

Politically meaningful entities, with real followers and real leaders, begin with extended families and the clans they blend into. With this, we leave behind the far larger ethnic groupings that alas are mere labels, to enter the world of amoral familism—the only possible organizing principle, in the absence of functioning parties that can effectively coalesce diverse interests and represent them, or the much worse alternative that is all too present-arbitrary and fragmented warlord rule.

Because each cohesive clan or community is in effect a kingdom of its own, Afghanistan cannot be conquered by winning a great battle in the Clausewitzian manner, or even a series of battles. There is no unitary army that can be defeated decisively to finally win the war. Instead there are many kingdoms, each of which must be subdued, or destroyed, or won over and co-opted with inducements as well as threats. It was this multiplicity of kingdoms that the Taliban finally could not co-opt fully nor extinguish, and indeed the "Northern Alliance" was a gathering of them, more or less kept together by the downward flow of resources from the leaders who still received some meager help from abroad: Ahmad Shah Massoud, Haji Abdul Qadir, Hussain Anwari, and others. The one entity in it that was not a gathering of families and clans was the Uzbek mercenary army of Abdul Rashid Dostum, nominally the militia of his very own *Junbish-i-Milli Islami Afghanistan* political party, of which it can be said that it is neither a movement (Junbush), nor is it national (Milli), nor even Islamic, and certainly not a political party.

Because of its sheer lack of means, the Northern Alliance could not defeat the well-funded Taliban, which in addition was directly supported by regular Pakistani troops. But given decent funding, a new voluntary gathering of anti-Taliban forces, including the Kabul kingdom of Karzai, could do very well in fighting the Taliban, certainly more so than the Afghan national army. Given decent funding, moreover, there should be no great problem of command and control, Afghan style, because the leaders would have the wherewithal to ensure that the large and small militias under them keep pointing their weapons in the right direction. The scope for funding is in fact more than decent, because *1 percent* (!) of what the United States now spends in Afghanistan each month on indigenous security forces (about 80 million dollars), would provide $800 for each one of 100,000 militiamen, a princely monthly salary by Afghan standards, and that for service where one lives, to defend one's own people. There is no point in doing the numbers because the upkeep of US forces in Afghanistan is so enormously costly—it works out at a million dollars a year per uniformed head—that their replacement would offer much scope for both large savings and ample funding for militia forces that should in any case be materially supported by China, Russia, and India as well. In the end it is a matter of comparative advantage: landlocked, pre-national, and Muslim Afghanistan is both the worst place to keep US troops and the best place to sustain the militias that can advantageously replace them.

Notes

1 Not an anachronistic attribution: it was first made by J. J. M. De Groot in *Sectarianism and Religious Persecution in China*, vol. 2 (New York, NY: Paragon Book Gallery, Ltd., 1963), 311–29.

2 Alex Spillius, "The US has spent $648 million on 31 civilian M-17s; it can now buy aircraft ready for military use directly from Russia," in "U.S. to buy Russian helicopters for Afghan Air force, September 7, 2010. www.iraq-war.ru/article/229060.

3 "Concept of Peace and Condemnation of Terrorism in Islam," Darululoom Deoband-India, Preaching and Teaching of Islam, www.darululoom-deoband.com/english/index.htm.

4 The $180 million Salma Dam development in Herat is the single largest project.

5 Mark Mazzetti and Eric Schmitt, "Pakistanis Aided Attack in Kabul US Officials Say," *New York Times*, August 1, 2008.

6 Of Afghanistan, not the so-called Pakistani Taliban, the latest name for armed rebels in chronically rebellious areas. Pakistani officials naturally try to obfuscate the difference so as to claim that they are "fighting the Taliban."

7 Human Rights Watch, "*The Massacre in Mazar-I-Sharif*," vol. 10, no. 7 (November, 1998).

8 Apologists for Islam habitually deny the currency of the death penalty for apostasy, in spite of numerous contemporary instances. Regarding the Hazara, the newly installed Taliban governor Mulla Manon Niazi reportedly declared: "Hazaras are not Muslim, they are Shi'a. They are *kofr* [infidel]". After the massacre, in a more genial mood ("What has happened has happened") he told Hazaras: "You either accept to be Muslims or leave Afghanistan." See document cited in note 3; section VI.

9 US air-rescue planning reportedly presumed Iranian overflight permission.

10 The simplest explanation for Ismail Khan's devolution from Emir of Herat and master of the very profitable Islam Qala customs barrier on the Iran road (and less profitable Kara Tepe customs on the Turkmenistan road) to minister in Kabul in Karzai's cabinet (with the added comic touch of his aviation portfolio), given the man's aversion to flying machines. Regarding the profitability of Islam Qala, see Anna Paterson, "A Study of the Market in Second-hand Cars," *Afghanistan Evaluation Unit Case Study Series*, October 2005, Sect. 6.1: "Some importers said that they had sometimes been forced to pay customs taxes on imported vehicles twice: once in Herat and once in Kabul. It is possible that during the period when Ismail Khan was governor of Herat, and some customs duties from Herat were not reaching central government."

11 On April 15, 2011, in The Hague, I shared a conference platform with Amrullah Saleh, Karzai's former National Security Directorate chief. He argued with vehemence that "the West" is morally obligated to help Afghanistan. I agreed to support his plea if he would swap his watch for mine. But he refused to relinquish his gold Rolex.

12 Judging by desertion rates; though allowances should be made for the 17 Afghans who deserted from Lackland Air Force Base. Innocents until then exposed to nothing more risqué than pubescent boys dancing in gowns were assaulted by San Antonio's "Graham Central Station" multi-night club featuring "scantily clad women" rolling around in Jell-O. www.foxnews.com/us/2010/07/20/exclusive-awol-afghans-bmw/#ixzz1Dzsad8wB.

13 More detailed numbers would only mislead. But see Congressional Research Service, 7-5700 (RL33110) Amy Belasco: *The Cost of Iraq, Afghanistan, and Other Global War on Terror Operations Since 9/11* (September 2, 2010): "If the FY2011 war request is approved, total war-related funding (since 2001) would reach almost $1.3 trillion, including $455 billion for Afghanistan."

14 The ethnographic information is derived more from my widely traveled Afghan relatives than from my personal observations; I have tried to cross-check data with the extant literature, chiefly Thomas Barfield, *Afghanistan: A Cultural and Political History* (Princeton, NJ: Princeton University Press, 2010).

15 The Ismai'lis (Sevener Shi'a) of the Kayan valley near Doshi in western Baghlan province, traditional devotees of the Sayyid Naderi family, who call their chief a *Pir* (in spite of the lack of Sufi associations). Because of his politics, the nearby northern end of the Salang tunnel was tranquil during the Soviet occupation and even after.

16 Aside from the exotic terminology *Melmastia* (hospitality), *Nanawatai* (asylum), and more, it is identical to the the *mafia* code of the Western Sicily of my childhood; the *uomini d'onore*, were just as likely as any Pashtun to kill their errant females for their own honor's sake. They no longer do that, but their *ospitalità* still outdoes *Melmastia*. See Anton Blok, *La Mafia di un vilaggio Siciliano 1860–1960*, (Edizioni di Communita, 2000). One Afghan parallel is that the pseudonymous village, actually Contessa Entellina, well-known to me when donkeys still prevailed, is of exotic Arbëreshë ethnicity. Kundisa is the arbërisht name.

CHAPTER 8

Beyond Victory and Defeat

Scott Sigmund Gartner and Leo Blanken

As a goal or end state, winning hearts and minds provides the wrong focus for operations ... [it should be] giving the people faith they are going to a better future, that things will continue to improve, that we, the United States will not leave prematurely ... and the situation will not revert to the chaos of the 1990s.

—Former commander 3rd Brigade Combat Team, 1st Infantry Division

Introduction

The outcome of the war in Afghanistan will likely resemble neither victory nor defeat. Eliminating the prospect of an outright "victory" would recognize the inability of the United States to do all of the following: neutralize the Taliban, create a sustainable Afghan national government, develop a viable Afghan economy, and tamp down regional instability. Conversely, outright military defeat is also avoidable, as the political decision to withdraw US forces resides solely in Washington, given that the Taliban are unable to defeat American units in the field. Given the low likelihood of outright victory or imposed defeat, then, what might war outcomes actually look like?

We propose the notion of an "oscillating outcome" to reconceptualize the likely strategic endgame for the United States in Afghanistan. Counterinsurgency thinking tends to be fixated on the idea of repressing the enemy, keeping violence levels low, and raising opinions of the local government to higher levels. But what if the end result were not to be construed as static—win or lose—but rather as an oscillating outcome consisting of up-and-down cycles of conflict? That is, outbreaks of violence among Afghans, even large and somewhat sustained, might be acceptable if measures of a successful outcome are associated with the development of an Afghanistan resilient enough to absorb considerable levels of violence and avoid descending into the chaos of an ungoverned space, one that would be attractive to groups such as al-Qaeda. The goal of a resilient Afghanistan contrasts with the more standard objective of pursuing an outcome that is inherently peaceful and static. A state resistant to the chaos that attracts al-Qaeda, however, encapsulates the core mission of the United States in Afghanistan: denying Afghan territory as a base for transnational terrorism.

One way to characterize such thinking is to consider violent crime in New York City. The goal of the New York City Police Department is not to eradicate crime outright, because that would be unattainable. Instead, its objective is to restrain the pattern of criminal activity within acceptable limits. At one extreme, if crime were allowed to run rampant, tourism, investment, and residents's quality of life would collapse. At the other extreme, the resources dedicated to fighting crime are characterized by declining marginal returns, and the costs of reducing violent crime to zero would not only be prohibitively high, but would turn the city into a "police state." Instead, officials create ranges of acceptable criminal behavior, and only become concerned when crime seems to be growing "out of control." By rethinking the end of the war in Afghanistan analogously, we allow for a fundamental reassessment of US goals and operational benchmarks.

Recasting the definition of "victory" allows us to rethink strategy as well. Recognition of the likelihood of an oscillating (also called dynamic) outcome suggests the question: What does it take to get Afghanistan to a resilient place where violence stays within a set range?, rather than What does it take to eradicate the enemy? We argue that forming a resilient Afghanistan requires a different type of American strategy, one that focuses on small units, locally deployed, in a force commitment that is sustainable in the US domestic political arena for the long term (which we describe as *Going Small, Going Local,* and *Going Long*). Such a change in strategy would help to address concerns about a number of current, critical national security problems, most notably:

1. *US Public War Support*. A major reduction in US troops in the region would decrease American casualties and relieve political pressure for total US withdrawal.
2. *South Asian and Middle Eastern Public Opinion.* Reducing the US footprint in-country reduces the perception in South Asia and the Middle East that the US military is an occupying force.
3. *US Financial Duress*. Reducing the US footprint creates monetary savings in a time of American fiscal duress.
4. *US Military Overstretch*. The drawdown of forces would reduce strain on US units, many of which are in desperate need of rest and refitting after numerous deployments.
5. *Afghan National Army (ANA)*. Going small and local minimizes reliance on the ANA and reduces the dangers of possible Taliban control of the Afghan military.

These changes also represent a better match for US goals and interests with:

1. *Afghanistan Conditions*. Implement a strategy more in accordance with constraints created by weakness of central institutions, tribal culture, and the rugged topography.

2. *NATO/Allied Capabilities*. Allow allied militaries to reduce or restage their presence, thereby easing strains among NATO partners.
3. *US Special Operations Forces (SOF) Capabilities*. Match strategy with US unconventional warfare assets.
4. *Global War on Terror*. Reshape strategy in the "Global War on Terror" into a new, long-term, and sustainable grand strategy.

We now proceed to lay out the argument previewed above. First, we provide a more detailed analysis of the "oscillating outcome" concept, with historic illustrations. Next, we briefly summarize the relevant aspects of the Afghan war, paying particular attention to how the conflict is contextualized within changing realities at the grand strategic level. Then, we elaborate on the *small, local, long* strategy features noted above. Finally, we discuss the process of strategic assessment and the importance of anticipatory indicators, and we close with a discussion of the challenges that may arise from following both current and the proposed polices.

War Outcomes Are Patterns

In Afghanistan the United States and its allies have focused on static outcomes, eliminating the Taliban, minimizing violence, and improving perceptions of the Kabul government. However, we believe that patterns of oscillating violence that cycle between intense and more moderate levels are likely to occur. Further, outbreaks of cyclic violence might well be acceptable if US measures of performance capture the conditions that lead to a more "resilient" Afghanistan rather than a nation-state that is characterized by a static peace. An acceptable oscillating outcome means a situation where we observe occasional outbreaks of sharp violence, but the system in place remains capable of restoring the equilibrium once it has been disturbed. The question then is: What kind of continued American presence, support, and involvement is required to improve resiliency? We next develop each of these vital concepts and apply them to the war in Afghanistan.

Oscillating Outcomes

Some wars lead to static outcomes that narrowly and uniformly constrain behavior. For example, following World War II, the United States had extremely positive relations with Germany. In fact, for America's next major dispute, the cold war, West Germany became one of its staunchest and most important allies. Clearly, the military battle between the United States and Germany ended in spring of 1945 for both countries and has never resumed. If we were to graph the level of violence between the two countries from 1941 to today we would observe a dramatic and brief surge during World War II, followed by virtually zero bilateral conflict for the next sixty years, during which time the level of violence has remained fixed and unchanged. This type of conflict outcome is a *static outcome*: since 1945, it has not varied.

In contrast, we look at Israel. Founded in 1948, Israel fought major wars in 1956, 1967, and 1973, and has also fought in conflicts such as the War of Attrition, the Intifadas, the invasions of Lebanon in 1982 and 2006, the battle in Gaza, and so on. At the same time, one would be profoundly mistaken to say that Israel or even the Middle East was consumed by war. Israel stayed out of the 1991 Gulf War, withdrew from Lebanon and the Sinai, and granted partial autonomy to the occupied territories. Furthermore, major peace efforts involving Israel, Egypt, and Jordan dramatically decreased the likelihood of regional war. This increased level of interstate peace, however, seemed to be followed by increased intrastate violence, first with the Palestine Liberation Organization (PLO) in Jordan, then with Hamas and Hezbollah in Israeli-occupied territories and in Lebanon, and most recently in Egypt, Libya, Syria, and Tunisia. A graph of Israeli conflict behavior over time would show a high level of military operations in general, but a sine-wave-like pattern that varied from intense military conflicts to low-level violence. This graph would be bounded both below (there is rarely absolute peace going on between all the actors) and above; there is rarely total war occurring. The conflicts around Israel represent an *oscillating outcome* that shifts regularly among intermediate levels of violence.[1]

Unlike the US-Germany relationship, which was highly conflictual during World War II and then became increasingly cooperative with little to no fundamental variation, the Israel-Arab-Palestinian outcome varies between intensity levels over time. A slice at any one time (1979 Camp David Accords: peace; 2009 invasion of Gaza: war) does not adequately reflect the temporal pattern that oscillates episodically between more pacific and more conflictual situations, a dynamic outcome.

Oscillating outcomes represent a fundamentally different way of thinking about war and power than static approaches.[2] Thinking about dynamic outcomes rather than static outcomes is especially useful when "conflict behavior has a perpetual action-reaction component in addition to being influenced by the current power distribution."[3] In oscillating systems the key question is: "Under what conditions is such behavior likely to oscillate repeatedly, or become unstable?"[4] That is, when does the bounded system explode into chaos?

Stable and Unstable Outcomes

Oscillating outcomes largely follow two types of patterns: *stable* and *unstable*.[5] First, as shown in figure 8.1, the pattern can cycle around the same level over time. For example, Afghanistan civilian casualties might average 100 per month, but some months that figure is 50 and other months it is 150. The variation might be seasonal; driven by weather, the poppy harvest, or more reasons that are human-based. For example, villagers might oppose Taliban restrictions, which results in violence and many casualties. Following the violence the village is quiet and peaceful (few casualties). After a while, the villagers once again rebel against the Taliban's imposed restrictions and generate the cycle anew. This type of oscillating pattern, despite its significant change and movement over time, is called a *stable outcome* because it cycles around a constant expectation (its equilibrium).

Oscillating patterns can also change radically. As shown in figure 8.2, the pattern can begin to cycle unevenly, with greater degrees of amplitude, to the point where the system is no longer able to contain the swings and spins out of control. This type

FIGURE 8.1. Stable Oscillating Outcome

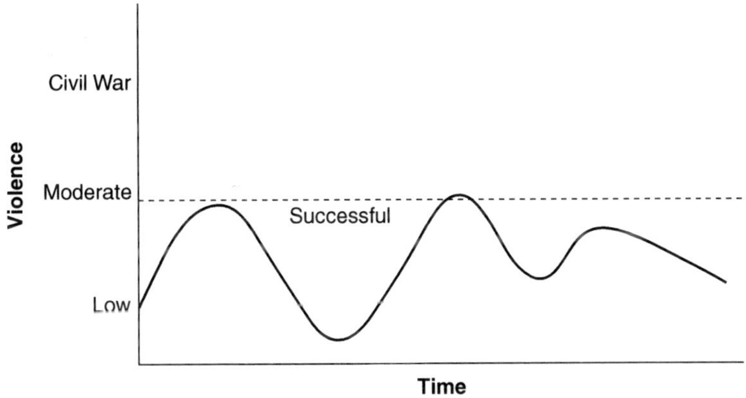

of oscillating pattern is called an *unstable outcome*: the swings become so extreme that "the system explodes," leading to chaos and structural failure.[6] Figure 8.2 shows all three possible states:

1. *Successful.* The pattern remains stable around a constant level of violence.
2. *Unsuccessful.* The cycle needs to return to the previous cycling pattern to be successful.
3. *System Failure.* The pattern becomes unstable and explodes, leading to system collapse.

The US fear in Afghanistan is not just that efforts to constrain the Taliban and bolster the national government will be slow or will go through unsuccessful periods, but that the oscillations will grow increasingly severe and exceed the ability of the system to reset. Should Afghanistan prove unable to recover from increasingly higher levels of violence, the major concern is that the system will explode and

FIGURE 8.2. Unstable Oscillating Outcome

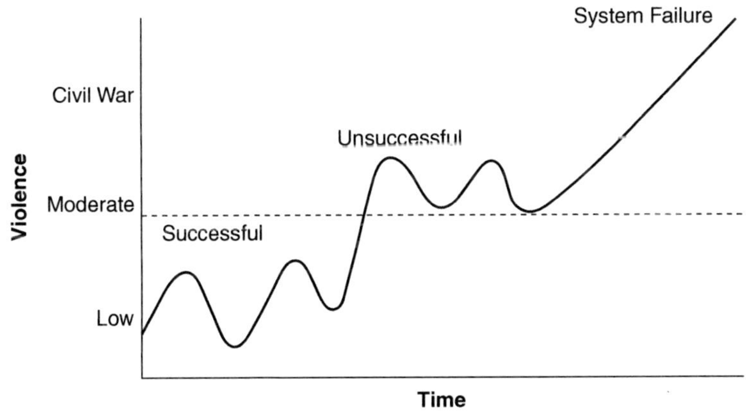

decay into civil war, creating an ungoverned space that could be capitalized on by transnational terror groups such as al-Qaeda. Thus, as shown in figure 8.2, the deepest American fear is that the violence swings grow increasingly severe and reach the point of civil war where the government and country collapse and chaos ensues.

Resilience

We argue that an oscillating system is a likely result of the war in Afghanistan. Therefore, the essential concern is whether such an oscillating system will be stable or unstable. Thus the United States needs to rephrase its key question from: What does the United States need to do to win in Afghanistan? to What does the United States need to do to sustain a stable outcome in Afghanistan? If the American and allied efforts create a stable outcome—a cycling steady-state—then the next question is: What can be done to reduce the levels of violence around which the patterns of conflict oscillate? That is, once the United States is certain that the unstable dynamic shown in figure 8.2 is unlikely to occur, the next question to ask is: How does it reduce the average level of violence central to the pattern?

Thinking about the end result in Afghanistan as an oscillating (as opposed to a static) outcome, and rephrasing the main question of the US intervention from what wins to what creates a stable outcome, fundamentally alters one's perspective on the war. Rather than being focused on static victory and fixed goals, the focus is more fluid, seeking to create an Afghanistan resilient enough to resist extreme spikes in violence. A resilient Afghanistan oscillates from low (or more realistically medium) levels of violence to high levels and yet has a stable equilibrium that is robust enough to return to the previous cycling pattern once it has been disturbed.

Creating a more resilient Afghanistan, as opposed to eradicating the Taliban, requires changes in the American strategy and strategic assessment. The United States needs to:

1. *Go Small.* Deploy small units within a thin web of air and logistical support.
2. *Go Local.* Focus on working with local forces to improve local security.
3. *Go Long.* Recognize that transforming a nation like Afghanistan takes decades.
4. *Use Anticipatory Indicators of Success.* Capture civilian expectations of security.

Before making our case for these four approaches, we briefly review the Afghanistan situation.

The Afghan Conflict in the Context of US Grand Strategy

Given our discussion of the oscillating outcomes concept, it is necessary to characterize briefly the ongoing conflict in Afghanistan. In so doing, we cover both the conflict in that theater of operations as well as its import for broader issues of grand strategy. We do so to set the stage for offering the policy prescriptions of going "small, local, and long."

The War in Afghanistan

After the attacks of September 11 (9/11), the United States responded by attacking the Taliban regime in Afghanistan. In the decade since the initial invasion, the war has evolved through at least four distinct phases. The first stage was the air power campaign that immediately followed the 9/11 attacks. The second stage was the marriage of small American special operations forces (SOF) and the Northern Alliance that dislodged the Taliban regime by the end of December 2001. The third phase was a transition to heavy general purpose forces (GPF), which began with Operation Anaconda in March 2002. With the publication of the army counterinsurgency manual FM-3-24 in 2006, the United States began to implement a two-pronged approach: (1) conduct a more targeted counterinsurgency strategy (most clearly reflected by the killing of Osama bin Laden on May 1, 2011), and (2) the latest phase, pursue a broader array of goals that requires a massive conventional military footprint in-country. It is against the backdrop of this recent strategic situation (as of spring 2011) that we set our approach in contrast.

We briefly examine three relevant aspects of the current military strategic situation: the large size, cost, and complexity of the US-led International Security Assistance Force (ISAF) order of battle, the challenge of performance measures, and the problem of defining strategic goals. We think that, together, these problems make a strong case for a fundamental reassessment of strategy and performance evaluation.

As of December 2011, the United States had ninety-thousand troops in Afghanistan (out of an ISAF total of roughly 125,000), having steadily increased from fifty-two hundred in 2002.[7] The United States has justified building up such a large conventional presence in Afghanistan based on two presuppositions that we think are highly questionable. First, the surge in Iraq troop levels was seen as crucial to changing the tide in that theater of operations. More recent analyses of the Iraq surge, however, question whether the increased troop levels were necessary, or even related to success, arguing that the "awakening" of Sunni militias was the turning point in the conflict, rather than the increase in US troop levels.[8] The second, and more troubling, reason for the large and growing conventional footprint in Afghanistan was the inherent nature of the US military and what has been termed loosely an "American way of war," which emphasizes mass, technology, heavy logistic efforts, and the liberal application of firepower to annihilate enemy forces.[9] Metz, for example, argues that "[t]here is an old saying that, 'when all you have is a hammer, every problem looks like a nail.' America has an amazing hammer—its military—which is very good at seizing and controlling territory."[10] To summarize this argument, large numbers of GPFs are in Afghanistan because it is in the nature of the US military to do so, rather than as the result of strategic reasoning.[11] Organizational culture and bureaucratic inertia have a powerful influence on strategy.[12] We argue, however, that such a large conventional force, if it was ever an efficacious choice, is no longer sustainable.[13]

The second relevant aspect of the Afghan conflict is the challenge of metrics. The current strategic situation on the ground has proven so fluid and poorly measured as to be almost impossible to characterize with any degree of certainty.[14] Despite being one of the most polled, interviewed, and discussed groups of people on the planet, the population of Afghanistan remains a mystery. Each week offers a flood of blogs, editorials, and government reports that reverse the conclusions of the week before. There are two reasons for this confusion. The first is common knowledge: that the types of metrics needed to assess progress and agent performance in a counterinsurgent campaign are inherently difficult.[15] The second is less understood: that the type of standardization and quantification necessary to monitor and evaluate agents in a large bureaucracy is problematic for the subtle professional judgment necessary in a counterinsurgency environment.[16] This aspect is important because the inherently complex environment is not suited for the types of GPFs currently operating within it.

The third relevant characteristic is that there are a multitude of disparate, and sometimes conflicting, goals being articulated by the political leadership. A December 2010 press release from the White House argues that: "[t]he core goal of the U.S. strategy in the Afghanistan and Pakistan theater remains to disrupt, dismantle, and eventually defeat al-Qa'ida [*sic*] in the region and to prevent its return to either country."[17] Given that there is widespread recognition that US efforts largely eliminated al-Qaeda from Afghanistan (as demonstrated by the revelation that Osama bin Laden lived in Pakistan), why is the United States still fighting in Afghanistan? The conflicts in Iraq and Afghanistan demonstrate that wars can be self-sustaining in their generation of new and varied goals.[18] Since 2001, many other strategic goals and indicators of success have emerged in, and disappeared from, the debate: Taliban insurgents killed, civilians protected, economic development, democratization, centralized governance, local governance, "safe" territory, human rights established, narcotics interdicted, and so on. Some of these are strategic, some are operational or tactical, and yet it has never been made clear how these fit together. Former Secretary of Defense Robert Gates attempted to summarize:

> We are in Afghanistan because we were attacked from Afghanistan, not because we want to try and build a better society in Afghanistan. But doing things to improve governance, to improve development in Afghanistan, to the degree that it contributes to our security mission and to the effectiveness of the Afghan government in the security area, that's what we're going to do.[19]

In other words, the "clear" military mission that Gates attempts to describe is actually a complex, nation-building effort that currently encompasses both the creation of a centralized state and the significant remaking of its economy. We think it is time to return to a more narrowly delineated military mission scope that supports more restricted and more obtainable political objectives, ones that are assessed through more meaningful measures of actual impact, and which focus more on legitimacy and less on centralization.[20]

US Grand Strategy beyond Hegemony

Any proposed military strategy in Afghanistan must be assessed in light of its implications for overall grand strategy. With the exit of the Bush administration's neoconservatives and their mixed grand strategy of aggressive unilateralism coupled with optimistic nation-building, strategic thinking seems to have been left adrift in President Obama's White House. This has raised the serious question: "How could a global hegemon like the United States lack the *sine qua non* of a coherent national security strategy?"[21] That is, how does the Afghanistan conflict fit within a strategic orchestration of policy that includes all aspects of national power? Millett, Murray, and Watman provide a framework for evaluating the effectiveness of national strategy, and argue that effective wartime policy must display (among other things) consistency between strategic means and political ends, risk weighed against stakes, and supportability by the nation's economic base.[22] Using these criteria, we discuss the relevant aspects of the Afghan conflict within the grand strategic concept, highlighting the issues of the US fiscal crisis, American domestic political support, the broad spectrum of US military capabilities, and strategic opportunity costs.

Fiscal Constraints

The United States is in a state of serious fiscal distress. This situation can either be viewed as a temporary challenge[23] or a grave and irreversible trend.[24] Grand theories of international relations do not bode well for the United States, as they largely predict that hegemonic powers tend to take on more political and military commitments while the economic advantages that made them powerful diffuse to other actors in the system. This process is exacerbated as domestic pressure increasingly leans towards consumption, rather than toward investment in innovation and improved production techniques.[25] Regardless of whether the United States is doomed to inevitable erosion or not, the fact of the matter is that current rates of spending in Afghanistan (averaging well over one million dollars per year, per soldier, which is double the figure for operations in Iraq) are simply not sustainable.[26]

Public Opinion

A second domestic constraint on the future of US operations in Afghanistan is the collapse of political support at home. Despite the remonstrations of the war's supporters, who argue that the "US cannot remain a superpower if the suspicion takes root that we are a feckless nation that can be stampeded into surrender by a domestic caucus of defeatists,"[27] the reality is that support is collapsing. A November 18, 2010, poll shows that, for the first time, half of respondents decided that the United States should no longer be involved Afghanistan.[28]

Studies repeatedly show that war and its attendant military casualties affect election outcomes in the House of Representatives, the Senate, and the presidency.[29] Military casualties influence elite views, media coverage, and most profoundly and importantly, public opinion.[30] As a result, except in rare situations when the homeland is seen as threatened (e.g., World War II), the deployment of tens of thousands of US troops to fight a costly war will eventually rapidly generate strong and active opposition. As fighting continues in a conflict and military personnel are injured and killed, the American public and its leaders will increasingly oppose a war. This effect is robust and well documented across a variety of wars. The negative relationship of military casualties and support suggests that:

1. *Selection*. Leaders need to be extraordinarily selective when using US force abroad.
2. *Support*. Force should only be used when the US public strongly values the objective.
3. *Low Cost Is Long-term*. Deployments that are smaller, less deadly, and cheaper are more likely to last longer and be less opposed than those that are larger, more lethal, and expensive.

For example, by being "small" and "local," US counterinsurgency efforts in the Philippines have also been able to be "long."[31] Most Americans are unaware of the mission, and the few casualties resulting have had minimal public impact.[32] Small forces, given the right strategy and enough time, can be highly effective.

Strategic Opportunity Costs

Foreign policy requires resources. State resources can reflect a broad spectrum of factors that support foreign policy, from economic, military, and technological to public opinion and leader attention. One thing that remains clear, however, is that states, even as powerful as the United States, have finite capacity. As a result, pursuit of one foreign policy objective limits the remaining resources available to pursue alternative foreign policy objectives. Put simply, national security actions have opportunity costs.

There is a broader military strategic debate that has arisen from operations in Afghanistan, which involves the continued ability of the general purpose forces to face contingencies *other* than counterinsurgency operations (COIN). As Colonel Gian Gentile warns, "Skills and core competencies [other than COIN] have ... atrophied significantly.... If you have an army optimized for combined arms warfare it still can do other kinds of missions. However, if you optimize an army to do nation building and small wars it becomes much more problematic to step into the direction of doing fighting at the high end of the spectrum."[33]

A recent internal US Army white paper, for example, reveals that a stunning 90 percent of Army artillery personnel are unable to execute their core mission of providing accurate fire support.[34] The sum of this critique is that future missions across a broader spectrum of contingencies (such as concerns about China as a global competitor) will be crippled by creating a military that has overadapted to the idiosyncrasies of the Afghanistan conflict.[35]

We turn next to the Vietnam War to identify alternatives to today's COIN strategy. We are especially eager to discover strategies that have fewer human, economic, and opportunity costs, and thus are more sustainable for the complex challenges faced in Afghanistan.

Vietnam War Lessons

The United States pursued a variety of strategies in the Vietnam War. An early difference in strategy manifested between the Army, which primarily deployed large units in search-and-destroy missions, and the marine corps, which because of its smaller size and unique history, pursued a unique counter-insurgency approach.

CAP Strategy

In 1940 the marines developed the *Small Wars Manual*, which stated that in counterinsurgency wars:

> [T]he goal is to gain decisive results with the least application of force and the consequent minimum loss of life. The end aim is the social, economic, and political development of the people subsequent to the military defeat of the enemy insurgent.[36]

When marines arrived in Vietnam, therefore, the corps had a well-articulated counterinsurgency strategy that emphasized local pacification.[37] The army, instead, continued its Korean War approach of focusing on the physical destruction of the enemy and measuring success through enemy body counts.[38]

In Vietnam, the marine corps initiated a "Combined Action Platoons" (CAP) strategy in contrast to the army's search-and-destroy policy.[39] The CAP mission statement identified its primary objective as "local defense."[40] The CAP strategy dispersed small units of a dozen or fewer US Marines to villages for long periods of time.[41] The idea was to work with local forces to foster local security. Unlike previous advising relationships, in the CAP Program, US and indigenous forces worked extremely closely together: As Major Richard Braun told the corps' commandant, General Lewis Walt, CAP would be "a combined unit, a group of Marines and Viets who would eat, sleep, patrol and fight as one unit—not two."[42]

The goal was to improve security to the point that Vietnamese hamlet leaders could ignore Viet Cong (VC) demands to provide men, food, and supplies because the VC would have lost the ability to terrorize the villagers. Villagers recognized previously that as soon as American forces left, the VC would return and punish them for cooperating with the United States. Thus it was vital to convince local leaders that the CAP units were long-term insertions. Marine Corps Captain Jim Cooper summed up this strategy, when he told the people of a Vietnamese village that "henceforth the people would be protected from the VC, for he had come to stay."[43]

CAP Assessment

Combined action platoons and search-and-destroy strategies could not be more different. The CAP strategy focused on creating a permanent village presence, while the search-and-destroy strategy emphasized movement to find, fix, and destroy enemy forces. Given these disparate objectives, the two organizations chose very different performance indicators.[44] The marines measured success by looking at indicators of village expectations of future security and stability, such as rice production: "The marines [*sic*], through their rice-protection program dubbed Golden Fleece prevented the VC from seizing part of the local rice crop."[45] Rice production represents an *anticipatory performance indicator*: it looks at civilians' anticipation of their future security. If the villagers felt secure enough to invest their scarce capital in rice seed, invest four months of back-breaking labor to nurture and harvest the rice, and then risk not turning it over to the VC, they clearly had an expectation of ongoing security. Furthermore, as Marine Corps General Walt points out, "Each catty of rice … not going into Viet Cong bins meant that another catty had to be grown in North Vietnam and brought over the hundreds of miles of mountain trails by human bearers."[46] Finally, the marine corps' strategy resulted in lower casualties: General Richard Clutterbuck stated that CAP casualties were "only 50% of the casualties of the normal infantry or Marine battalions being flown around by helicopters on large-scale operations."[47]

If the CAP strategy was successful, then the VC would be deterred from attacking CAP villages, resulting in less combat, more rice sown, and fewer enemy casualties. Given its focus on the enemy body count as the measure of success, the Army considered the CAP strategy a failure.[48] Major General Depuy stated that, "the Marines came in and just sat down and didn't do anything. They were involved in counterinsurgency of the deliberate, mild sort."[49] While the marine corps determined that their strategy was successful (rice production went up in CAP villages), the Army saw it as failing.[50] The CAP program was canceled "because of its *low* [*sic*] success rate—it did not kill enough Communists."[51]

Vietnam War Lessons

While the historic ability of the CAP program to change the Vietnam War's outcome remains unclear, the CAP program provides important counterinsurgency lessons.

1. *How Organizations Measure Success Matters*. Different performance indicators can lead to fundamentally divergent assessments of success and failure.
2. *Anticipatory Indicators of Success Work*. The CAP program's reliance on the amount of rice sowed reflected villagers' expectations of their local security and stability.
3. *Small and Local Strategies Work*. Small and local counterinsurgency isolates insurgents from the domestic population, separating them from their logistics base.
4. *Going Small and Local*. This strategy can result in both improved stability and lower US casualties.

Strategy

Strategy is the policy through which a military pursues political goals given imposed constraints. In the war in Afghanistan, we believe that American and Afghan political and economic constraints put a premium on strategies that rely on small units that focus on local objectives using anticipatory indicators of success in a way that facilitates a long-term commitment.

Going Small

The proposed application of US military force must be small in scale to make our proposed strategy work. This is true for two reasons. The first reason is that such a choice accords with the fiscal and public opinion constraints outlined above.

In this line of reasoning, the reduced footprint reduces the human, economic, and thus political costs for US leaders. A smaller footprint can take the conflict out of the public "spotlight," allowing longer and more effective interventions. In this way the scale of effort is a necessary condition for the ability of the United States to stay for the long haul, as discussed below.

The second reason that a "small" choice is appropriate is due to the varying quality and skill sets of US military forces. The US military has developed units, small in number but high in quality, which have been designed and trained to fit the mission requirements for this proposed strategy: the SOF community. These selective, highly trained, elite, and special units can apply unconventional warfare strategies to "win a war by working with, as opposed to neutralizing or fighting around local populations."[52] Tucker and Lamb go to great pains to show that, in their capacity to do such things, these SOF troops "are not only *elite* but *special* because they conduct missions that conventional forces cannot perform, at least not at acceptable levels of risk and cost."[53] Spulak elaborates on this distinction between conventional and SOF forces: "Conventional forces attempt to lower the risks by … force protection, very lethal platform-based weapon systems, dispersion of forces, technology-based intelligence, deliberate planning, networking, economy of force, large numbers, uniformity and rigidity in doctrine and training, reserve, and caution."[54] Turnley notes that the nature of SOF forces allows for an entirely different approach to missions:

> SOF are organized and act in small groups because their comparatively homogenous, highly capable personnel allow small relatively undifferentiated teams to exercise flexibility and creativity, which mitigates friction in a fundamentally different way than the relative certainty of behavior exhibited by GPF [general purpose forces], whose large manpower base with a wide range of distribution of critical attributes and capabilities requires large, functionally differentiated groups to be effective.[55]

Small in this case is not only politically and financially expedient, but matches up better with US SOF assets, and provides a better outcome in the physically remote and politically sensitive operating environment. Rothstein summarizes the case for choosing a select few forces over "surging" large numbers of general purpose forces thus: "[h]aving boots on the ground are important, but more important is having smart boots on the ground."[56]

Going Local

Political realities in Afghanistan necessitate engaging the polity at the local level. This is true for two reasons. First, it fits with the traditional culture of the country, and second, it will prove to be more militarily effective in the counterinsurgency effort. The cultural traditions and political history of Afghanistan rarely include a place for a centralized state with strong sovereign rule, "National security forces have never been sufficient to establish security in Afghanistan. This strategy reflects a Western understanding of the 'state.'… As illustrated during Afghanistan's most recent stable period, from 1929 to 1978, security has historically required a synergy of top-down efforts from the central government and bottom-up efforts from local tribes and other communities."[57]

The effort to force a rigid centralized government on the Afghan people is not only culturally alien, it is beyond the means of the United States and its allies to accomplish. As Henriksen notes, the topography interacts with societal divisions to create a patchwork rather than a monolithic state: "The mountains and valleys of Afghanistan enforce territorial compartmentalization, making intertribal cooperation difficult among the fragmented tribes and their internecine and overlapping conflicts."[58] As one tribal elder from Kandahar stated: "My allegiance is to my family first, then to my village, sub-tribe, and tribe" and that the government played no meaningful role in his life.[59] Therefore, continuing to push for a centralized model of governance and security goes against the grain of the environment, and is one of the major problems hampering efforts to secure a stable and realistic outcome in the conflict.

Going local—at the village or district level—will also be a more effective way of securing the countryside. Currently, the Afghan National Army is failing to reach the at-risk population in the more remote areas of the country; its "soldiers are typically deployed in battalion-sized elements and centrally located. In fact, the rural areas generally do not benefit from the existing array of these forces [...]."[60] Efforts to train and improve the Afghanistan army have clearly proven challenging and a big part of the problem is the lack of a national Afghan identity to mobilize the forces. Alternatively, local forces sanctioned by *shuras* and *jirgas* face no problem with incentives, as they are focused on defending their families, homes, and villages.[61] Local defense also plays to the Afghan people's tactical, intellectual, and logistical strengths; it puts a premium on firefights, local knowledge of their own area, and small arms.

In villages that would not support the Taliban without the threat of violence, small, highly trained US units working with larger, local units to defend their villages provides an effective means for separating Taliban insurgents from their logistics bases. Marine Gen. James Mattis (head of the US Central Joint Forces Command) sums up the case clearly when he states that: "cohesive small units, well trained in more than fire and maneuver, and living among the people, are fundamental to victory."[62]

Going Long

In terms of the pacification of Germany and the elimination of the Nazi threat, the Allied victory in defeat of World War II was total, complete, and permanent. When richer, more powerful North Korea invaded the South in 1950, it was only with US assistance that South Korea remained independent. The United States has continued to provide major military assistance (tens of thousands of US troops per year are based in South Korea), massive foreign aid, and a security guarantee—all of which many argue is required to deter another North Korean attack. Thus, war in Germany and Korea both resulted in stable outcomes, but the nature of that stability and whether it requires additional assistance differs markedly.

Afghanistan's poor infrastructure, abject poverty, weak government, and social and ethnic divisions, in the face of a strong and effective enemy, soundly suggest that even if desirable outcomes are reached, Afghanistan will require continued, long-term US support. Two factors will determine the ability of the United States to remain in Afghanistan: US public opinion (driven by military casualties) and allied support (discussed in the conclusion).

Strategic Assessment

Strategic assessment represents one of, if not *the* most important aspect of war, affecting how militaries fight, train, and allocate resources.[63] Assessing success in war is like playing a game without being able to see the score. When it is over, winners and losers will be clear, but while it is ongoing, both sides remain in the dark. In order to shed light on their performance, militaries establish strategic assessment mechanisms. The nature of a conflict's outcome, however, represents a vital and underappreciated factor influencing performance evaluation systems.

Dynamic Outcomes

Assessments of oscillating outcomes require fundamentally different approaches than static outcomes. Evaluations of static outcomes are straightforward: Is the outcome desirable (e.g., allied US victory over Germany in World War II and the establishment of NATO allied relationship)? Since the outcome is static, no additional assessment efforts are required after the initial evaluation. Evaluation of oscillating outcomes is more complex. When the outcome represents a dynamic pattern, one not only wants to assess current conditions but also other parts of the pattern. The desirability of the outcome is a function of the current and likely future conditions, as indicated by the pattern of the past.

Assessing performance in counterinsurgency warfare, however, is even harder: "Because of its complex nature, devising measures that do gauge progress in a counterinsurgency can be difficult."[64] We believe that part of the challenge is the frequency of dynamic, oscillating outcomes in insurgent conflicts.

Oscillating Outcome Assessment

Recognizing an oscillating outcome requires three essential aspects of strategic assessment:

1. Avoid over- and underestimation of violence.
2. Reduce reliance on violence-based indicators of performance.
3. Employ anticipatory-based indicators of performance.

First, violence levels will vary from medium to high, making it important that assessments do not over- or underestimate violence levels because of conditions resulting from the timing in the cycle one observes. That is, looking at a trough suggests lower-than-actual levels of violence, whereas looking at a peak suggests higher-than-average levels. It is necessary to recognize that oscillating indicators change. Instead of absolute levels, one wants to observe whether a pattern remains stable or unstable, and if stable, evaluate the cycle's equilibrium set point.

Second, we anticipate that all Afghanistan outcomes will remain violent for years to come. The existence of violence itself, much like the existence of crime for the police chief, by itself does not indicate failure. We believe that recognizing the bloody nature of Afghanistan politics and society in the near future encourages reliance on strategic assessment indicators that do not measure violence (e.g., attacks, US casualties, civilian casualties, IEDs, etc.).

Third, rather than employ violence-based metrics of strategic assessment (which are predominantly driven by the insurgents), we advocate the use of anticipatory indicators of success, like the "amount of rice planted" indicator used by Combined Action Platoons in Vietnam. Anticipatory indicators capture how civilians assess their security situation. For example, an important anticipatory indicator is the percentage of boys sent to school. Parents will only let their children go to school if they anticipate that their village or neighborhood is safe. Since boys attend schools at higher rates than girls in Afghanistan, it is better to look at male enrollment rates. As the percentage of boys sent to school increases, the suggestion is that the civilian population anticipates stability and security in the near future. Another effective and similar measure is the number of businesses open in the local bazaars. Local businessmen typically have few goods. To have them out on display at the local bazaar indicates that they have a high expectation of security and stability for the future.

Policy Recommendations

The best outcome of America's war in Afghanistan will likely not be static but rather dynamic, oscillating between violent conditions of bad and worse. The American goal then is to create a resilient Afghan societal fabric that will not be ripped apart by these cycles of violence, or descend into civil war and provide an opportunity for transnational terrorists like al-Qaeda. Resiliency will come from the ground up, facilitated by small American military units, locally oriented, in a long-term US commitment. Evaluating these efforts requires that the United States shift from indicators of success that focus on national levels of violence (e.g., attacks per week) or ANA structural measures (e.g., number-ready companies) and instead look at indicators that capture civilian expectations of security and stability (e.g., children in school). In order to be successful the US effort will need decades, which requires a low-casualty conflict and a new way of incorporating allies. Understanding the characteristics and range of likely Afghan outcomes provides a more detailed roadmap of the conflict's likely future and allows us to understand better the requirements of US strategy, assessment, and policy.

We have four main policy recommendations. The United States in Afghanistan should:

1. Go local.
2. Go small.

3. Go long.
4. Employ anticipatory indicators of success.

Current strategic analyses suggest that American strategy in Afghanistan is in dire straits: "If the essence of strategy lies in making choices under constraint, the American approach is certainly inefficient and possibly ineffective."[65] If implemented, our research suggests that the recommendations we propose could dramatically improve the situation for the United States in Afghanistan.

Allies

If a long war is necessary to create a resilient Afghanistan that can resist Taliban takeover, then not only will it be vital to minimize US casualties, it will also be critical for American decision makers to recognize the low likelihood that ISAF allies will stay the course and remain in Afghanistan for decades. We recommend reconceptualizing allied help. Today, there are many allies *simultaneously* assisting the United States in Afghanistan. Should the war continue for a decade, however, it is hard to conceive that any allies would support the United States ten years from now. Allies do, however, provide international legitimacy that, while it may not mean much to the Afghan people, does mean something to people in other (especially Western) nations throughout the world. In order to retain allies and fight a long war, we recommend shifting from this simultaneous allied support to *sequential allied support*. Allies would still be involved in joint decision making, but their troop deployments would be staged across time—one after another in an agreed-upon sequence.

Proposed Policy versus Current Policy

It is important to recognize the impressive efforts US forces have made in counterinsurgency in Iraq and Afghanistan. Beyond the substantial improvement over previous thinking shown by the current COIN doctrine, US forces have demonstrated innovation and openness to experimentation in dealing with complex and difficult situations. For example, in Delaram (Helmand District), marines have created a new school for Afghan police officers, brought in a Muslim marine chaplain to pray with local imams, employed female marines to connect with the local female population, and patrolled on foot. The result has been "to turn former insurgent strongholds along the Helmand River valley into reasonably stable communities with thriving bazaars and functioning schools."[66] This line of effort is being implemented most fully in the "village stability operations" (VSO), in which ISAF forces are deployed in small numbers to contested villages to establish security, raise and train local defense forces, encourage traditional governance mechanisms, and foster sustainable development.[67] We heartily encourage the expansion of such operations. We also point out, however, that without agreed-upon indicators of success, VSO operations, like the CAP operations before them, may face bureaucratic challenge from those whose preferred strategies assess performance differently. Thus, expansion of VSO operations not only requires additional resources, but also necessitates the understanding and acceptance of anticipatory indicators of success.

US policy continues, however, to focus on building up the Afghanistan National Army and Afghan government and striving to use these centralized institutions to defeat the Taliban.[68] Many of us believe the task of improving the ANA is unlikely to succeed, however, and instead diverts resources away from local security efforts that we see as more likely to improve resilience and thus as more critical. But, should the ANA become an effective fighting force and develop the ability to project power, this would represent a weapon that could be used against US interests in the region, and therefore has the ability to increase, not decrease, US regional distress. That is, if the ANA becomes capable, while corruption, illegitimacy, and inefficiency so cripple the Afghan national government that it collapses internally, then the Taliban would control an effective military that could project force and influence throughout the region.

Efforts to strengthen local militias and defenses would improve villages' and towns' capabilities for resisting Taliban incursion, but would fail to produce an ability to project power (special care would need to be taken to insure that these militias do not "go rogue" and attack neighboring towns to remedy long-standing grievances). The government and economy would remain weak, with political legitimacy, economic activity, and aid primarily operating at local and provincial levels. Communications might also be localized with low-power radio broadcasting. Violence would never be eliminated and instead would oscillate within an acceptable range. Yet, with US and allied help, the country could remain sufficiently resilient to survive costly conflict spikes and remain stable. Given the tremendous problems involved in training, equipping, and improving the Afghan national army and the severe corruption, inefficiency, and illegitimacy of the central government, we think that this local approach is much more likely to result in a desired outcome than the top-down approach advocated by current US policymakers.

It is hard to imagine a stable Afghanistan war outcome that does not involve long-term American security assistance. Given Americans' consistent and negative reaction to American casualties suffered, it is equally hard to imagine sustaining the continued deployment of the current number of US troops given their human and economic costs. Dramatically decreasing the number of US forces in Afghanistan through shifting the force structure to focus on SOF and small units represents the only viable political option for maintaining a long-term US military presence in Afghanistan. By working with local militias (creating "one" unit out of "two"), small numbers of SOF can help to direct a large number of forces. Local troops may not be adequate to conduct search-and-destroy missions for insurgents, but they can effectively defend their villages and homes and thus deny the Taliban access to people and supplies. Additionally, fundamentally shifting ISAF deployments from simultaneous to sequential allied support can help to guarantee that the United States does not fight alone years from now when domestic public support inevitably wanes.

The Future

Since 9/11, Americans have shown US service men and women tremendous support. This support is clearly visible; it is common to observe Americans clapping as armed forces personnel enter airports and people frequently walking up to service men and women and personally thanking them for their efforts. These behaviors contrast sharply with many public reactions to personnel during the Vietnam War. At the same time, the war in Iraq and increasingly the war in Afghanistan, like the Vietnam War, have become highly unpopular and politically costly to the leaders who initiated them. Given the unpopularity of the war in Afghanistan and its growing human and economic costs, there is going to be tremendous domestic political pressure on the Obama administration and on other US leaders to withdraw American forces from Afghanistan. In order to preempt this pressure, the United States needs to implement a new, innovative set of strategies that pursue a more narrowly defined goal in a more reduced way. Otherwise, the United States will withdraw without achieving anything.

Going small, local, and long represents a way to fight that we think will be more effective in Afghanistan, the wider region, and domestically in the United States. Implementation requires careful calculation of the right number, mix, and location of US troops. Some areas of Afghanistan are either so supportive of the Taliban or so opposed to the Taliban that the insertion of US units would lead to high costs or be unnecessary. Like all strategies, execution requires that the United States be strategic in its approach and take into account variations among regions, provinces, and villages as well as conditions on the ground. Furthermore, suggesting this type of change in strategy and performance assessment does not address the key, initial question of whether the United States should have been in Afghanistan in the first place. Our notion of oscillating outcomes, however, does shed light on the utility of initiating wars like the one in Afghanistan.

Wars in poorly developed countries like Afghanistan are highly likely to result in insurgency. Unlike the defeat of major countries like Germany and Japan, the institutional structure of developing countries is too feeble to enforce a surrender treaty.[69] As a result, defeat is not a definitive, institutional endstate (like General MacArthur accepting the Japanese surrender on the deck of the battleship *USS Missouri*), but rather the cessation of one type of fighting and the initiation of another: insurgency warfare. Furthermore, these types of insurgencies result in two unique conditions. First, their outcomes tend to be oscillating, as the absence of decisive force often removes the options of clear victory or defeat. Second, these conflicts are hard to assess, as appropriate indicators remain ambiguous. As a result, these conflicts are likely to result in long and costly involvements. Oscillating outcomes and unclear indicators are thus signs of costly and indecisive wars.

Summary

In the post-cold war world the United States reigns militarily supreme, in terms of traditional measures of power. It is vital for American decision makers, however, to recognize the long-term and total costs of wars against weak states, and not to be deluded by their seemingly low initial costs. The *ability* to use force represents a fundamentally different concept from the *need* to use force. Decision makers need to be cautious when contemplating projecting force, especially the deployment of troops, into peripheral conflicts. This caution should include recognition that determining the complete costs of a conflict is challenging, especially when the opposing state is weak. Decision makers would do well to keep in mind that defeating a weak state is cheap and easy; transforming it into a stable ally is costly and hard.

Notes

John M. Spiszer, "Counterinsurgency in Afghanistan: Lessons Learned by a Brigade Combat Team," *Military Review* (January–February): 73–74.

1 For a related topic, see the literature on "enduring rivalries": Gary Goertz and Paul F. Diehl, "Enduring Rivalries: Theoretical Constructs and Empirical Patterns," *American Political Science Review* 37, no. 2 (1993): 147–71; D. Scott Bennett and Timothy Nordstrum, "Foreign Policy Substitutability and Internal Economic Problems in Enduring Rivalries," *The Journal of Conflict Resolution* 44, no. 1 (2000): 33–61.

2 Charles Doran and Wes Parsons, "War and the Cycle of Relative Power," *American Political Science Review* 74, no. 4 (1980): 947–65.

3 Kelly Kadera, *The Power-Conflict Story: A Dynamic Model of Interstate Rivalry* (Ann Arbor: University of Michigan Press, 2001).

4 Diane H. Felmlee and David F. Greenberg, "A Dynamic Systems Model of Dyadic Interaction," *Journal of Mathematical Sociology* 23, no. 3 (1999): 155–80.

5 Diane H. Felmlee, "Application of Dynamic Systems Analysis to Dyadic Interaction," in *Oxford Handbook of Methods in Positive Psychology*, ed. A. D. Ong (New York: Oxford University Press, 2007).

6 Felmlee, "Application of Dynamic Systems Analysis to Dyadic Interaction."

7 Amy Belasco, *Troop Levels in the Afghan and Iraq Wars, FY2001-FY2012: Cost and Other Potential Issues* (Washington, DC: Congressional Research Service, 2009).

8 Julian E. Barnes, "Battle Centers on Surge," *Wall Street Journal*, August 27, 2010.

9 Russell F. Weigely, *The American Way of War: A History of United States Military Strategy and Policy* (Bloomington: Indiana University Press, 1973/1977); for a critical reassessment of this argument see Brian M. Linn, "'The American Way of War' Revisited," *Journal of Military History* 66, no. 2 (2002): 501–33.

10 Steven Metz, *America's Flawed Afghanistan Strategy* (Carlisle Barracks, PA: US Army War College, 2010).

11 Andrew F. Krepinevich, *The Army in Vietnam* (Baltimore: Johns Hopkins University Press, 1988).

12 Scott Sigmund Gartner, *Strategic Assessment in War* (New Haven: Yale University Press, 1997).

13 See Arquilla and Rothstein, "Assessing the Strategic Alternatives," chapter 12, this volume.

14 For debate over the most recent "National Intelligence Estimate," see Elisabeth Bumiller, "Intelligence Reports Offer Dim View of Afghan War," *New York Times*, December 14, 2010.

15 David J. Kilcullen, *Counterinsurgency,* chapter 2 (New York: Oxford University Press, 2010); Shon McCormick, "Primer on Developing Measures of Effectiveness," *Military Review* (July–August 2010): 60–66; Nancy E. Blacker and Charlie H. Kim, "Measuring Economic Development in a COIN Environment," *Military Review* (November–December 2010): 11–18.

16 Henry Mintzberg, *Structure in Fives: Designing Effective Organizations* (Englewood Cliffs, NJ: Prentice Hall, 1993); Leo Blanken and Justin Overbaugh, "Looking for Intel…or Looking for Answers? The Role of Military Intelligence in a Counterinsurgency Environment," *Intelligence and National Security* (summer 2012).

17 Office of the Press Secretary of the White House, *Overview of the Afghanistan and Pakistan Annual Review* (Washington, DC, 2010).

18 Also see Scott Sigmund Gartner and Marissa M. Myers, "Body Counts and 'Success' in the Vietnam and Korean Wars," *Journal of Interdisciplinary History* 25, no. 2 (1995): 377–96.

19 Eugene Robinson, "The No-Win War," *Washington Post*, August 3, 2010.

20 Hy Rothstein and John Arquilla, "Understanding the Afghan Challenge," chapter 1, this volume.

21 John T. Kuehn, "Talking Grand Strategy," *Military Review* (September–October 2010): 74; Andrew J. Bacevich, "Obama's Strategic Blind Spot," *Los Angeles Times*, July 6, 2009.

22 Allan R. Millett, Williamson Murray, and Kenneth H. Watman, "The Effectiveness of Military Organizations," *International Security* 11, no. 1 (1986): 37–71.

23 Michael Fullilove, "Smart Power: Exaggerating America's Decline," *International Herald Tribune*, June 18, 2008.

24 Gideon Rachman, "American Decline: This Time It's for Real," *Foreign Policy* 184 (January–February 2011): 59–63.

25 Paul Kennedy, *The Rise and Fall of the Great Powers: Economic Change and Military Conflict from 1500 to 2000* (New York: Random House, 1987); Robert Gilpin, *War and Change in World Politics* (Cambridge, UK: Cambridge University Press, 1981): 156–85.

26 Todd Harrison, *Estimating Funding for Afghanistan* (Washington DC: Center for Strategic and Budgetary Assessment, 2009); Todd Harrison, *The Fiscal Commission and Defense: Strategy in an Age of Austerity* (Washington DC: Center for Strategic and Budgetary Assessment, 2010).

27 Bret Stephens, "Is Afghanistan Worth It?" *Wall Street Journal*, August 3, 2010.

28 Quinnipiac University Polling Institute, "Support for War in Afghanistan Collapses," last modified November 18, 2010, www.quinnipiac.edu/x1295.xml?ReleaseID=1537.

29 Jamie L. Carson, Jeffrey A. Jenkins, David W. Rohde, and Mark A. Souva, "The Impact of National Tides and District-level Effects on Electoral Outcomes: The US Congressional Elections of 1862–1863," *American Journal of Political Science* 45, no. 4 (2001): 887–98; Scott Sigmund Gartner and Gary M. Segura, "All Politics Are Still Local: The Iraq War and the 2006 Midterm Elections," *PS: Political Science* 41, no. 1 (2008): 95–100; Erik Voeten and Paul Brewer, "Public Opinion, the War in Iraq, and Presidential Accountability," *Journal of Conflict Resolution* 50 (2006): 809–30.

30 Gartner, *Strategic Assessment in War*; Scott Sigmund Gartner, "Making the International Local: The Terrorist Attack on the USS Cole, Local Casualties, and Media Coverage," *Political Communication* 21, no.2 (2004): 139–60; Gartner, "Making the International Local"; Scott Sigmund Gartner, "The Multiple Effects of Casualties on Public Support for War: An Experimental Approach," *American Political Science Review* 102, no. 1 (2008): 95–106.

31 For a discussion of US counterinsurgency efforts in the Philippines, see Thomas H. Henriksen, *Afghanistan, Counterinsurgency, and the Indirect Approach: JSOU Report 10-3* (Hurlburt Field, FL: Joint Special Operations University, 2010).

32 If the number of US troops in the Philippines seems too small to matter, remember that these figures are approximately the same as the number of US forces who toppled the Taliban government. For a brief comparison of these two conflicts, see Henrikson, *Afghanistan, Counterinsurgency, and the Indirect Approach.*

33 Quoted in Octavian Manea, "Thinking Critically about COIN and Creatively about Strategy and War: An Interview with Colonel Gian Gentile," *Small Wars Journal*, 2010.

34 Guy Raz, "Army Focus on Counterinsurgency Debated Within," *National Public Radio*, May 6, 2008.

35 For a broader discussion of this issue, see Evan Braden Montgomery, *Defense Planning for the Long Haul: Scenarios, Operational Concepts, and the Future Security Environment* (Washington DC: Center for Strategic and Budgetary Assessment, 2009).

36 Cited in Krepinevich, *The Army in Vietnam*, 172.

37 Larry Cable, *Unholy Grail: The US and the Wars in Vietnam* (London: Routledge, 1991).

38 Gartner and Myers, "Body Counts and 'Success' in the Vietnam and Korean Wars."

39 For a deeper discussion of the CAP program and the marine corps' organizational dispute with the Army, see Gartner, *Strategic Assessment in War.*

40 Combined Action Platoon, *Cap Mission Statement*, www.capmarine.com, accessed February 1, 2011.

41 This mirrored, to some extent, Viet Cong strategy. See Morris Janowitz, *The Professional Soldier* (New York: Free Press, 1971), xiv.

42 Bing West, *The Village* (New York: Simon and Schuster, 1972), 10.

43 Krepinevich, *The Army in Vietnam*, 173.

44 Gartner, *Strategic Assessment in War.*

45 James J. Wirtz, *The Tet Offensive: Intelligence Failure in War* (Ithaca, NY: Cornell University Press, 1991), 43.

46 Krepinevich, *The Army in Vietnam*, 174.

47 Ibid.

48 Gartner, *Strategic Assessment in War.*

49 See Krepinevich, *The Army in Vietnam*, 175.

50 The Army saw the marine efforts as failing as their body counts declined. See Douglas Kinnard, *The War Managers* (Wayne, NJ: Avery Publishing Group, 1985), 61.

51 Deborah D. Avant, "The Institutional Sources of Military Doctrine: Hegemons in Peripheral Wars," *International Studies Quarterly* 37 (1993): 420.

52 Hy S. Rothstein, *Afghanistan and the Troubled Future of Unconventional Warfare* (Annapolis, MD: Naval Institute Press, 2006), 175.

53 David Tucker and Christopher J. Lamb, *United States Special Operations Forces* (New York: Columbia University Press, 2007), 146, emphasis added.

54 Robert G. Spulak, *Innovate or Die: Innovation and Technology for Special Operations: JSOU Report 10–7* (Hurlbuit Field, FL: Joint Special Operations University, 2010), 6.

55 Cited in Spulak, *Innovate or Die,* 8.

56 Rothstein, *Afghanistan and the Troubled Future of Unconventional Warfare,* 169. There is evidence that some GPF units, such as the Army's 173rd Airborne Brigade Combat Team and US Marines in Delaram under General Nicholson, may develop the skills and unit-cultures necessary to handle CAP-like missions, which would increase considerably the population of deployable soldiers (Michael Moore and James Fussell, *Afghanistan Report I: Kunar and Nuristan, Rethinking U.S. Counterinsurgency Operations* [Washington, DC: Institute for the Study of War, 2009]; Rajiv Chandrasekaran, "Marines Going Rogue or Leading the Fight?" *The Washington Post,* March 13, 2010).

57 Seth G. Jones, "Community Defense in Afghanistan," *Joint Forces Quarterly* 57 (2010): 9.

58 Henriksen, *Afghanistan, Counterinsurgency, and the Indirect Approach,* 15.

59 Cited in Jones, "Community Defense in Afghanistan."

60 Michael R. Fenzel, "The Maneuver Company in Afghanistan: Establishing Counterinsurgency Priorities at the District Level," *Military Review* (March–April 2010): 37.

61 Seth G. Jones and Arturo Munoz, *Afghanistan's Local War* (Santa Monica, CA: RAND, 2010).

62 Tony Perry, "Marines in Afghanistan Take 'The Village' to Heart," *Los Angeles Times,* January 8, 2010.

63 Gartner, *Strategic Assessment in War.*

64 Jonathan J. Schroden, "Measures for Security in a Counterinsurgency," *Journal of Strategic Studies* 32, no. 5 (2009): 716.

65 Rothstein and Arquilla, chapter 1, this volume.

66 Chandrasekaran, "Marines Going Rogue or Leading the Fight?"

67 This line of effort is being implemented by Combined Forces Special Operations Component Command – Afghanistan (CFSOCC-A). See Ty Connett and Bob Cassidy, "VSO: More than Village Defense," *Special Warfare* 24, no. 3 (2011): 22–27; and Brian Petit, "The Fight for the Village: Southern Afghanistan, 2010," *Military Review* (May-June 2011): 25–32.

68 As of July 2010 the ANA had 134,028 members and the Afghan National Police (ANP) had 115,525. In the opinion of the Office of the Secretary of the Defense, however, the "quality" of these forces remains "a serious challenge" that "if not adequately addressed…poses significant strategic risk and threatens to delay the upcoming transition". See Office of the Secretary of Defense, *Report on Progress Toward Security and Stability in Afghanistan* (November 2010).

69 Leo Blanken, *Rational Empires: Institutional Incentives and Imperial Expansion* (Chicago: University of Chicago Press, in press), Chapter 2.

PART III

Other Perspectives

CHAPTER 9

The Ethics of Exit: Moral Obligation in the Afghan Endgame

Russell Muirhead

Over the past decade, just war theory has been extended to include a new category: postwar justice, or *jus post bellum*. In its most ambitious formulations, *jus post bellum* requires victorious nations to meet demanding and expensive duties before they can ethically disengage from a postwar situation. This would highly constrain NATO, for example, as it winds down the occupation force in Afghanistan. Against this view, what follows will argue that postwar justice does not require NATO or the United States to remain in Afghanistan until it successfully establishes a stable democratic state that enforces individual rights, nor does it require that the United States fully develop the Afghan economy. The demands of postwar justice are lesser: It may be enough if the Afghan state that emerges from this war is legitimate rather than democratic, and relatively secure, even in the absence of full prosperity. What postwar justice does require, I argue, is meeting the specific responsibilities to particular groups and individuals that have been accrued over more than a decade of fighting.

According to the tradition of just war theory, wars are judged twice: once with respect to the cause, and again with respect to how they are fought.[1] Over the past decade, a number of observers have focused on the possibility that wars ought to be judged a third time as well. On this view, we should judge the way wars are settled or ended on terms that do not entirely derive from whether the cause was just or whether the war was justly fought. This third category, *jus post bellum*, now vies for inclusion among the ancient categories of *jus ad bellum* and *jus in bello*. Although the claims of *jus post bellum* are more familiar than the novelty of the category might suggest, it is not easy to get clarity on the demands (and, just as importantly, the requests) it makes. Various advocates of the concept have specified it quite differently, although it is possible to group advocates of *jus post bellum* into two rough groups (*maximalists*, who argue that postwar justice requires a great deal, and *minimalists*, who argue that it only makes more basic demands).

In a perfect world we might hope that moral reasons would trump all other sources of motivation: In the ideal world, morality always comes first. But in the familiar world peopled by the "crooked timber" of humanity, prudent action depends on entertaining considerations beyond moral ones. The rule of morality, where moral reasons overwhelm every other kind of reason, is not likely to lead to humane conditions. Maximal understandings of postwar justice subtly invite us to imagine that morality might dictate, rather than constrain. Among other things, this will make morality less forceful by making it less worldly. Even more important, moral reasons are often not singular—morality involves many reasons which conflict. These conflicts are especially evident in the scenarios that arise in postwar situations. To suppose that morality might, even in the ideal and unworldly case, dictate action is to privilege one narrow kind of moral idea—obligation—over all other moral reasons.

Thus the maximal image of postwar justice should be resisted, and postwar justice should instead focus on more minimal yet urgent considerations, such as peace, stability, legitimacy, and the responsibilities to protect specific groups and persons within the defeated or host nation who contributed to and who shared the (just) goals of the victors, even and especially when those goals proved too costly to fully realize. To abandon one's friends is reprehensible, even when protecting one's friends is very expensive. Protecting those who have worked and risked all to create institutions and practices that reflect our greatest ideals should be the focus of postwar settlement. This is of urgent relevance in the endgame that the United States considers as it prepares to exit Afghanistan.

Is *jus post bellum* Something New?

Jus post bellum is not one of the traditional categories of just war theory: Michael Walzer's classic *Just and Unjust Wars,* for instance, does not contain an explicit account of the matter.[2] Some people point to a 1994 proposal by Michael Schuck as the starting point for an explicit category of *jus post bellum.*[3] Kosovo, Bosnia, and the problem of peacekeeping raised the specter of extended occupations in the name of justice, but it was the invasion of Iraq in 2003 that brought scholars (but not only scholars) to concentrate their concern on the justice of what happens *after* combat operations come to a close.[4] Conventional combat operations were a small part of the story in Iraq; in Afghanistan, the moment that demarcated combat and postcombat has never been clear, although traditional just war theory seems mostly concerned with the causes of war and the manner of fighting war—in short, with combat—considerations about justice do not come to a stop once combat operations stop.

If it is a new category, from a deeper perspective *jus post bellum* reflects a familiar kind of evaluation. Not entirely novel, its essentials follow from the more familiar categories of *jus in bello* and *jus ad bellum.* If war is only justified as a last resort of self-defense, and if it must be fought in a manner that respects the distinction between combatants and noncombatants, then it only makes sense that the kind of peace we most approve of would be constrained by the very moral considerations that inform what counts as a just cause of war and a just manner of fighting it. As many advocates of *jus post bellum* note, the basic idea that the justice of war depends in part on the kind of peace it produces goes back to Aristotle.

What happens after combat operations have ended profoundly influences our evaluation of the war itself. The ancient practice of victor's justice—according to which, after Rome sacked Carthage, all the men were killed and the women and children sold into slavery—has no hold on our intuitions. More recently, the way we commonly evaluate the world wars of the twentieth century is educational. World War II is sometimes called a "good war" and the word "good," in contrast to "victorious" or "effective," is instructive. If indeed it was a good war, it was good in that our cause seems to have been good, and the cause of our enemies, evil. But in addition, it was a "good" war because its settlement laid the foundation for a peaceful society of states in which individual rights could be secured and nations could prosper. Other wars have brought victory, from a military or political point of view, such as the 1991 Gulf War. But the first Gulf War will not go down as a good war because its settlement was both morally ambiguous (leaving in place the enemy dictator) and unstable. World War I is perhaps the most familiar case of a war that gave way to an unstable peace, in no small measure because its victors imposed punitive terms on the defeated. The unstable peace of the 1920s and 1930s, and the cataclysmic war that followed, vitiated the sacrifices of World War I, and amplified its senseless quality.

We engaged in the analysis of *jus post bellum* before the category became current. Just as inevitably as we will judge the cause of war or the manner in which it is fought, so we will also judge the kind of settlement that represents the end of war. To be sure, the category of *jus post bellum* brings more urgent attention to the moral importance of the way wars are ended—an attention that in any case is highlighted by the kinds of conflicts that certain countries, like the United States, find themselves in at the moment. If it is a new category for arranging our moral understanding, it is not new in its substance. It is already present in our arguments, evaluations, and judgments.

What Does Postwar Justice Entail?

To say that postwar justice is already present in our arguments and evaluations does not mean that we agree about what it means. On the contrary, there is much disagreement about what postwar justice entails. The recent literature, for instance, reveals a broad difference between what Alex Bellamy calls "minimalist" and "maximalist" conceptions of *jus post bellum*.[5] The restricted conception of *jus post bellum* focuses, in brief, on refraining from violating basic rights and quickly exiting so as to allow the subject nation to carry on with its political life: There is a presumption, as Gary Bass argues, "that victorious states should seek to limit their occupation of conquered countries to the shortest time possible."[6] The focus on respecting elemental rights insists that even once fighters stop fighting, they continue to follow the laws of war and the moral principles that invest even those on the "wrong" side (or merely the "losing" side) with rights. In the minimalist understanding of *jus post bellum*, the responsibilities that follow combat emanate from the logic of just war theory. The main moral imperatives of minimalist *jus post bellum* are negative: Do not harm innocents, respect the sovereignty of the defeated nation, and lay a foundation for a durable peace. This is the *jus post bellum* that we know before we name it, since it is implicit in ordinary judgments and evaluations. This understanding of *jus post bellum* does not necessarily present a severe constraint on the ethics of exit—on the contrary, the ethical thing is to exit, and allow the defeated people to resume their sovereignty.

Maximalist conceptions, by contrast, encompass the more ambitious agendas of political reconstruction, social and civic rehabilitation, and economic rebuilding. They ask not merely that victors obey the laws of war even in peace; they envision prosecuting those guilty of war crimes (and the violation of rights that made war necessary in the first place) in war crimes tribunals. In this view, victors have a responsibility to reconstruct the political order on a basis that puts the positive enforcement of rights on a secure foundation; ideally, victors would also rebuild civil society and reconstruct the peacetime economy.

Maximalist understandings of *jus post bellum* grow out of the very same concerns that give rise to minimalist understandings. The central goal of minimalist *jus post bellum*—exiting so as to allow the polity to carry on its collective political life (in a manner that does not threaten others)—is born of respect for the rights of nations to rule themselves. But the right of self-determination derives from individual rights: The rights of political communities or states "derive ultimately from the rights of individuals."[7] Taking individual rights seriously, however, makes stopping at a minimal understanding of *jus post bellum* unstable; if defending rights is what justifies going to war and if observing rights is what defines fighting a war justly, then it is a short step to saying that postwar justice is essentially about securing individual rights for *both* winners and losers. This is precisely what maximal understandings of *jus post bellum* assert. As one account of *jus post bellum* summarizes this understanding, "A just peace is one that vindicates the human rights of all parties to the conflict."[8]

The contemporary confidence in the universality of basic human rights reflects a post-Kantian morality, where the imperatives of morality are categorical. Indeed, some *jus post bellum* advocates look explicitly to Kant for both grounding and inspiration. In Brian Orend's view, for example, Kant was the first to offer a sustained understanding of postwar justice. In his reading, "Kant favored widespread internal regime change in the direction of human rights realization." The goal of postwar justice is to establish a "minimally just" or "legitimate" society, which he defines as one that seeks recognition of its legitimacy in the international community, subscribes to rules of international justice and citizenship, and satisfies the "human rights of its individual members (to security, subsistence, liberty, equality, and recognition)." "Vindicating rights," Orend says, "not vindictive revenge, is the order of the day."[9] Maximalist *jus post bellum* makes a policy of regime change morally respectable (if not also morally obligatory). What counts as a "minimally just polity" reflects universal standards of justice: A minimally just society, as Orend says, is "in every individual's self interest," and "respects everyone's potential for autonomy and self-direction," and "thus has universal appeal."[10] It is not much of an exaggeration to say that, in this view, the basic principles that define the minimal threshold for a just polity represent the "end of history," understood as the most justifiable goal of human action that all human beings will come to grasp over time.[11]

The force of maximalist conceptions of *jus post bellum* is seen most clearly not in wars of self-defense (it is odd for successful self-defense to generate a *duty* to sponsor the aggressor's political, social, and economic reconstruction), but in humanitarian interventions. For instance, Orend argues that regime change is a justified cause for war if the regime in question has so woefully violated the rights of its own citizens that it cannot be seen as a "minimally just regime," *and* if the interveners undertake the process of building at least a minimally just regime in its place.[12] This process will necessarily engage the forces fighting for regime change deeply into the affairs of the host society. The process should include, for instance, purging the old regime and prosecuting its criminals, demilitarizing the society, providing security for the whole society, constructing a rights-respecting constitution, nourishing civil society, and rebuilding the economy.[13]

In this view, the kinds of duties that arise depend on the nature of the regime one is fighting. Bass, for instance, argues powerfully for a hybrid understanding of *jus post bellum,* where the default position advocates a limited occupation of defeated regimes but requires something more ambitious in cases of "extreme" genocidal states. "Genocidal states," Bass argues, "fall into a special category."[14] In Bass's view, we not only have a duty to intervene to protect innocents against the atrocities committed by extreme genocidal regimes, but we also possess a corresponding duty to assist the sovereign people in their effort to reconstruct a decent sovereign state. And the longer onlookers wait to intervene against genocidal regimes, "the greater the obligation to a reconstruction program that aids the victims."[15]

For Walzer too, wars of humanitarian intervention motivate new and more ambitious moral duties. "Imagine a humanitarian intervention that ends with the massacres stopped and the murderous regime overthrown; but the country is devastated, the economy in ruins, the people hungry and afraid," he asks. "The forces that intervened did well, but they are not finished." We acquire new responsibilities, Walzer argues, in the course of a successful humanitarian intervention. It may not seem fair that in the course of doing one good thing (at great sacrifice) one acquires new responsibilities to do more good things (at more cost). But that, Walzer insists, is what fighting justly requires. We simply would not praise a humanitarian intervention that left its beneficiaries in poverty and anarchy as successful or good. Walzer is not certain of exactly what duties arise in humanitarian interventions—to know that, we would need a more fully developed theory of "justice-in-endings ... that engages the actual experience of humanitarian (and other) interventions." But such a theory, when worked out, should, Walzer says, detail what the responsibilities of intervening forces "will be if they win." Ideally, he says, an international agency "could stipulate and enforce these responsibilities."[16]

Orend too would ideally like to invest the maximal *jus post bellum* responsibilities in international law, enforced by international authorities. "There should be another Geneva Convention," he says, "this one focusing exclusively on *jus post bellum*—that is, on what the winners of war may and may not do to countries and regimes they have defeated."[17] Ideally, there would be "firm and objective guidelines against which to measure achievements and to create timelines for both progress and eventual withdrawal."[18] Orend says that "There needs, in short, to be an ethical 'exit strategy' from war, and it deserves at least as much thought and effort as the purely military exit strategy so much on the minds of policy planners and commanding officers."[19] With respect to Afghanistan, Walzer, too, holds that "we have incurred obligations from fighting for eight years [over a decade] in someone else's country." Walzer notes that those who say "This is a mess, and we should simply get out" are uttering a view that, given the concrete responsibilities and commitments we have undertaken, is "simply immoral."[20]

The Ethics of Exit in Afghanistan

How the ethics of exit bear on the Afghan endgame will depend on whether minimalist or maximalist criteria apply to the war in Afghanistan. If we apply the minimal understandings of *jus post bellum*, then the central goals are to get out quickly after the threat is neutralized and restore sovereignty to Afghanistan. In the maximal view—akin to what Orend or Walzer would recommend—the United States would fail in its obligations if it were to exit Afghanistan before a stable, responsive, rights-respecting, accountable government; a vital civil society; and a promising economy are in place.

The difference between minimal and maximal understandings bears directly on whether it is right to differentiate between the Taliban and al-Qaeda (and identify the latter as more of a threat to American national security than the former). Some suggest that a speedier path to stability requires tolerating some Taliban presence, or at least a willingness to negotiate with representatives from the Taliban.[21] In this view, it is in the interest of the United States to hammer out an informal accommodation with the Taliban that permits NATO and the United States to exit without inviting civil war—as long as there is assurance that the Taliban would not again tolerate al-Qaeda in Afghanistan. Protecting Afghans from Taliban rule is a lesser priority, in this view. In the minimalist version of postwar justice, such a strategic accommodation might even be *required*, especially if it allowed the United States to exit Afghanistan and return full sovereignty to the Afghan state.

But on the maximal understanding of *jus post bellum*, this kind of exit would be immoral. A theocratic regime by definition violates individuals' right to conscience; furthermore, a regime that severely restricts women's civil, political, and economic rights multiplies the injustice. What Orend calls a "minimally just" regime requires equality, freedom of religion, and equal opportunity, all of which Taliban rule in one way or another would likely violate. The same would likely hold if the United States exited with a regime like Karzai's in power: Again, a corrupt central government that, though less repressive than the Taliban, devolves power to patriarchal tribes at the periphery also falls short of the equality, liberty, and recognition that Orend's minimally just state demands. Perhaps *any* regime that devolved extensive powers to traditional tribal authorities would fail to satisfy a minimal version of Western understandings of individual rights and political justice.

This points to the central difference between minimal and maximal understandings of postwar justice: Where minimal understandings place a premium on exiting quickly and restoring the autonomous political life of the defeated nation, maximal understandings endorse long-term occupations, which are necessary to restructure the political culture. For instance, establishing a regime in Afghanistan with the enforcement powers to uphold individual rights would require building a central government with the capacity to regulate social practices throughout the country. It would require a central government that could enforce women's rights to equal education and career choice. The only acceptable solution, in this view, would be a centralized democratic government with enough immunity from local power structures to rewrite local practices. Creating a stable state of this sort, capable of resisting local opposition and recasting traditional modes of legitimacy, would likely require an occupation lasting for decades and costing many billions of dollars.

Although advocates of the maximal view do not advocate that occupying powers sponsor and guide a social revolution from above, the logic of the argument points in this direction. In the maximal conception of *jus post bellum*, morality is not merely a *constraint* on strategic action, as it is in traditional just war theory. It is rather a guide that displaces strategy; ultimately, it replaces political judgment. Morality—not a prudential assessment of what is necessary for peace—dictates the goals of war, and morality sets the terms for what kind of war settlement is acceptable. Morality dictates that the old regime be purged, that the society be demilitarized, that the victors supply police security, that a "rights-respecting constitution which features checks and balances" be established, that the economy be rebuilt, that the educational system be revamped and "new values" be inculcated.[22] All things considered, any of these goals might in fact prove desirable in Afghanistan, Iraq, or elsewhere. Or perhaps they might not: Sometimes tolerating the old regime rather than purging it conduces to postwar stability; sometimes allowing significant segments of society to retain their militias and arms is more prudent than demilitarizing (such as with the Kurds); sometimes a single constitution fails to produce a governing majority (Iraq in 2010); sometimes it is more respectful to let people design their own educational institutions according to values they actually believe in. What policy best conduces to peace cannot be decided by consulting a list of human rights or universal moral principles.

When morality takes priority over political judgment and military strategy, the tyranny of morality displaces all other modes of reasoning. This in turn endangers the ultimate goal of morality: a decent society. The minimal understanding of *jus post bellum*, grounded in the traditional understanding of just war theory, aims to allow a defeated people to get on with their collective life—to make and to remake their own society and their own politics, consistent with respecting the rights of other peoples. This is why its focus is on observing the negative duties that protect those who do not present a direct threat to one's life, forging a workable and durable peace, and then *getting out*. In the new maximalist interpretation, however, *jus post bellum*, grounded in a utopian image of the end of history, morality rules.

In theory, the rule of morality should be agreeable. That is, people should embrace it—after all, it is, in theory, "in every individual's self-interest" and "thus has universal appeal."[23] But what if, by chance, everyone does not agree to the imposition of a minimally just state? As a matter of fact, *everyone* will not agree to the principles that define a minimally just polity as Orend describes them (at least not everyone in Iraq and Afghanistan). Should dissenters be coerced, or forced to accept what (we say) is in their interest? How can we be so certain that it is in their interest, if they say it is not?

The answer to this question points to a distinctive feature of the neo-Kantian morality that supports maximal conceptions of postwar justice. What gives moral principles their force, in this view, is not that people in fact accept them, but that they are justifiable *in principle*. Some philosophers will supply an argument that shows how their conclusions are rationally justifiable; but many forgo this trouble, and more or less assert the justificatory force of what they propound. There is, of course, a danger here: To believe that our basic principles of political morality are rationally justifiable means it does not really matter whether people *actually* agree to the principles. Because the principles are justifiable, people *should* agree. When we stop noticing whether people agree because we assume they would agree if they were exercising their faculties of moral reasoning correctly, morality threatens to become tyrannical.

The tyranny of morality is dangerous not only to defeated peoples in postwar occupations. It is also a threat to the democratic life of the victor's domestic politics. What, for instance, is the right course of action if *jus post bellum* morality dictates that we reconstruct a defeated people's politics and rebuild their economy *and* at the same time, the citizenry of the victorious country does not support the expenditures required to pursue these goals? For some, this is an easy question—akin to whether a government should enforce equal citizenship on a population that contains many (even a majority of) racists. In this case, the moral principle of equality should trump public opinion. That morality rarely has such power does not disturb the principled view that it should. Mere public opinion, in this view, has no moral standing. The same is true of maximalist *jus post bellum*: Ideally, a victorious country will fulfill its moral duties irrespective of public opinion at home. "Weakness of will" might explain a failure to do your duty—but it does not *justify* such a failure.[24]

This is why the advocates of maximal *jus post bellum* are not satisfied with resting responsibility for postwar duties on the shoulders of victorious parties in war. The "real-world realization of morality through law" requires a "ratified legal document," enforceable through international agencies.[25] The rule of morality requires, in short, a moral ruler. One might shudder to imagine what kind of enforcement powers international bodies must possess in order to compel victorious parties to carry out extremely expensive and long-term economic, political, and military aid programs *against the wishes of their own populations.* Even if such a power were possible, it is hard to imagine how it could be desirable, for there is no such thing as an impartial moral ruler. Every worldly power will have its own worldly interests, and will be supported by its own coalition of worldly powers. To imagine that such a power would act well when it is not accountable to the peoples it affects (the victorious peoples and defeated peoples) is to be utopian in the worst way. Nothing human is pure—not even international institutions.

At stake here is a deeper philosophic question: whether there are, in theory, standards of political morality that can be applied across borders and cultures? Even if one believes that there are very general universal principles of justice and morality, it is a further question whether our moral yardsticks are so finely calibrated that we can confidently describe a regime type that is "minimally just" for all peoples of the world. In the West we express our basic principles of political morality in the language of rights, and this language has enough currency to supply the basic vocabulary of the UN's universal declaration of rights. But we should not be fooled by universal declarations into thinking that rights are easily made universally acceptable. In the Western nations, where such rights are taken as foundational, their exact specification and application is always disputed. Perhaps underlying these disputes is a baseline of agreement, perhaps not. We do not usually need to plumb the philosophic depths of our disputes because concrete and urgent matters make pragmatic accommodations possible in the absence of complete philosophic agreement. The fact that our own principles of justice are the subject of intense disputation should give us pause in supposing that we can construct a regime type that reflects a universal substratum of "minimal justice."

This "pause" is what informs the minimalist understanding of *jus post bellum*, which counsels that victors should do as little damage as possible and equip the defeated people to get on with their national life in a manner that does not threaten their neighbors or the international world. The idea is not that there are no universal principles of morality or justice. Perhaps there are, and perhaps we know what they are. Rather, we should not be overly confident that we can know exactly how they should be specified, adapted to local circumstances, and approximated in enduring institutional arrangements. This is why minimalist *jus post bellum* puts a priority on national self-determination over imposing even a "minimally just regime." Every just regime is, in practice, only minimally just. It is up to the defeated peoples in the wake of a just war to work out their own version of a minimally just polity.

The Special Case of Genocidal Regimes

Some views of *jus post bellum* are a hybrid where minimal postwar justice applies in most cases, while maximal postwar justice requirements apply in a few special cases—namely, in cases of genocidal regimes. For instance, Gary Bass aims to preserve the humanity of the minimal understanding (the goal of which is essentially to equip the defeated people to take responsibility for their own national life) while carving out an exception for maximal understandings that only applies in "extreme" cases of intervening to overturn genocidal powers.[26] Bass is aware of the disincentive that such weighty duties present, and is reluctant to "add to the burden" that already dissuades states from engaging in humanitarian interventions. Still, he says, "if a state has satisfied the demands of *jus ad bellum* and *jus in bello* in its war against a state committing a genocide, but did not reconstruct the genocidal country afterward, then a strong case can be made that the justice of the overall effort would be compromised."[27] In addition, failure to reconstruct the genocidal country would raise suspicions that the intervening country was only acting out of a sense of its strategic interests, perhaps compromising the justice of the cause of war.

From this perspective, the critical question for the United States and NATO exiting Afghanistan concerns whether the Taliban ought to be regarded as posing an "extreme" genocide risk, thus justifying further intervention as needed. Abhorrent as Taliban rule was and would likely be if the Taliban were to come to power again, their record reflects that they did not engage in one-sided mass murder with the intention of annihilating a tribal, ethnic, national, or religious group. In short, the Taliban regime violated basic human rights and liberties, but was not a genocidal power.[28] Thus, on the "Bass standard," the war in Afghanistan cannot be understood as the kind of emergency humanitarian intervention that warrants applying the most extensive *jus post bellum* responsibilities. Rather, the Afghan war is better understood as a self-defensive conflict where the United States had reason to remove the threat and to ensure that the conditions nourishing the threat in the first place were ameliorated, all while following the laws of war and causing as little destruction as possible—and then, to get out.[29]

The difficulty with this combination (that applies minimalist understandings of postwar justice in most cases, and maximalist understandings in the case of genocidal regimes) is that the category of "genocidal regime" is a very low standard. Rulers can steal from their people, oppress large segments of the population, and impoverish their people without being genocidal. So it is tempting to argue that if there is a strong reason to reconstruct polities in genocidal regimes, there must be some reason (perhaps less urgent) to reconstruct very bad and unjust regimes that stop their crimes short of genocide. This is sensible, as far as it goes. Going further requires entertaining the notion that not all moral reasons generate obligations.

It may not always be wrong to undertake more than what minimal postwar justice asks—but it also may not be required. Postwar justice needs to make sense of the idea that there is some kind of moral reason to intervene in and contribute to the reconstruction of unjust regimes, without resorting to a brittle requirement to intervene, occupy, and reconstruct at all costs. This argument invokes a moral category that is too often overlooked in accounts of postwar justice: This is the category of what it is good or even honorable to do, rather than what it is obligatory or required to do. Not all moral reasons generate *duties*. Duties are severe obligations of a very specific sort. For instance, the cashier at the coffee shop has a duty to give you your change. If he does in fact give you your correct change, he should not be applauded: it would be strange to say, "My change—and all of it! How very good of you!" Honesty, in this case, is not an option; it is an obligation. But in other cases, morality endorses options rather than requirements. To say that countries with airlift capacity and robust military force would do well to intervene to prevent atrocities—or to build stable democratic institutions and flourishing economies in the postwar phase may be plausible. But to say in addition that they are *obligated* to overturn unjust regimes and replace them with better ones, no matter how long it takes and how much it costs, is far less plausible. Were they to reconstruct a polity in a rights-respecting way that laid good foundations for a durable and decent regime, this would be a very good thing. But they would not be merely meeting a moral obligation; a full and successful reconstruction would seem to go well beyond what any people are required to do for any other.

The term that moral philosophers use for actions that go beyond duty is "supererogatory." If that term is unfamiliar, the actions it describes are not: They are common and essential to a decent society. Supererogatory acts are superior to or beyond obligation; in colloquial terms, the word we use to describe these acts is "good," as in, "it was good of you to do that." You didn't have to, one might say—but you did. And the proper response when someone treats you well or does you a good deed is gratitude. We do not have to thank people for doing their duty, any more than the landlord thanks us for paying the rent. But we do thank those who do more than their obligations require. It is a good thing for one country to intervene in another to arrest or prevent grave injustices—a very good thing. And it is a better thing still to reconstruct the country's politics and nourish its economic life. Nations that undertake such efforts deserve gratitude and praise (unlike the shopkeeper who gives you correct change). Nations that succeed in such ventures deserve glory. But that which we honor is not necessarily that which is obligatory or required.

Jus post bellum is not simply about obligation. It contains a great number of moral reasons that do not underwrite obligations, but that instead endorse acts that it would be good to do. These reasons may conflict with each other, and they may even conflict with moral obligations: We may be obligated to return responsibility for the political life of a nation to a defeated people even though they seem destined to fail, and even though at some level it would be good to oversee their politics longer, such that they might have a better shot at success. Moral reasons do not form a coherent whole, where each reason is consistent with and ordered alongside every other. The moral world is home to intractable conflicts and dilemmas, which is why navigating it requires judgment. This judgment includes prudence, or an awareness of how things are likely to work out in practice, given all the various causes that bear on the situation. Morality is not its own special province that ideally would rule over politics and strategy (with the help of international institutions). Moral reasons ought to be weighed alongside other kinds of reasons, sometimes taking priority, sometimes not, allowing for the possibility that second-best is often best in practice. Moral responsibilities do not crowd out political judgment. Political judgment is not only about fitting particulars (particular actions or policies) under general categories (like universal moral imperatives). It involves a weighing of various kinds of reasons, and is not separate from moral reasoning, but is part of moral reasoning.

Morality seems to have its greatest force in the realm of obligation, which is why it is tempting to reduce all moral reasons to obligations, and then to insist that moral obligations take precedence over every other kind of reason. Decent people who want to reduce evil and improve the world want to make moral reasons more forceful, and thus they may be tempted to make all morality equivalent to the most forceful kind of morality: Everything moral becomes a moral obligation. This may not lead to a more decent world, but rather to the tyranny of morality and the displacement of political judgment. Good political judgment is always a kind of moral judgment—and it entertains, as it must, moral reasons that go beyond obligation.

Specific *jus post bellum* Duties in Afghanistan

The extensive duties posited by many advocates of *jus post bellum* do not apply to the United States as it contemplates exiting from Afghanistan. Rather, the minimal understanding of *jus post bellum* applies, and the United States should be focusing on equipping Afghanistan to carry on its national life while eliminating the threat that al-Qaeda poses internationally from its base there. It would be consistent with the demands of postwar justice for the United States and NATO to focus more on stability and legitimacy than on democracy and the enforcement of individual rights. Legitimacy is a lower standard for politics than justice, and it does not require democratic institutions. Legitimacy refers to a condition where a state is stable because it enjoys voluntary support from most of the social groups that constitute the population. Justice is a more demanding condition, one that, as it is generally understood in the West, looks to whether every individual within a population could (in principle) agree to the basic structure of society.[30] To construct a regime that is just in this sense might be a good thing to do in Afghanistan, but it is likely to require an occupation that lasts many decades and in the end renovates many local understandings and customs. Such an undertaking, which would require a great deal of policing and violence, is not required by postwar justice. Postwar justice rather requires leaving a *legitimate* regime, one whose stability derives from the support of social groups within the society. A legitimate state may not enjoy support from *every* group or *every* individual. It may not be a just regime, in the fullest sense. But it should house a domestic politics in which Afghans themselves can work out their own understanding of a just polity.

To say that postwar justice is not entirely a matter of obligation does not mean that obligations are irrelevant. On the contrary, occupying powers can incur specific obligations to groups and persons by the agreements they make and the commitments they take up in the course of a war or occupation. Moral obligations arise, as Michael Walzer says, by "choosing to fight in someone else's country" for many years.[31] Walzer has in mind the achievements that have emerged over the past decade in public health, health care, education, civil society, and politics. "A version of democratic politics has emerged," Walzer says. As he sketches it, our duty is in part to protect and sustain these works. But to say that we are bound to defend and advance these achievements might be to embrace unlimited intervention in Afghan affairs. The emerging vision of democratic life, after all, might be quite fragile, the possession of a very small minority. What would be required to sustain it might be expensive, intrusive, and ultimately ineffective. To sustain these achievements would be a good thing, but to say that it is a duty is another and more severe matter. Postwar justice does not require that we establish the sort of state we would want to live in, but instead that we leave it to Afghans to build the sort of state they would like to live in.

But building a state is rarely an entirely peaceful enterprise, which points to the greatest moral calamity associated with exiting Afghanistan: a civil war between the Taliban and non-Pashtun tribes. From one perspective, both the United States and NATO could be seen as implicated in such a war, given that they have trained a very large army that would be party to the combat. Aside from bearing some responsibility for the destruction and killing that such a war would entail, both Europe and the United States would be obligated to assist the millions of refugees that such a war would inevitably produce. The question is whether the prospect of such a civil war entails a duty to continue occupying Afghanistan while stabilizing and rebuilding the Afghan polity until the prospects of such a war are remote. If this were the case, then in practice the goals of minimalist postwar justice might require the same ambitious policies as maximalist postwar justice.

But this is not necessarily the case. First, it is important not to overstate the responsibility of the United States and NATO for Afghanistan's civil strains: The conflict between modernists and traditionalists in Afghanistan antedates the US invasion, and is not a product of the war against al-Qaeda. Outside powers do not have blanket permission to intervene in civil wars, as terribly violent and intractable as civil wars tend to be. To say that the United States or NATO has an obligation to prevent any possibility of civil war in Afghanistan because it invaded in self-defense would be to issue a blanket permission to intervene in Afghan domestic politics. Finally, recognition that it is not a moral obligation to prevent an Afghan civil war at all costs should direct attention to ways of minimizing the possibility for civil war that fall short of sustaining a massive occupation that aims to wholly renovate the Afghan polity. The parties to civil conflict may not be able to afford a war, for instance, in the absence of outside funding. The United States might more efficiently meet its moral obligations by policing the stream of money flowing to Afghanistan, especially to the Taliban.

If the United States does not have an absolute obligation to prevent civil war, it might nonetheless have obligations to specific people and parties in Afghanistan that have worked with the United States to create a democratic state that protects individual rights and liberties. Our obligation is to specific people, our allies in the cause of building an open, liberal, and democratic society.[32] This is a different and more specific kind of obligation, and it should be central in any plans for exiting Afghanistan (and Iraq, for that matter). The questions are, "Who has helped us; who has taken risks to advance our goals; who has made our goals his or her goals—who shares the cause; and who among these friends is likely to be punished or worse after we exit as a result of their help?"

For instance, thousands of Iraqis assisted coalition troops, especially but not only, in interpretation and translation. They did so at enormous risk, and many suffered kidnapping, torture, and death.[33] To abandon Iraqi employees in the wake of an exit would be to condemn hundreds or thousands of people to death—it would be to abandon our political friends. If we cannot stay in Iraq and protect them and we cannot—we should give them US citizenship and generously enable their transition to American society. Indeed, the United States has done far too little to assist its Iraqi employees in obtaining not merely visas, but citizenship, and in making the resettlement to the United States successful. A special immigrant visa program was established in the 2008 Refugee Crisis in Iraq Act that created twenty-five thousand slots for Iraqi employees of the US government over five years, but better implementation and more slots will be required if we are to avoid a catastrophic abdication of duty to the Iraqis who worked for coalition troops.[34]

The United States and NATO have a similar duty in Afghanistan to Afghans who directly worked for International Security Assistance Force troops. But the special duties that arise in a just withdrawal do not stop with those who were directly employed by NATO troops. The two million Afghan girls who have attended schools, and the teachers who run these schools, are all potentially exposed to retaliation after the exit of NATO troops. In a case like this, it is even less feasible to resettle each girl and her extended family in the United States, and a more determined diplomatic approach with both formal and informal rulers of Afghanistan will be necessary. It is not unimaginable that negotiations with the Taliban might elicit enforceable guarantees of security for Afghan schoolgirls, and something like that seems already to be developing.[35] The moral obligation to protect Afghan girls who attended school at our urging and with our protection is so urgent that it should be at the center of any withdrawal plans and should constrain strategic actions so that they conform with whatever is necessary to accommodate the duty.

This kind of duty, to Afghan schoolgirls and Iraqi translators, is a special and specific duty—and it is a duty. It would not merely be "good" to protect our friends and allies; it is essential. Reprisals following our exit would reflect a moral failing and a human catastrophe, not to mention a strategic error in that it would harm the reputations and credibility of NATO and the United States. If one were to ask where these specific duties come from, we could liken them to the idea of a promise. We made an implicit promise to both Afghan schoolgirls and Iraqi translators that we would construct a certain kind of society, one where the values of equality and freedom would prevail. If we exit without having made good on our grandest promise for social and political reform, we should not let those who believe in us suffer rape, torture, and death as a consequence of our own failure.

Some might argue that the moral obligations involved in such promises do not generate an urgency to do whatever is necessary to protect those who relied on us. After all, some would insist that in the real world, parties to contracts should "beware" and take due precautions against the possibility that the other party may not be able to make good on its end of the deal. This argument might hold that so long as the United States made a full and good faith effort to keep up its end of the deal, then it has done its part. If it proved inadequate to fully realize its grandest intentions, well, this argument might say, so it goes. In politics, nothing is certain.

But what is at stake here is not merely a promise. It is a cause. The Iraqi translators may have worked for coalition troops because it was a well-paying job and the Iraqi economy, destroyed by both tyranny and war, produced very few other jobs. But no doubt many joined not only for this reason but also because they shared the goal of creating a rights-respecting democracy in Iraq. Our vision was also their vision. The same is true of the feminists, teachers, and even schoolgirls in Afghanistan: They were not opportunists looking for a check to cash, but believers in a society that treats women with respect and invests in each person's growth and potential. These people are not merely self-interested agents standing on the other side of a promise; they are our allies, our political friends, our fellow partisans. The obligations at stake are political and partisan. Every cause in politics is a partisan cause, because there is *no* cause that is in everyone's interest or commands universal assent. Accomplishing anything in the political world, no matter how good it may seem, requires a team, because every cause is embattled. Political action takes friends, or partisans, who stand by you as you stand by them. And partisans, or political friends, owe something to each other. In particular they owe loyalty, for without it, nothing—no matter how good—can ever be done.

We have inspired—and hired—allies, political friends, fellow partisans. In both Iraq and Afghanistan, our allies have risked all to help us and to help their own politics on the way to something more open, liberal, and democratic. These friends should be at the center of any plans for exit, whenever exit may come. To abandon them is to show ourselves unworthy of our own cause.

Trying to meet the specific obligations that I've described might easily invite a creep from the minimalist standard towards a maximalist norm. After all, the Taliban will not differentiate between the schoolgirl and the provincial governor who has supported the coalition–fully meeting our specific obligations to local allies who have worked for the cause of creating a rights-respecting, accountable government, might well mean that we occupy the country permanently. In the end, it may not be possible to fully respect the political rights of defeated countries on one hand, and to fully meet our responsibilities to local allies on the other. There may be no morally pure way of exiting Afghanistan, and negotiating this tragic dilemma will require creativity and political judgment. At best, such judgment will be guided by the competing moral reasons at stake even if it cannot fully satisfy any of them taken individually.

Notes

1 Michael Walzer, *Just and Unjust Wars: A Moral Argument with Historical Illustrations,* 4th ed. (with Preface) (1977; repr., New York: Basic Books, 2006), 21.

2 Ibid.

3 Doug McCreedy, "Ending the War Right: *Jus Post Bellum* and the Just War Tradition," *Journal of Military Ethics* 8, no. 1 (2009): 66–78, at 70.

4 For instance, Brian Orend, "Justice After War," *Ethics and International Affairs* 16, no. 1 (2002): 43–56; Orend, "*Jus Post Bellum:* The Perspective of a Just War Theorist," *Leiden Journal of International Law* 20, no. 3 (2007): 571–91; Gary Bass, "Jus Post Bellum," *Philosophy and Public Affairs* 32, no. 4 (2004): 384–412; Louis Iasiello, "*Jus Post Bellum*: Moral Obligations of the Victors of War," *Naval War College Review* 16, no. 1 (2004): 33–52.

5 Alex Bellamy, "The Responsibilities of Victory: *Jus Post Bellum* and the Just War," review of *International Studies* 34 (2008): 601–25; and Mark Evans, "Moral Responsibilities and the Conflicting Demands of *Jus Post Bellum*," *Ethics and International Affairs* 23, no. 2 (2009): 147–64.

6 Bass, "Jus Post Bellum," 387.

7 Walzer, *Just and Unjust Wars,* 53.

8 Robert Williams and Dan Cadwell, "*Just Post Bellum*: Just War and the Principles of Peace," *International Studies Perspectives* 7, no. 4 (2006): 313, 317; Orend, "*Jus Post Bellum,*" 578.

9 Orend, "*Jus Post Bellum,*" 580.

10 Ibid., 582.

11 Francis Fukuyama, *The End of History and the Last Man* (New York: Free Press, 2006).

12 Orend, "*Jus Post Bellum.*"

13 It is not entirely clear whether interveners are morally bound to undertake this process, in Orend's view, or whether the process is a "historically grounded recipe," or ultimately a contingent recipe, for achieving the morally necessary goal of building a "minimally just society" (Orend, *Jus Post Bellum*, 584).

14 Bass, "Jus Post Bellum," 398.

15 Ibid., 401.

16 Walzer, *Arguing about War* (New Haven: Yale University Press, 2004), 20–22.

17 Orend, "*Jus Post Bellum,*" 575.

18 Ibid., 577.

19 Ibid., 581.

20 Walzer, "Is Obama's War in Afghanistan Just?" *Dissent*, December 3, 2009, available at www.dissentmagazine.org/online.php?id=314.

21 Stephen M. Walt, "Negotiate with the Taliban?" *FT*, May 8, 2009, accessed at http://walt.foreignpolicy.com/posts/2009/05/08/talking_with_the_taliban.

22 Orend, "*Jus Post Bellum,*" 584–86.

23 Ibid., 582.

24 Evans "Moral Responsibilities," 162.

25 Orend, "*Jus Post Bellum,*" 572.

26 Bass, "Jus Post Bellum," 399.

27 Ibid., 400.

28 Thomas W. Simon, "Book Review: Defining Genocide," 15 *Wisconsin International Law Journal* 243, no. 15 (Fall 1996).

29 Bass, "Jus Post Bellum."

30 Rawls, *Political Liberalism* (New York: Columbia University Press, 1993), 35.

31 Walzer, "Is Obama's War in Afghanistan Just?"

32 Walzer "Is Obama's War in Afghanistan Just?" Also see, Robert Mackey, "'Just War' Theory and Afghanistan," *New York Times*, in "The Lede: Blogging the News with Robert Mackey," December 10, 2009, available at http://thelede.blogs.nytimes.com/2009/12/10/just-war-theory-and-Afghanistan/.

33 Phil Sands, "Interpreters Used by British Army 'Hunted Down' by Iraqi Death Squads," *The Independent*, November 17, 2006, available at www.independent.co.uk/news/world/middle-east/interpreters-used-by-british-army-hunted-down-by-iraqi-death-squads-424660.html.

34 "Tragedy on the Horizon: A List of Just and Unjust Withdrawal," The List Project to Resettle Iraqi Allies, May 2010, p. 12, available at www.thelistproject.org.

35 Jon Boone, "Taliban Ready to Lift Ban on Girls Schools," *The Guardian*, January 13, 2011, available at www.guardian.co.uk/world/2011/jan/13/taliban-lift-ban-girls-schools.

CHAPTER 10

Shaping Strategic Communication

Robert Reilly

Legitimacy is the main objective.

—Gen. David Petraeus and Gen. James Amos from Field Manual 3-24, *Counterinsurgency*

The mission of strategic communication, as presented here, is to convey purpose and to establish the moral legitimacy of that purpose in the eyes of those with whom one is trying to achieve it, that is, with those whose support is needed to fulfill one's purpose. The extent to which legitimacy is gained is the extent to which military force will not have to be used to achieve the goal. If the purpose is conceded, then the means can be peaceful. As Sun Tzu said, the ultimate victory is winning without fighting. In war, however, there are conflicting purposes and claims to legitimacy, which is the cause of the conflict in the first place. Strategic communication must then engage in a battle of ideas to advance the moral legitimacy of the cause at stake and to delegitimize the cause of the opponent, armed or otherwise. The conduct of the war of ideas is not something extrinsic to the shooting war; it is, or should be, intrinsic to it. It is in the minds of men (and women), after all, that wars are eventually won or lost.

When General Stanley McChrystal was senior military commander in Afghanistan, he said that "the conflict in Afghanistan is often described as a war of ideas and perceptions; this is true and demands important consideration."[1] This chapter examines the role of the war of ideas and of strategic communication in the Afghan conflict, America's longest war. What is its strategic purpose, and has its legitimacy been established during the past ten years?

This overall study considers the situation around the two axes of legitimacy and centrality. As the first chapter of this book suggests, centrality means control by the Kabul government, but in Afghanistan there is a congenital aversion to centralized control. Therefore, a highly centralized state may be, by definition, illegitimate in Afghan eyes. To the extent that this is so, extending the central government's authority broadens the opposition to the foreigners associated with this centralization.

Of course, when all order disintegrates, the issue of legitimacy evaporates as chaos takes hold. Chaos is never legitimate because man is a political animal in search of meaning. He will begin immediately to seek sources of legitimacy around which to form a community. The last time Afghanistan found itself in chaos, it was the Taliban, with Pakistani sponsorship, that emerged as the basis for that community. With the dysfunctional performance of the Karzai government, it is trying to do so again.

The word "legitimacy" is used here as a synonym for righteousness or the justice of one's cause. "Legitimacy" originally applied to rightful sovereignty by lineal descent, but also came to mean that which is in conformity with principle or law. Even when restricted to lineal descent, meaning born of *lawful* wedlock, the word "legitimacy" is essentially a term of *moral* reference. It, or "righteousness," is the single most important word in the arsenal of strategic communication. When Nabibullah Rabbani, from the Taliban's dispossessed Ministry for the Promotion of Virtue and the Prevention of Vice, proclaimed in December 2001 that "people understand we are the righteous ones and they know we could come back to power soon,"[2] he was attempting to seize this most powerful notion and put it to work for the Taliban cause.[3] Whoever wins the argument for justice wins the war of ideas and, concomitantly, the support of the people. This is the very substance of such wars: no legitimacy without justice. Of course, the claim to justice must be substantiated by the exercise of it, that is, by its administration.

It follows, then, that the pertinent questions about the war of ideas in Afghanistan are: Does the Taliban possess the requisite legitimacy to justify its return to power, as Rabbani insisted, at least over the areas it controlled in 2001, if not beyond? And can the Afghan government and US-led International Security Assistance Force (ISAF) retain or regain sufficient legitimacy to prevent this from happening? What respective sources of legitimacy are the various parties drawing upon, and are their actions consistent with their claims? The first part of this chapter examines the strategic communication of the United States regarding the legitimacy of its presence and purpose in Afghanistan. The second part considers the strategic issue of the legitimacy of the Karzai government in the struggle for the "hearts and minds" of the Afghan people, and then the Taliban side of the contest for legitimacy. The final section briefly examines and proposes specific actions in a strategic communication strategy to delegitimize the Taliban.

US Legitimacy

The United States cannot bestow legitimacy on an Afghan government, only Afghans can do that. But American presence in the country has to be itself justified by some association with Afghan legitimacy, otherwise it will be seen as malign. The US government has defined its main objective in Afghanistan as preventing the country from reverting to the Taliban and subsequently to a terrorist base. To do so, however, the United States seems to have adopted certain approaches that may undermine its own aims. In practice, the United States has identified success with the establishment of a Pashtun-led central regime, such as is headed by President Hamid Karzai today. But, as is discussed in part II, Mr. Karzai does not seem to be gaining long-term legitimacy for the Afghan central government or stability for his country. The failure on the part of the Afghan government to establish its legitimacy leaves the United States in a highly precarious situation.

Conflating the US goal of a nonterrorist Afghanistan with the establishment of a centralized, Pashtun-led government has not helped to produce consistent actions and messages. Is the United States conducting counterterrorism or counterinsurgency? Is it nation-building or not? Is it reinforcing the local rule of tribes and warlords who will work with it, or is it undermining them by extending the rule of Kabul? Is the United States departing or staying? Irresolution regarding the latter question has left the United States with the disadvantages of both positions ("we have been defeated"; "we are occupying your country"), but without the advantages of either ("we are not here to occupy your country"; "we will not abandon you").

As always, strategic communication has a particularly vital mission during war, when the peoples of other countries, whether adversaries or allies, need to know why we fight. There are, of course, multiple audiences for the articulation of an American "righteous cause." One audience is the troops themselves, for their inspiration and morale; one is the home audience, for its support of the troops; another is the people among whom one is fighting, to gain their neutrality if not support; and another is the enemy, to produce dismay among them from the delegitimization of its cause and the prospect of their defeat. Only the latter two audiences concern us here.

Is There a Strategy to Communicate?

So why does the United States fight in Afghanistan? After a decade of engagement there, the question may seem rhetorical, but it is not. It is important for the United States to answer this question if it wishes to use strategic communication as an aspect of its strategy in Afghanistan. Strategic communication cannot dictate an outcome, it can only assist in one. It can only be as good as the strategy it supports.

Frank Capra's "Why We Fight" films comprised one of the successful World War II strategic information campaigns to gain the support of the American people for the war and to explain to its troops the reasons and moral goals of the war. The campaign dwelt upon the legitimacy of the American cause and the illegitimacy and evil of the enemy cause. Since the launch of US and NATO military forces into Afghanistan some ten years ago, has there been, or is there now, something roughly analogous to explain "why we fight" to the people of Afghanistan so that they can understand the US presence there and identify with its purpose as their own?

Whatever efforts have been made in this direction have apparently failed. One might suppose that any justification for American presence in Afghanistan would necessarily begin with the fact that the United States was attacked from there on 9/11 by a terrorist group harbored by the Taliban government, which then refused to turn over the perpetrators. President Obama refers to Afghanistan as the "good" war because the justification for it seems so self-evident. When one has been attacked without provocation, is not the case for self-defense against the aggressor unassailable?

A barometer of how seriously the United States has failed in posing and answering this question was revealed in recent field research by the International Council on Security and Development (ICOS) located in Kandahar. The ICOS found that 92 percent of respondents (1,000 men) in the crucial southern provinces of Helmand and Kandahar were unaware of the 9/11 events; 9/11 is surely in the American vocabulary but apparently not in the languages of Afghanistan. An earlier July 2010 study by ICOS in the south found that a majority (of 552 men) had heard of 9/11, but that almost all were unable to state what took place during it or relate it to NATO/ISAF presence.[4] This failure would be equivalent to a World War II "Why We Fight" campaign that neglected to mention Pearl Harbor.

As a consequence, the general feeling among Afghans, as expressed by Kazem Ahang, dean of the Kabul University School of Journalism, is that, "The people don't know why the Americans are here. They only see that the more time goes by, the more American presence is growing…the only thing we have seen from Americans is their soldiers."[5]

Thus it appears that the United States may begin to leave Afghanistan without Afghans ever having understood why it was there in the first place, namely, why defeating the Taliban was key to making America safe. Without an explanation of 9/11, the default Afghan understanding of American presence is that it is an infidel foreign occupying force that has come to take their land. Nothing could make the United States look worse in Afghan eyes.[6] Not having heard a persuasive rationale, Afghans seek alternative explanations for the US presence in their country.

The vast majority of Afghans identify themselves above all as Muslims because Islam is the main source of significance in their lives.[7] A large portion of Afghans believe that foreign forces are in the country to destroy Islam, which is probably why a majority of them believe that it is wrong to work with foreign forces. To the extent that the United States emphasizes the inculcation and establishment of democratic principles, including women's rights, it is seen as assailing the Islamic identity of Afghans, which identity is at the core of their being, as it has been for centuries.

This plays well into the Taliban message of "foreign" forces undermining the Muslim religion and therefore justifying jihad. As was seen during the war against the Soviets, this is the one thing that has unfailingly worked in uniting the fractious Afghan tribes. According to the ICOS November 2010 study, "forty percent of those interviewed in the south believe the international forces are there to destroy Islam, or to occupy or destroy Afghanistan."[8] Forty-five percent of respondents in the south think that "foreign occupation" is the most important reason for young men to join the Taliban. In Marjah, the figure is 66 percent.[9] When Mullah Omar says, "The U.S. wants to prolong its occupation to pave its way for establishing itself in the region," he finds a ready audience.[10]

The failure to explain US presence (in a way Afghans can understand it) directly inflames the reaction against it. In fact, it serves to justify the opposition to it. As Matthew Hoh stated in his 2009 resignation letter as a senior civilian representative in Afghanistan, continued US military presence "greatly contributes to the legitimacy and strategic message of the Pashtun insurgency."[11] We become the cause of the problem we are trying to solve. Supporting this fact, one Helmand resident said that "Everybody wants to kill the foreigners, so they decide to join."[12] In its fall 2010 poll, ABC News, in exploring possible reasons for Taliban support, discovered that "68 percent say it could be because the Taliban are opposing the foreign forces; and 77 percent, say it could be for religious reasons."[13] As puzzling as it is for Americans to realize, they are seen as *kuffar*, nonbelievers, there to attack Islam and plunder the land.

The failure to explain and communicate "why we fight" is a failure to address the issue of righteousness. It is tantamount to surrendering in the war of ideas. According to a senior US official in Afghanistan, "The Taliban aren't just winning the information war—we're not even putting up that much of a fight."[14] Lt. Col. Shawn Stroud, former director of strategic communication at the US Army Combined Arms Center in Fort Leavenworth, Kansas, stated that "It's almost like we've surrendered the information battlefield."[15]

When the ICOS showed a photo of planes hitting the Twin Towers and the Pentagon on 9/11, and explained the event to five hundred interviewees in Panjshir and Parwan provinces (Tajik provinces), 59 percent subsequently said that "it justified the international presence in Afghanistan."[16] Only 16 percent said that it did not. No doubt, Pashtuns in the south would be a tougher audience, but surely more than 8 percent of them would get the point if it were presented to them, even this long after its occurrence. The ICOS study demonstrates that the American cause can be conveyed convincingly to Afghans who, either through tribal mores or Islamic law, can grasp the morality of self-defense and counterattack. The United States must not only transmit but ensure that the message is received. As Lawrence Freedman said, "Opinions are shaped not so much by the information received but the constructs through which that information is interpreted and understood."[17]

The legitimacy of America's presence must be accompanied by a firmness of purpose, a purpose that can be related to what the Afghan people themselves want. Together this would constitute the "narrative" that gives meaning to US actions in a way that is comprehensible and attractive to Afghans. As long ago as 2007, the US Defense Department Strategic Communication Plan for Afghanistan spoke of the "NATO-ISAF Master Narrative." The fact that there actually is no master narrative was reflected in the policy confusion over which strategy to pursue: counterterrorism or counterinsurgency; whom to kill, whom to advantage; over what period of time, and what good all of this will do. This state of confusion, as previously mentioned, conveyed mixed messages as to whether the United States is leaving or staying, and why. The cost of this indecision has been dear.

The effects of an expected American withdrawal, which commenced in the summer of 2011, have been enervating for those who oppose the Taliban and inspiriting for the Taliban and its supporters. As one discouraged member of Panjwayi's district council, Mohammad Rahim, expressed it, "The Taliban always leave, and the Taliban always come back."[18] The price of inconstancy is a lack of confidence in the United States and the demoralization of its supporters. As one villager said, "Now you say you will give me a gun—but tomorrow you will take it away, by then I will have even more enemies."[19]

This produces debilitating behavior in the government as well. "The border police chief for western Afghanistan, Brig. Gen. Malham Khan testified that one of his subordinates openly ordered his men to collaborate with the drug lords. His reasoning: 'This government and system would not last long, and we should not antagonize people and make enemies here.'"[20] Jelani Zwak, an Afghan student of Taliban propaganda, said, "People in provinces and tribal areas mostly accept this narrative, that [the Americans] are leaving and the Taliban is coming back."[21]

As for the Taliban, former Pakistani interior minister Aftab Kahn Sherpao stated that "The impression in the Taliban circles is that since now the Americans want to leave, what is the point of talking to them? This is a point of time where they haven't lost anything and in fact morale is higher."[22] Mawlawa Halimi, Taliban commander in Ghazni province, said,

> we hear that the Taliban attacked here and there and destroyed tanks and killed soldiers. Then in the next news item you hear that the Americans are calling for negotiations and of course you understand that these two news items are related. The second news item is the result of the first, and the Americans want to negotiate because they are losing. Why don't they just leave? What are they waiting for?[23]

Why should the Taliban negotiate seriously if the United States is already leaving? As the Afghan aphorism has it, "You have the watches; we have the time." And what is the difference between leaving in 2011 and 2014, for which men are willing to offer up their lives, and how is this difference to be expressed in a compelling way?

As long as the Taliban is perceived as winning and the United States as leaving, full engagement by the Afghan Army should not be expected, nor will efforts to raise militia be likely to succeed for the same reason. Villagers feel compelled to send one son to the Taliban and another to the Afghan Army because they are unsure which side will win.

Needless to say, American fickleness also encourages Pakistan to continue supporting the Taliban as a US departure would only increase Pakistan's influence through its Afghan proxies. In fact, US wavering encourages all the regional powers with a stake in Afghanistan—Russia, India, Iran, and so on—to line up their respective clients for another go at it.

To counter this and repair the damage, a clear, convincing message of enduring US commitment may be the single most important message to deliver, along with the seemingly contradictory signal that we are in Afghanistan only temporarily. Max Boot's clever line that "one way to leave Afghanistan faster is to promise to stay forever" is exactly right in psychology and substance, as long as the commitment to stay forever is credible.[24] Otherwise, the bluff will be obvious and will not work. The NATO announcement at the Lisbon conference in November 2010, that it will be in Afghanistan until the transition is completed at the end of 2014, and most likely beyond that in a supporting role, was very helpful in this regard. The change in the Obama administration's rhetoric has also been helpful, especially from Vice President Joseph Biden, as he was seen as an enthusiastic advocate for early departure.

What does staying mean? There are alternatives to the huge deployment of one hundred thousand troops and the expenditure of more than $120 billion annually.

What seems certain is that the surge at this level is not sustainable, either politically or economically, for the United States. Everyone knows this, including the Taliban. It nonetheless has created a breathing space in which the United States can reformulate and convey a coherent message, along with NATO, that sets forth a commitment that is realistic and therefore believable. The message of a credible commitment can help to influence a favorable outcome.

The payoff from the surge and the new emphasis on a long-term US/NATO commitment was already reflected in the Taliban reaction. "The Americans are more serious, and another thing that made people hopeful was when they said they would stay until 2014," a Taliban commander said in December 2010. "That has made people change their minds."[25]

By all means, the United States cannot be seen to have failed. If withdrawal from Afghanistan is perceived as a defeat for the United States—and an eventual Taliban victory will inevitably be seen as one—then the al-Qaeda and Islamist story line will be validated: that, by the power of Allah, they were able to defeat first the Soviet Union and then the American superpower. In his "End of History" article, Salman al-Awdah, one of bin Laden's spiritual mentors, said, "The oppressors are the swords of Allah on earth. First Allah takes his revenge by them, and then against them. The same as Allah has used, in Islamist eyes, the United States in order to destroy the Soviet Union, so he will take revenge against the Americans by destroying them."[26] It would be particularly apt in Islamist eyes that the venue for America's defeat should also be Afghanistan. This perception would energize and revitalize the global jihadist movement, as dispirited as it may temporarily be by Osama bin Laden's death.

It would be difficult to overestimate the effect of a US defeat. The ranks following the "strong horse" would swell considerably, not least in Pakistan, where groups like Lashkar-e-Taiba would be greatly strengthened, perhaps imperiling the Pakistani state itself with "Talibanization." As Indian strategic thinker Ajai Sahni said,

> I would ask you to try to project what the world would be in the case of a premature Western withdrawal. It would be a very difficult world, a world of Islamist triumphalism. This is not about Islam and never has been, but it is about a particular interpretation of Islam. There are tens of thousands of people who are currently sitting on the fence, whose sympathies are with the al'Quaeda [*sic*] and the Taliban. If they saw what they would interpret as Islam's defeat of the world's sole superpower, and of the coalition of the great powers of the world, they would switch over their allegiance and would become active Jihadists.[27]

Afghan Legitimacy

The first chapter of this book states that "even though President Obama has reiterated his determination to fight the 'good' war in Afghanistan, there exists grave doubt among both the Afghan and American people about the legitimacy of the government of Hamid Karzai and therefore the overall cause. This lack of a righteous cause, perceived or real, is not trivial." If anything, this is an understatement. Indeed, in June 2011, US Ambassador Karl Eikenberry, reflecting frustration with the Karzai government, said, "when we reach a point that we feel our soldiers and civilians are being asked to sacrifice without a just cause... the American people will ask for our forces to come home."[28] The legitimacy of the American presence has become tied to the legitimacy of the Karzai government or, at the very least, of the centralized, Pashtun-led conception of such a government, since it is on its behalf that the United States is acting. "Lack of a righteous cause" can leave American forces morally exposed, indeed, enervated. Without it, they would be, and are, seen as a sheer manifestation of physical force in pursuit of American self-interest. In terms of actual operations, it would be difficult, without a righteous cause, for the United States, as well as for everyone else, to comprehend what the political end state toward which Americans are fighting should look like. This is because moral principles provide the general orientation for the construction of that end state. If not in the moral difference between the conflicting conceptions of the end states, what has the fighting been all about?

As Stephen Carter and Kate Clark point out in their recent Chatham House study, "justice has a particular link to legitimacy in Afghanistan. Historically, the state has been minimalist, in terms of what Afghans wanted or expected from it. However, the 'legitimacy of the state and its ruler depended on the degree of justice the ruler delivered, as defined by Islam.'"[29] This raises two immediate problems. First, as mentioned earlier, the objective of US policy to create a strong central state is against the long-held traditions of the Afghan people. Second, the very least the Afghans expect from government is justice. A strong state that does not deliver justice is bound, then, to excite the deepest animosities of Afghans, as it does not meet their minimalist expectations while it makes maximalist claims. This seems to be getting the two most important things wrong.

What created the possibility of a Taliban comeback after its punishing defeat in 2001, and how has the Taliban seized the high ground in the war of ideas? For many, it is difficult to imagine that a war of ideas could be lost to the Taliban, considering its own abysmal record and primitive ideology. That it is winning, by the United States's own admission, is a measure of two things: the extent of the damage from three decades of war that, among other things, completely destroyed the infrastructure of government; and the incompetence and venality of the Karzai regime.

Hamid Karzai began his presidency with the affirmation of a *loya jirga*, a traditional Afghan means of reaching consensus, and then a 2004 presidential election, a far less familiar source of legitimacy in Afghanistan. As a Durrani Pashtun, he could also evoke some sense of legitimacy from the long Durrani line of Afghan rulers. However, Karzai was installed in a strong presidential system with powers to appoint officials down to the provincial, district, and subdistrict levels. This grated against Afghan tradition. Though he enjoyed a provisional legitimacy, Karzai undercut it through his attempts at centralization, attempts approved and instigated by the United States. Also, what little legitimacy was available through elections was compromised by the widespread fraud in Karzai's reelection in 2009.

Nonetheless, if Karzai had filled the vacuum created by the Taliban's departure with the minimal security and justice that historically successful Afghan governments have provided, the conditions for a Taliban resurgence could not have occurred. However, he did not have an "administration" to take over and, in the absence of governmental infrastructure, he chose or sanctioned the return of various predatory warlords as an alternative to maintain a semblance of order. Unfortunately, a number of them were associated with the depredations that had brought the Taliban to power the first time, and their version of order was closer to exploitation than administration. By sponsoring the creation of a strong central government, the United States identified itself with what was seen by many as oppression. And by flooding the country with amounts of money that Afghanistan could not possibly absorb in any normal way, the United States provided the fuel for massive corruption.

Through this combination of factors, an invaluable opportunity was squandered. "No one expected the Taliban to be back," said university student Luqman, a recent supporter of the Taliban in Kabul, "but when the normal people saw the corruption of the government, when they saw that the warlords are back, people started supporting the resistance."[30] In 2009, Transparency International found Afghanistan under Karzai to be the second-most corrupt country in the world after Somalia. The traditional Afghan patronage system is sometimes used to excuse or at least explain some of the corruption, but an ISAF officer noted, "This is not like a standard patronage system, where money flows down in exchange for loyalty, rather officials on the periphery move money upwards, in exchange for license [to commit crimes]."[31]

The general result was recently described by a graduate student at Kabul University who works for the US Agency for International Development (USAID) mission. He said that average Afghans "don't even know that we have a constitution and certainly don't know what their rights are, while the rich and powerful, who know that we have laws, don't pay any attention to them."[32] Consequently, "there is not even security in property. If a person owns, for example, a house, and the local strongman wants it, he just tells the owner to get out. The owner has no choice. If he does not obey, he is apt to be beaten or killed. There is no recourse through government even if the owner has all the proper papers." Government property suffers the same fate. Force rules. Force obtains. Corruption reigns. According to the ABC News Afghan poll mentioned earlier, "huge numbers continue to call corruption a problem at the provincial, national and local levels alike—93, 88 and 85 percent, respectively." In the same poll, "when asked why some people may support the Taliban, 71 percent say 'too much corruption in the government.'"[33]

What about the justice system of the Afghan government? Why is there no recourse through it? "Although there is a state system of justice in operation in all provinces," said Frank Ledwidge, who recently served as the first Justice Advisor to the United Kingdom's Provincial Reconstruction Team (PRT) in Helmand, "the reality is that this is, at best, ramshackle and inefficient, at worst criminally corrupt on a huge scale."[34] According to the International Crisis Group, "Afghanistan's legal system is broken…courts are either nonexistent or are in disrepair. The majority of Afghans view justice institutions as the most corrupt in the country."[35] Government officials usually require a bribe to register a complaint and it can then take years to get a judgment. As *Washington Post* reporter Ernesto Londoño describes it: "The country's criminal justice system is among the weakest links in a system of deficient institutions. It is beset by widespread corruption, shoddy police work, a presumption of guilt and subservience to the politically powerful."[36] Judges and prosecutors often do not appear and, when they do, are without access to copies of the laws and statutes.

The beneficiaries of this dysfunction are the Taliban. As related by *The Guardian* reporter Ghaith Abdul Ahad from Wardak Province, "Many say the civilian apparatus of the Taliban-run districts operates a more effective justice system than the government's, which is corrupt and inefficient."[37] Even an Afghan USAID employee admits, "There is no corruption where the Taliban are in control."[38] Karzai's failure to establish a bare minimum of justice left the winning issue of righteousness lying in the gutter for the first insurgent to pick up.

This left the Taliban not only with a vision of justice as compared to none, but a vision of justice compared to predatory abuse by the government. This has slowly overcome the deep reluctance of Afghans who otherwise would not have turned back to the Taliban because of its abysmal record of misrule in the 1990s.

The Taliban has also been successful in monopolizing the all-important religious issue because of the failure of Karzai or ISAF to engage with religion constructively in the last decade. The Taliban used the local religious networks of mullahs, madrassas, and mosques, and its shadow administration of parts of the country is based on these networks. Because of the centrality of religion to the lives of Afghans, whoever provides the interpretation of daily events through Islamic eyes wins the audience's allegiance. "They've co-opted the religious narrative for the last several years," said Rear Adm. Greg Smith, NATO's communications chief in Afghanistan. "They've used that narrative locally very effectively."[39]

The Taliban Claim to Justice

The Taliban has made the highest kind of claim to justify its rule: It is doing God's will. Mullah Mohammed Ghaus, the foreign minister of the Taliban, said, "We believed we were working with Allah as His pupils. We have got so far because Allah has helped us."[40] As Carter and Clark state, "Justice is central to the self-image of the Taliban."[41] It is a vision of justice and a concomitant outrage at injustice that impels the Taliban and attracts people to it. It is not, of course, the only thing, but it is the main thing. God's will embraced all of Afghanistan, not simply the Pashtuns. Because its purported religious authority was larger-than-tribal, the Taliban has a claim for controlling Afghanistan in its entirety, which it came very close to achieving. Even for those not attracted to the Taliban version of Islam, Taliban rule was at first preferable to what preceded it.

What followed, however, made it seem less preferable and helps explain how the Taliban was so easily overthrown in 2001. The Taliban's primary asset, its religiosity, was also a liability because its Deobandi brand of Islam is not native to Afghanistan. It was rather the product of the hundreds of *madrassas* that had been set up in Afghan refugee camps in Pakistan, where several generations of Afghans, with little or no experience of their native land, had been educated during and following the war with the Soviets. Sponsored by fundamentalist Pakistani religious parties, these *madrassas* inculcated in their students a puritanical view of Islam that excludes ideas that are not obviously Islamic and brooks no compromises with modernity. It is also antithetical to mystical Sufism, which has traditionally enjoyed a broad and deep following in Afghanistan, and to folk Islam, also popular among Afghans. An aide to Mullah Omar, Mullah Wakil, expressed the vision emanating from this kind of indoctrination: "We want to live a life like the Prophet lived 1,400 years ago and jihad is our right. We want to recreate the time of the Prophet."[42] Osama bin Laden was so pleased with the results that he is purported to have said, "Afghanistan is the only country in the world with a real Islamic system."[43]

Unlike any other Muslim country, Taliban Afghanistan banned kite flying, card games, girls' schools, dolls, music at weddings, most sports, clapping at sports events, lobster, nail polish, firecrackers, statues, sewing catalogs, pictures, Christmas cards, priceless Afghan historical art treasures, Sufi shrines, photography, and television, among other things. Imitating its Saudi supporters, the Taliban initiated a Ministry for the Promotion of Virtue and the Prevention of Vice, whose officers ensured that men were not shaven, that women wore full burkhas, and that no female would be seen unescorted by a male relative. They also made sure people were at prayers. As for a social and political program beyond this, the Taliban thought it presumptuous, as Allah would provide everything else, including food to those whom He wished to feed. These strictures alienated many Afghans whose version of Islam was less radical and more accommodating to folk and Sufi ways. Many began to chafe under the strict Taliban version of shari'a rule and became disillusioned because the Taliban had no program beyond the literal imposition of its ideology.

The ease with which the Taliban was overthrown in 2001 and the jubilation in the cities over its downfall would seem to make its return in the past several years hard to comprehend. As late as 2006, ABC News polls showed 88 percent of Afghans said that it was good that the United States had invaded Afghanistan, though that figure declined to 74 percent in late 2010. Yet the Taliban's resuscitation, again sponsored by Pakistan, has been in the same terms as its initial rise: Islamic justice.

Causes animated by righteousness are not as easily subject to the normal forces of exhaustion as are purely political ones. This is because of what is at stake in them. Wars of ideas concern the very reason for existence. They touch upon the source of meaning in life. When that source of significance is threatened, people take arms, either metaphorically or literally, to defend it. Rather than live without it, they prefer to kill or be killed. As Mullah Omar has declared, "the Islamic Emirate [of Afghanistan] is not a foundation, the leaders of which you can buy with money or could deceive with your phony processes and fatuous slogans—but that their personalities are overwhelmed with the Islamic faith and real Afghan spirit. They have a strong resolve to forge ahead with the jihad and keep on the face-off with the enemy. Either they will lay down their lives or compel the enemy to flee the territory of the Afghans."[44]

As mentioned earlier, the issue of justice is paramount in winning the war of ideas, and it is why the Taliban is winning and has been able to overcome, at least partly, its legacy of oppression. When civil authority has collapsed and tribal structures have weakened, the default position in Afghanistan is shari'a, which is the

Taliban specialty. This works in Afghanistan as it has in Pakistan, where the late Abdul Rashid, deputy leader of the Red Mosque in Islamabad, said, "the Islamic system takes action wherever the state fails."[45] As a Taliban leader explained, "One of the main reasons for our popularity is the failure of this government."[46] The first force to enter a chaotic area, bring miscreants to justice, and establish legal order wins.

The Taliban can enter an area with its mobile courts and quickly hear a few court cases to establish credibility. The courts' verdicts are taken seriously as enforcement is harsh and sure. As a result, Afghans will actually travel into Taliban-controlled areas specifically to seek out a Taliban court. According to the ICOS study, "59% of southern interviewees would like the Taliban to provide justice."[47] An elder from the Dhani Ghorri district told *The Guardian* newspaper: "In the courts of the Taliban there are no bribes and no corruption. Even the people from the government come to the Taliban to solve their problems. Problems that take years to be solved in government courts take a few days in the Taliban courts."[48]

Despite the rough justice of the Taliban's literal version of shari'a rulings, Afghans often find it better than no justice at all, and preferable to the slow and corrupt court system of the government. Though they are primarily Pashtun, the Taliban courts eschew tribal loyalties in delivering verdicts, as opposed to the government officials who often favor their own clan or tribe. They do not take bribes. Taliban courts are impartial enough to have even found against their own commanders in certain cases. This deeply impresses the populace with their impartiality. In order to spread its jurisdiction, the Taliban also assassinates government judges, leaving itself as the only alternative.

The Taliban's success in delivering justice is perhaps its single most effective means of undermining the Karzai government and appropriating legitimacy. Every judgment rendered by a Taliban court is a successful usurpation of sovereignty. It is such a powerful symbol and exercise of legitimacy that it is the first thing the Taliban undertakes when it moves into an area. Sometimes, it is the only thing it does. By itself, it is enough to establish its control and split the people away from the government, and by just doing this one thing well, the Taliban gains allegiance. Whoever administers justice will *be* the state. The Taliban knows this and it is why the issue of justice is stressed so prominently in its propaganda.[49] "The main two problems we deal with in the Taliban courts are bandits and land disputes," said Abdul Halim, a Taliban mosque leader, who divides his time between fighting and his job as a preacher. "When we solve these problems we win the hearts of the people."[50] In her research on Taliban propaganda, Joanna Nathan found that justice is the most popular motif: "Justice is very central to how they try to depict themselves and how they depict the current regime.... Justice is what people are longing for—therefore they use it. It's the highest priority in terms of how they portray themselves—the Emirate had justice and the government today doesn't."[51]

In short, Afghans believe that under the Taliban, despite the negatives, their property will be safe and they will have access to fair trials. The Taliban is also saying that it has learned from its past errors, which made it so broadly unpopular. "The Taliban that will return will not be like the old Taliban," claims a Taliban leader. "We have learned from the old mistakes. We will accept others."[52] Unless the government of Afghanistan finds a way to compete in this area, it will be impossible for it to establish legitimacy or to gain allegiance. By default, the Taliban will win.

Unless this issue is addressed in a compelling way, the buildup in Afghan security forces, including military and police, to roughly 305,000 by late 2011 and possibly as many as 378,000 by 2012, will not be enough to ensure the government's survival or the United States's successful withdrawal. To whom or to what will the security forces owe their allegiance? Will the army disintegrate when its foreign sponsors leave? Or will it be tempted to take over in a military coup? The ICOS report notes that there is a clear "potential for the Afghan security forces to switch sides" after being trained by NATO.[53] As it is, according to one report, "the ANA (Afghan National Army) is now evaporating every year through desertions (18%) and non-reenlistment (60%)."[54]

If the Afghan government fails to develop legitimacy, why should security forces give it their fealty? Though the words "irreversible transition" are used by the US military to justify the increased numbers of Afghan security forces, the term itself contains about as much political wisdom as did "government in a box" when applied to the surge in Marjah. Government does not come in a box, and there is no such thing as an "irreversible" transition secured by sheer numbers of security forces. Regarding the increase in police, Jukka Savolainen, the head of the European Union Police Training Mission in Afghanistan, cautioned that "Policing is ineffective until you have rule of law. You need courts where you can have a fair trial and a fair and functional corrections system."[55] In other words, no justice, no legitimacy, no "irreversible transition." The lesson from the failure of the Afghan government to secure a minimum of justice is that you cannot establish legitimacy with the aid of strategic communication if you are not acting legitimately. David Ogilvy's saying applies: Nothing kills a bad product faster than good advertising.

Taliban Illegitimacy

This makes it all the more important to delegitimize the Taliban. How can this be done? The Taliban's strong points are justice and religion. Since the righteousness of its cause rests upon these principles, they must be called into question and undermined in an aggressive information and action campaign. Perhaps the government could be encouraged to compete with Taliban courts by fielding its own circuit-riding shari'a courts, utilizing judges with unquestioned integrity who would be protected by Afghan Special Forces. These courts could offer a more lenient interpretation of shari'a more compatible with Afghan tradition. Finally, the Taliban gains great advantages from the congenital Afghan antipathy to foreigners, especially *kuffar* (nonbelievers or infidels). For this reason, it is essential that the attack on Taliban legitimacy be conducted by and for Afghans.

The Taliban operates an effective network of information activities by radio, Internet (www.shahamat.info/english/), print publications, videos, cell phone text messages, rumors, and night letters. It is particularly adept at fashioning its military activities for propaganda purposes. It also responds speedily in order to put out its version of events first. Michael Doran, former deputy assistant secretary of defense said that when US forces carry out an operation in Afghanistan "within 26 minutes we've timed it—the Taliban comes out with its version of what took place in the operation, which immediately finds its way on the tickers in the BBC at the bottom of the screen."[56]

Taliban messages emphasize:

- That it is already governing by providing security and justice.
- That it is winning—demonstrated by Taliban ability to strike almost anywhere and destroy at will.
- That Karzai is a puppet (the United States has done major damage in reinforcing this impression by holding Karzai up for public ridicule over corruption, arresting those whom he patronizes, and by providing him with American bodyguards, an image which cements in people's minds the idea that he is an American puppet).
- That the Taliban represents traditional Afghan values and true religion versus Western corruption.
- That the Taliban has changed—an impression it tries to reinforce by broadcasting music and poetry.
- That Western forces are there to attack Islam and violate the country.
- That time is on its side.

Gen. David Petraeus, when he was commander of US and international forces in Afghanistan, issued operational guidelines in 2010, stressing that the "information war" must be fought aggressively to ensure insurgent propaganda is not just promptly challenged but also beaten to the punch. "Turn our enemies' extremist ideologies, oppressive practices and indiscriminate violence against them. Hang their barbaric actions like millstones around their necks," the guidelines say. "Be first with the truth."[57]

The success of the surge in the south was essential to rebut the Taliban narrative that it was winning. It showed clearly that the insurgents could lose. Apart from the tremendous value of successful military operations with respect to delivering this message, information operations regarding the subjects below can reinforce this success and greatly expand upon it precisely in the way that General Petraeus recommended.

First, it should be noted that Afghanistan has developed a very rich media environment since 2001, one that was completely lacking under the Taliban, that banned television and allowed only its own radio station, Radio Voice of Shari'a, to dominate the airwaves. There are now one hundred or so privately and community-owned radio stations in the country, twenty-six TV stations based in Kabul, and another nine in the provinces. As electricity spreads, TV will continue to gain market share, though radio still remains the most influential. According to a report on the Afghan media landscape, a 2009 Asia Foundation poll discovered that "81 percent of people surveyed owned a radio, 41 percent owned a TV and 52 percent owned a mobile phone—only 6 percent, on the other hand, owned a computer."[58] Print media are also flourishing, though their reach is restricted by Afghanistan's high illiteracy rate. These media are generally against the return of the Taliban as they know their operation would be outlawed. They are the means through which to reach the Afghan population. NATO has been slow to realize this and only belatedly took the step of ensuring that its press releases were available in Dari and Pashtu.

The US embassy in Kabul is demonstrating some smart media initiative by supporting the creation of new TV programs with the right messages. For instance, "Eagle Four," about a fictional police unit, reports *The Wall Street Journal*, is "the first of several television shows funded by the US government as part of a strategy to galvanize Afghans behind their security forces. The show's first episodes debuted on Tolo TV, one of Afghanistan's largest stations. Tolo will follow up with 'Birth of an Army,' a reality show that follows recruits from their first training missions to their battles with insurgents." To illustrate what can be accomplished, Pakistan has already begun to air a similar TV action series dramatizing the role of the Pakistani armed forces in fighting the Taliban called "Beyond the Call of Duty." It has proven to be very popular, especially with the rural population. As one viewer said, "Most people, including me, initially thought Pakistan was fighting a US war. But when I watched the drama, I came to the conclusion that those guys [i.e., the terrorists] are a cancer for the whole country and should be cut out."[59]

"The US-backed shows are part of a broad allied effort to counter a Taliban propaganda offensive against coalition and Afghan forces, a push that runs parallel to the surge of forces on the ground. TV is seen as an effective way for the United States to spread its message to Afghanistan's largely young and illiterate population. A cop show appeals to the core demographic: impressionable young men."[60]

Programs like these are relatively inexpensive to make in Afghanistan and are even less expensive in radio format.

Anti-Taliban Themes

The Taliban needs to be attacked through its distorted notion of Islam, its dreadful legacy, its atrocities, and its foreign-based control. At a minimum, failure to challenge its narrative effectively endorses it.

Religion: Mistaken Notion of Islam

As Pakistani journalist Ahmed Rashid noted, the Taliban ideology "fitted nowhere in the Islamic spectrum of ideas and movements that had emerged in Afghanistan between 1979 and 1994.... The Taliban represented nobody but themselves and they recognized no Islam but their own.... Before the Taliban, Islamic extremism had never flourished in Afghanistan."[61]

To the extent to which it is recognizable, the Taliban version of Islam is a vulgarization of Deobandi teaching, which is native to India, not to Afghanistan. However, even Deobandi teaching from India can be used to discredit Taliban terrorist activities, like suicide bombings.

The single most effective weapon against the Taliban is to defeat it spiritually by calling into question the chances for salvation of its members, and by demonstrating that it has been manipulated into pursuing a violent path that is un-Islamic and that redemption lies in renunciation of the Taliban ideology. Since the Taliban is primarily a religiously motivated organization, sowing doubt at the theological level would be devastating. This would be literally demoralizing. This work obviously must be done by Afghan Islamic scholars.

This approach was used so effectively in Egypt that its most violent terrorist group, al-Gama al-Islamiyya, publicly and officially foreswore violence as un-Islamic. It even removed the sword from its emblem. Theological and Qur'anic scholars were able to achieve this renunciation after intensive, lengthy dialogue and debate with leading al-Gama figures, who then themselves wrote revisionist tracts. The publication of these revisions further unnerved any remaining al-Gama members and their families, who quivered at the prospect that they were jeopardizing their immortal souls or that the souls of their expired compatriots had been lost.

With the right members of the *ulemma* such an approach could begin in Afghanistan with captured Taliban members and could also be carried out publicly through all the media and in the mosques. This would require a sustained, sincere, comprehensive effort. It would be the work of years. It must have the backing of the *ulemma* and the government. Its success would be more decisive than a military victory, as no organization can survive a spiritual defeat—its loss of meaning. This is the ultimate demoralization.

This objective can be partly achieved with the proper kind of Qur'anic duels, modeled on Judge Hamoud al-Hitar's effort in Yemen. The premise of his challenge to militants was: "If you can convince us that your ideas are justified by the Koran, then we will join you in your struggle. But if we succeed in convincing you of our ideas, then you must agree to renounce violence."[62] The potential for generating broad public interest in this approach is significant. The war of ideas can be very good theater. When properly refined, such "duels" could be dramatized on radio, TV, and in print.

The British magazine *Prospect* reports on an effective example of how this can work: "The Voice of America's Radio Deewa, broadcasting in Pashto to the badlands of the Pakistan-Afghan frontier, has shown how much potential there is here: in the past two years, the number of pro-Taliban callers to popular daily phone-in programs in the region has declined after their views were very publicly and successfully challenged on air. Many Islamic militants have a sketchy knowledge of their religion, and their views often do not stand up to serious scrutiny."[63]

The Taliban premise that it "has the time" to wait out the length of any US/NATO commitment largely rests upon the existence of its secure sanctuaries in Pakistan to which it can safely retreat at any time. However, ideas do not have borders, and their ideology can be struck from anywhere. What the Taliban needs above all is a theological safe haven. This should be denied through a theological assault.

In summary, Attack Taliban *takfiri* ideology—dedication to violent jihad against other Muslims, which is forbidden by mainstream Islam. Just as there was an Amman Message against terrorism and *takfiri* ideology produced under the sponsorship of

King Abdullah of Jordan, so there should be a repeated Kabul message from the *ulemma* of Afghanistan to the same effect. Both Saudi Arabia and Egypt produced effective TV programs revealing the deception of al-Qaeda jihadi teaching and on the deprogramming of jihadis. Afghan media can do the same.

Taliban Legacy

Many Afghans are skeptical that the Taliban has changed. More than six in ten reject the notion that the Taliban has adopted a more moderate stance.[64] Reinforce this skepticism by reporting on and emphasizing current behavior that shows it has not changed: for example, burning down school houses, throwing acid on school girls, executions, attacks on Sufi shrines, and so on. Therefore, it is necessary to keep the memory of prior failure alive.

- Film and radio dramatizations of the Taliban's five years of misrule should be used. Use anniversaries and radio dramas to accompany them.
- Memorialize the Taliban massacres against ethnic minorities after the fall of Mazar-i-Sharif in September 1998 and the fall of Bamiyan in October 1998. UN officials documented "15 massacres" between 1996 and 2001. They also said, that "[t]hese have been highly systematic and they all lead back to the [Taliban] Ministry of Defense or to Mullah Omar himself."[65]
- Republication of Taliban decrees after the capture of Kabul, 1996. What follows is a partial Taliban translation from Dari in the original English handout:

  > "Women should not step outside your residence."
  > "Sitting and speaking between male and female doctors are not allowed."
  > "To prevent music . . . cassettes and music are prohibited."
  > "Anyone observed who has shaved and/or cut his beard, they should be arrested and imprisoned . . ."
  > "To prevent kite-flying. The kite shops in the city should be abolished."[66]

- Clear message to the Afghan people: Do you wish to live like this again?
- Emphasize the Taliban destruction of *insaniyat*—the traditional Afghan understanding of the shared humanness of all people. Use traditional Afghan poetry to counteract and rebuke the Taliban dehumanization of its opponents.
- Dramatize the indifference of the Taliban to general welfare, to anything but shari'a enforcement of the most literal and severe sort.

Taliban Atrocities

As Mullah Omar wrote in *The Islamic Emirate* magazine in December 2001, "We know that taking a Muslim's life is a cause of defeat."[66] The Taliban also knows that its chief vulnerability, like al-Qaeda's, is the "loss of the justice of our cause."[67] In Islam, the greatest offense, aside from apostasy, is the killing of another Muslim. By this very measure, the Taliban should be defeated. The Taliban is the primary source of civilian casualties, three times as many as the number from ISAF actions. Therefore, the Afghan media should be encouraged to dramatize and publicize civilian casualties from the Taliban.

Remarkably, before the arrival of General Petraeus, the policy was not to emphasize Taliban civilian casualties because it might present a propaganda victory for the Taliban. It would illustrate the inability of the Karzai government and ISAF forces to protect civilians. Thus, one of the Taliban's greatest vulnerabilities was transformed into a Taliban asset by mistaken US information policy. People still knew they were not being protected but were deliberately not stirred to outrage by the Taliban atrocities. The net result was a gain for the Taliban, which benefited from the fear it generated without suffering from people's moral obloquy. General Petraeus immediately reversed this shortsighted policy:

- Dramatize the victims of the Taliban in print, photo essays, radio, and film documentaries. In Iraq, the US Defense Department supported a series of documentaries on "The Victims of Saddam's Regime," which were then incorporated into a weekly hour-long TV show called "Overcoming the Legacy of Evil." This program, also supported by the Department of Defense, became the second-most popular TV show on al-Iraqiya, the state channel. Something like this could and should be done in Afghanistan.
- The Taliban has destroyed more Qur'ans than anyone. By killing the governor of Kunduz in 2010, it destroyed a mosque in the adjoining province of Takhar where he was in attendance. It uses mosques to hide arms.
- Taliban attacks on Afghan cultural heritage, from the destruction of the Bamiyan Buddhas to the bombing of Sufi shrines. The March 5, 2009, bomb attack on the shrine of the great Pashtun poet Rahman Baba (born around 1605) on the outskirts of Peshawar, by a group believed to be affiliated with the Taliban.
- Talibanization is destroying Afghan culture (folk and otherwise), most especially Pashtun culture.
- Attempted genocide against the Shi'a Hazara minority community in Afghanistan. The Taliban does not consider Shi'a to be Muslims.
- Suppression of Sufi orders (just like the Soviets), mainly Naqshbandiya and Qaderiya; methodical destruction of Sufi shrines (inspired by alien Deobandi and Wahhabi ideology).
- As Council on Foreign Relations Senior Fellow Stephen Biddle suggests, "create a political narrative that puts the Taliban on the outside, killing innocent Afghans, and ourselves on the inside, defending them."[68]

The Biddle strategy naturally suggests the next Taliban vulnerability.

Foreign Influence

The Taliban is very susceptible to charges that it is under the control of the Pakistani ISI, and the charge that Karzai is a puppet should be thrown back at the Talibs. Fifty-seven percent of the respondents in Panjshir and Parwan believe that Pakistan controls the Taliban.[69] And a large portion of the population in Helmand (20 percent) and Kandahar (40 percent) believe this as well.[70] The United States, through Afghan sources, should reinforce the impression that the Taliban is a foreign puppet and in foreign pay. The combination of unfavorable views of Pakistan with Pakistan control of the Taliban should be parlayed into a potent campaign against the Taliban. The Taliban can be made to be the outsiders. An example would be a fictional radio drama of the Quetta Shura, portraying Mullah Omar and senior Taliban operatives receiving their instructions from the ISI to carry out operations harmful to the people of Afghanistan, serving the purposes of Pakistani foreign policy and living securely in Pakistan.

Conclusion

The only antidote to the enemy narrative that the United States is in Afghanistan to occupy the country and to destroy Islam is a lower profile and a reduced presence: fewer irritants, fewer targets. The United States should provide support in the background and for the long haul. As Field Marshal Frederick Sleigh Roberts, Lord Roberts of Kandahar (commander of the Kabul and Kandahar field forces, Second Anglo-Afghan War, 1879–80) counseled, "We must not be afraid of Afghanistan and would profit by letting it be the master of its own fate. Maybe it is not the most attractive solution for us, but I feel that I am right in asserting that the less they are able to see us, the less they are likely to hate us . . . we will have a much greater chance of getting the Afghans on our side if we abstain from any interference in their internal affairs whatsoever."[71]

The United States might be wise to adopt this latter statement as doctrine, and broadcast its adherence to it widely, as it has no business interfering in the internal affairs of Afghanistan as long as its strategic goals are met. Those goals are more likely to be met if it does this and abandons the idea that an internal reconfiguration of Afghanistan and its culture are prerequisites for its success. This latter idea has brought the United States close to disaster.

Recent strategy seems to reflect the wisdom of Lord Roberts' advice. In Helmand province, Maj. Gen. Richard Mills, the commander of US and NATO troops in southwestern Afghanistan, said, according to the *The Washington Post*, that his "forces have gradually pulled back to the fringes of many stabilized districts and are letting Afghan police and soldiers patrol those areas. In many parts of the province," he said, "things are progressing along at a very steady and satisfactory rate."[72] In November 2010, President Karzai said that the time has come to "reduce the intrusiveness into the daily Afghan life."[73]

At least one of the US objectives in Afghanistan seems to have been conceded by the Taliban. Abdul Salam Zaeef, the former Taliban ambassador to Pakistan, who now resides in Kabul, said, "The Americans have one right only, and that is their right to be assured that Afghanistan will not be used against them and that is something the Taliban should give. Apart from that they have no rights, they have no right to tell us about democracy and human rights. That's an Afghan issue and it will be decided by the Afghans."[74] Lord Roberts would probably have had no problem with this message. Perhaps neither should we.

Regardless of any change in strategy to achieve a stable Afghanistan that will not harbor terrorist groups, the general outlines of the war of ideas will remain the same in terms of the competing claims of legitimacy. A reduced American profile and presence, necessary for long-term success, would nonetheless sustain the sense of urgency about the need to win this war. With this in mind, the United States ought to consider every action it undertakes in Afghanistan, including military ones, in light of whether it advances the legitimacy of the Afghan government and the American presence there, or if it contributes to delegitimizing the Taliban. If it does neither of these things, it ought not to be done because "legitimacy is the main objective."

Notes

1 Global Security, "Initial United States Forces - Afghanistan (USFOR-A) Assessment," www.globalsecurity.org/military/library/report/2009/090830-afghan-assessment/090830-afghan-assessment-02.html, accessed August 5, 2010.

2 John Pomfret, "For a Feared Taliban Officer, Few Worries about Reprisals," *The Washington Post*, December 23, 2001.

3 Note the Pakistani terrorist group's attempt at the same claim in its name of Lashkar-e-Taiba, "Army of the Righteous." Also, most Islamist parties have the word "Justice" in their names, as in the Prosperous Justice Party in Indonesia (PKS) or the Muslim Brotherhood party in Egypt, the Freedom and Justice Party.

4 Norine MacDonald, *Afghanistan: The Relationship Gap* (London: The International Council on Security and Development, July 2010), 53, www.icosgroup.net/2010/report/afghanistan-relationship-gap/, accessed August 2010.

5 Yaroslav Trofimov, *Faith at War: A Journey on the Frontlines of Islam, from Baghdad to Timbuktu* (New York: Picador, 2005), 209.

6 Norine MacDonald, *Afghanistan Transition: Missing Variables* (London: The International Council on Security and Development, November 2010), 48, www.icosgroup.net/2010/report/afghanistan-transition-missing-variables/, accessed December 2010.

7 Thomas Barfield, *Afghanistan: A Cultural and Political History* (Princeton, NJ: Princeton University Press, 2010).

8 Ibid.

9 Ibid.

10 Mullah Omar's Letter to Taliban Militants, MEMRI, www.memrijttm.org/content/en/blog_personal.htm?id=4167&param=UPP, accessed December 2010.

11 Matthew P. Hoh resignation letter, *The Washington Post*, September 2009, www.washingtonpost.com/wp-srv/hp/ssi/wpc/ResignationLetter.pdf?sid=ST2009102603447, accessed October 2009.

12 Jean MacKenzie, "The Battle for Afghanistan. Militancy and Conflict in Helmand," *New America Foundation*, September 2010, http://counterterrorism.newamerica.net/sites/newamerica.net/files/policydocs/helmand2.pdf, accessed November 2010.

13 ABC News, "Afghanistan Poll: Where Things Stand 2010," November 30, 2009, http://abcnews.go.com/Politics/Afghanistan/afghanistan-poll-things-stand-2010/story?id=12277743, accessed December 2010.

14 Yochi J. Dreazen and Siobhan Gorman, "Pentagon Jams Web, Radio Links of Taliban," *Wall Street Journal*, April 18, 2009, http://online.wsj.com/article/SB124001042575330715.html, accessed April 20, 2009.

15 Greg Bruno, "Winning the Information War in Afghanistan and Pakistan," Council on Foreign Relations Backgrounder, May 11, 2009, www.cfr.org/publication/19330/winning_the_information_war_in_afghanistan_and_pakistan.html, accessed June 2, 2009.

16 MacDonald, *Afghanistan Transition*.

17 Lawrence Freedman, "The Transformation in Strategic Affairs," *The Adelphi Papers* 45, no. 379 (International Institute of Strategic Studies, 2006): 610.

18 Joshua Partlow and Kaarin Bruliard, "U.S. Operations in Kandahar Push Out Taliban," *The Washington Post*, October 25, 2010, www.washingtonpost.com/wp-dyn/content/article/2010/10/25/AR2010102505658.html, accessed October, 27, 2010.

19 Stephen Grey, "Afghan Gang Wars in Helmand and US Policy," *Le Monde Diplomatique*, August 8, 2010.

20 Yaroslav Trofimov, "Karzai Divides Afghanistan in Reaching Out to Taliban," *Wall Street Journal*, September 10, 2010.

21 Ernesto Londoño, "Taliban Steps Up Propaganda War," *The Washington Post*, October 2, 2010, A7.

22 David Nakamura, "Pakistani Security Officials Want Role in Afghan Talks," *The Washington Post*, October 25, 2010, www.washingtonpost.com/wp-dyn/content/article/2010/10/24/AR2010102403135.html, accessed October 27, 2010.

23 Ghaith Abdul-Ahad, "Talking to the Taliban about Life after Occupation," *The Guardian*, November 26, 2010, www.guardian.co.uk/world/2010/nov/26/taliban-afghanistan-occupation, accessed December 4, 2010.

24 Max Boot, "One Way to Leave Afghanistan Faster Is to Promise to Stay Forever," commentary, January, 13, 2011, www.commentarymagazine.com/blogs/index.php/boot/386500, accessed January 2011.

25 Carlotta Gall and Ruhullah Khapalwak, "NATO Push Deals Taliban a Setback in Kandahar," *New York Times*, December 15, 2010.

26 Fawaz A. Gerges, *Journey of the Jihadist* (Orlando, FL: Harcourt Books, 2007), 103.

27 Ajai Sahni, "The Dynamics of Terrorism in the AfPak Conflict," London, The Henry Jackson Society, July 22, 2010, www.henryjacksonsociety.org/stories.asp?pageid=49&id=1696, accessed August 2010.

28 Don Nissenbaum, "U.S. Envoy Rebukes Karzai," *Wall Street Journal*, June 20, 2011, A11.

29 Stephen Carter and Kate Clark, *No Shortcut to Stability: Justice, Politics and Insurgency in Afghanistan* (London: Chatham House, 2010), 20.

30 Ghaith Abdul-Ahad, "Face to Face with the Taliban," *The Guardian*, December 14, 2008, www.guardian.co.uk/world/2008/dec/14/afghanistan-terrorism/print, accessed December 15, 2010.

31 Carter and Clark, *No Shortcut to Stability*, 11.

32 William R. Polk, "August in Kabul," *The American Spectator*, November 2010, 34.

33 ABC News, "Afghanistan Poll: Where Things Stand 2010."

34 Frank Ledwidge, "Justice and Counter-insurgency in Afghanistan: A Missing Link," *The RUSI Journal* (February 2009): 8.

35 "Reforming Afghanistan's Broken Judiciary," Asia Report No. 195, International Crisis Group, November 2010.

36 Ernesto Londoño, "American Former Beauty Queen Defending Foreigners Stuck in Afghan Legal System," *The Washington Post*, October 22, 2010, www.washingtonpost.com/wp-dyn/content/article/2010/10/22/AR2010102204250.html.

37 Abdul-Ahad, "Face to Face with the Taliban."

38 Polk, "August in Kabul," 34.

39 Londoño, "Taliban Steps Up Propaganda War."

40 Ahmed Rashid, *Taliban: Militant Islam, Oil and Fundamentalism in Central Asia* (New Haven, CT: Yale University Press, 2001), 22.

41 Carter and Clark, *No Shortcut to Stability*.

42 Rashid, *Taliban*, 43.

43 "Deobandi Islam: The Religion of the Taliban," *Global Security*, October 2001, www.globalsecurity.org/military/library/report/2001/Deobandi_Islam.pdf.

44 "Islamic Emirate of Afghanistan Reiterates Opposition to Peace Talks," MEMRI, December 2010, www.memrijttm.org/content/en/blog_personal.htm?id=4168&param=UPP, accessed December 2010.

45 Zahid Hussain, *The Scorpion's Tail* (New York: Free Press, 2010), 107.

46 Ibid.

47 MacDonald, *Afghanistan Transition*, 46.

48 Ghaith Abdul-Ahad, "Five Days Inside a Taliban Jail," *The Guardian*, November 25, 2010, www.guardian.co.uk/world/2010/nov/25/taliban-afghanistan-prison-special-report?intcmp=239, accessed December, 2010.

49 Carter and Clark, *No Shortcut to Stability*, 22.

50 Abdul-Ahad, "Face to Face with the Taliban."

51 Carter and Clark, *No Shortcut to Stability*, 23.

52 Ghaith Abdul-Ahad, "Talking to the Taliban about Life after Occupation."

53 Paul Tait, "Study: Few Afghans Know about 9/11, Reason for War," *Reuters*, November 19, 2010, www.reuters.com/article/2010/11/19/us-afghanistan-report-idUSTRE6AI2OX20101119, accessed November 25, 2010.

54 Larry Goodson and Thomas H. Johnson, "Parallels with the Past," *Foreign Policy Research Institute*, April 2011, www.fpri.org/enotes/201104.goodson_johnson.afghanistan.html, accessed May 5, 2011.

55 Joshua Partlow and Ernesto Londoño, "Plan Calls for More Afghan Security Forces," *The Washington Post*, January 18, 2011, A7, www.washingtonpost.com/wp-dyn/content/article/2011/01/17/AR2011011704404_2.html.

56 Ibid.

57 Jason Motlagh, "Afghan Radio Wars: Combating the Taliban's Message Machine," *Time*, November 28, www.time.com/time/world/article/0,8599,2032811,00.html, accessed December 2010.

58 Dominic Medley, "The Growing Media Landscape in Afghanistan," *The RUSI Journal* (February–March 2010): 31.

59 Tom Wright, "Pakistan's Army Is Ready for Its Close-Up," *Wall Street Journal*, June 18, 2011, C2.

60 Maria Abi-Habib, "U.S. Courts Afghans Through Television," *Wall Street Journal,* November 17, 2010, http://online.wsj.com/article/SB10001424052748703628204575618573846693534.html, accessed November 20, 2010.

61 Rashid, *Taliban*, 18–19.

62 James Brandon, "Koranic Duels Ease Terror," *The Christian Science Monitor*, February 4, 2005, www.csmonitor.com/2005/0204/p01s04-wome.html, accessed March 2006.

63 Gordon Adams "Could the Media Save Afghanistan?" *Prospect-172*, July 2010, www.prospect-magazine.co.uk/2010/07/could-the-media-save-afghanistan/, accessed July 2010.

64 ABC News Fall poll, 2010.

65 Edward A. Gargan, "Taliban Atrocities," *Newsday.Com,* October 12, 2001, www.papillonsart-palace.com/massacre.htm, accessed October 2010.

66 Trofimov, *Faith at War*, 204.

67 "Captured al-Qaeda letter to Ayman al-Zawahiri," Iraq, 2005.

68 Bruno, "Winning the Information War."

69 MacDonald, *Afghanistan Transition,* 62.

70 MacDonald, *Afghanistan,* 55.

71 Quoted in Artyom Borovik, *The Hidden War* (New York: Grove Press, 1990), 12.

72 Craig Whitlock, "On Afghan Trip, Gates Says War Strategy Is Working," *The Washington Post*, December 9, 2010, www.washingtonpost.com/wp-dyn/content/article/2010/12/08/AR2010120806354.html, accessed December 2010.

73 "Karzai: US Should Cut Back Afghan Military Operations" *VOA News*, November 14, 2010, www.voanews.com/english/news/Karzai-Wants-US-to-Cut-Back-Afghan-Military-Operations-107921714.html, accessed November 2010.

74 Abdul-Ahad, "Talking to the Taliban about Life after Occupation."

CHAPTER 11

Civil and Uncivil Society

Jade I. Rodriguez and Rebecca Lorentz

Civil and uncivil society networks will play integral roles in shaping the future of Afghanistan. Civil society is represented by the general population, civilian government workers, private contractors, and nongovernmental organizations (NGOs). Uncivil society is comprised of warlords, illicit goods traffickers, and corrupt leaders. However, even these broad definitions have a Western slant. Is civil inherently good and uncivil inherently bad? In this case, no. It is critical to understand the potential benefits and problems that these groups bring, and to include roles for them in any exit strategy. Together, all these actors form the foundation on which a future Afghanistan will be built. Left unaccounted for, both civil and uncivil networks will have the potential to undermine the last decade's efforts toward achieving a peaceful end state.

President Obama's "civilian surge" in 2009 increased the deployment of civilian workers supporting the counterinsurgency (COIN) strategy of "shape, clear, hold and build." They have created an environment in which civil society organizations have focused on the "build" phase of operations.[1] Despite the apparently overarching mission of nation-building, the reality on the ground illustrates a different dynamic. The lack of coordination and collaboration among the various players with regard to mission and strategy has constrained progress.

Multiple players are attempting to formulate solutions in an environment that is continuously changing and where chaos reigns within a subtle order imposed by a dynamic set of stakeholders. Traditional notions and definitions of civil society, particularly in relation to governance, corruption, and most importantly, who are the legitimate stakeholders in civil society, will be challenged. It is also necessary to keep in mind that, in Afghanistan, these themes and their "movers and shakers" may not always fit into clear parameters to which US and coalition forces may be accustomed. This chapter begins with an overview of the current state of civil society, followed by a discussion of the role that corruption plays in the overall political, social, and economic landscape. Identifying corruption as a possibly necessary evil leads into an analysis of alternative ways of looking at governance in Afghanistan and the potential need to explore the possibility of stabilizing the central government from the peripheries rather than from the core in Kabul. By strengthening local institutions and informal networks of stakeholders, both civil and uncivil, Afghan society will support a stable end state.

As an important component of civil society development, the youth of Afghanistan are viewed in this chapter as potential catalysts for change. Their inclusion can serve to bridge a generational gap, contributing to a more sustainable and stable foundation for future political processes and the creation of legitimate institutions. Despite an increasing presence across growing urban areas, youth have been largely understudied and, not surprisingly, ignored in the ongoing efforts of stabilization and reconstruction. As we have seen in recent events throughout the Middle East, youth are an important determinant of politics and provide a good overall measure of the future "health" of a country. Recommendations and the closing discussion will focus on their role in civil society.

Militarization of Aid

The humanitarian space, its development projects, and the aid that supports them, have operated under the notion that by "winning the hearts and minds" of the population, support and recruitment for the insurgency will be undermined and security will be brought to areas that are strategically important. The assumption that security can be increased via aid projects has resulted in a continuing flow of funds. Since 2002, over $17 billion in aid has flooded into Afghanistan.[2] This flow of cash has made aid a lucrative business, increasing the number of agencies vying for those dollars. An organization may be politically neutral and still have a financial incentive to provide services, even if the unintended consequences of those services are political in nature. Aid, after all, is a business. Before ideology, self-preservation is a priority for each aid agency. Whether the goal of self-sustainment is based on lofty ideals or on a capitalistic desire to run a business with potential for growth, the result is the same: a desire to remain a valid actor in the humanitarian aid space. If an aid organization were to leave Afghanistan in order to avoid being politicized, another would gladly take its place, as well as its funding. The window of opportunity that currently exists for NGOs creates a moral hazard; they are legally bound to be "nonpolitical" and yet, competition for grants combined with lack of governmental oversight leads to the strong possibility of politicking.

The likely alternative to the development of civil society is a continued motivation among the populace to support the insurgency. The responsibility lies with the government to use the aid fueling Afghanistan's redevelopment to attend to the needs of the populace. In 2000, the Taliban held that responsibility. At that time, Barnett Rubin wrote that the precarious humanitarian situation in Afghanistan meant that any decisions made by the Taliban in association with global policy would either lead to nation-building and legitimate government for Afghanistan, or to an even more illicit political economy, based on a "stigmatized" leadership.[3] More than ten years later, the options remain the same.

The potential for politicized aid is one dilemma for nongovernmental agencies operating in a war zone. Another lies in physical operations. Functioning in a war zone requires the creation of a military-like operation for these "unbiased" agencies, if for nothing else than self-preservation. Requiring this type of structural change in the agencies, and then further asking that they assist in the "shape, clear, hold and build" mission President Obama's "civilian surge" asks them to, now demands focus on both the "shape" and "build" phases of the operations. Too much of the end state relies on these humanitarian actors who are not experts at strategy. When foreign aid providers work too closely with government entities, it appears as though aid is guided toward the same mission as government operations, making them equally troublesome to both an insurgent group and to a government striving for independence from the strategies of others.

Adding to the militaristic impression, land and space shortages, along with security issues, often force NGOs to operate in locations alongside military operations, giving locals the impression of collusion. In fact, quite the opposite; the nonstate actors are more likely to cooperate with the illicit network actors for their own safety. The inclination to provide services to those who threaten harm in trade for guaranties of safety is part of human nature, and an unavoidable hindrance to impartiality. The result is large amounts of aid landing in the hands of warlords and politicians, doing little for the poor.[4] When aid is not distributed discriminately it will always end up in the hands of the powerful, prolonging conflict. In volatile environments, the effort to act impartially can prove dangerous for the aid provider.

The assumption that by meeting the basic needs of the population and "winning hearts and minds" the insurgency's support will be undermined, has, ironically, contributed to the rise of illicit and patronage networks that operate by means of bribes, nepotism, and contract flipping, contributing to the overall inefficiency in aid distribution and program implementation. The United States and NATO have taken a COIN approach; therefore, aid is a part of their strategic process. However, the ideal solution would have been to eliminate an insurgency from its inception. But in the case of Afghanistan, that moment has long since passed.[5] Where "shock and awe" proved sufficient to the task in 2001, the situation is now more of a battle of endurance. Insurgents are better suited for a long attritional struggle than centralized militaries.

It is clear that security will be necessary in order to avoid social collapse, a return to more intense conflict and/or a takeover by the Taliban. However, after more than ten years in Afghanistan, we have yet to understand the drivers of this war. Throughout history, few external players have ever seemed to gain that understanding in Afghanistan. What is evident is that in a conflict-ridden society, the erosion of human and social capital and the divisions within Afghan tribal society have been the price of war.

Corruption: A Necessary Evil?

According to the Corruption Perceptions Index (CPI), which measures the perceived levels of public sector corruption in 180 countries and territories, Afghanistan ranked 179th in 2009.[6] The ACSOR/D3 and Langer Research Associates poll in May 2010 found that corruption is broadly recognized; last December, Afghans almost unanimously called it a problem; 23 percent mentioned it as one of the top three issues (peaking at 31 percent in the south). That compares to 50 percent, as noted, calling security the single top issue, and 75 percent calling it one of the top three concerns.[7]

During thirty years of conflict and political unrest, Afghanistan has emerged as a major producer of illicit narcotics, an industry that thrives in weak or warring states, and a country that fuels instability and breeds corruption. According to UN statistics, Afghanistan has produced over 90 percent of the world's supply of illegal opiates for the past six years in a row. In 2008 and 2009, 98 percent of Afghanistan's opium was produced in seven provinces in southwestern Afghanistan, all of which are areas under contested control or under the influence of the Taliban or warlord organizations.[8] UN, US, NATO, and Afghan officials differ on how important income derived from drug trafficking is to the Taliban. The United States estimates that the insurgency stands to gain between $60 million and $100 million a year from the drug industry.[9] However, the late Richard Holbrooke, when he served as the US special representative for Afghanistan and Pakistan, declared that the Taliban made more money from donations from wealthy supporters in the Arab Gulf than from the drug trade.[10] Many Afghans believe it's the government, not the insurgency or the Taliban, that stands to gain from the drug industry, as high-level traffickers and businessmen tied to the government pay heavy donations for their continued political protection.

The drug business is not the only cause of corruption. It is unclear how much development aid has been funneled though patronage networks to corrupt officials and other illegitimate actors. This reality challenges us to redefine our notions about corruption and who can legitimately participate, or not, in governance and stabilization efforts in countries like Afghanistan. Those who have until now been defined by both the international community and the central government as legitimate actors are businessmen and tribal leaders who are allies in the war and who share a common disdain for the Taliban. In addition, many of them are part of long-standing patronage networks with tribal affiliations connected to Karzai's family and the Barakzai and Popalzai tribes. Governors, provincial councils, municipal governments, as well as provincial and district administrations, are either close to these tribes or have had to establish links to them.[11] These high-level professionals and their networks are only one element of what Afghans perceive as corruption by the central government. Their role in maintaining stability is sometimes questioned through their participation in power struggles for areas and resources. For example, Ghulam Haider Hamidi, the mayor of Kandahar, has been accused of working only with local businesses that ensure that profits go to the Karzai family. In a deal over a land project called Aino Mina, originally owned by the Ministry of Defense, Hamidi was accused of buying it for the city of Kandahar and then selling it to one of Karzai's brothers, who then used it to build a luxury community.[12] Critics have said that the interests of officials like Hamidi, the Karzai family, and the Taliban are the same because they include ensuring that stability and peace are not established since it would mean an end to a profitable war funded by aid money, contracts, and drugs.[13]

The patronage networks, their tribal and subtribal relationships, alongside the element of monopolization of resources, are what fuel corruption; yet with this corruption somehow comes a kind of legitimacy. Corruption is not easily defined in

Afghan life since it is informal, with unofficial channels that have the most influence and reach. The ability to provide for a group, whether it be one's own tribe or extended family, and/or the local community, ultimately defines whether an official is seen as corrupt or not. For those benefiting from the patronage networks, corruption is not a problem. Authors like Giustozzi point out that the presence of networks of warlords and/or militia leaders alongside officials in the central government has often reflected an ambiguous relationship resulting from an "enlightened elite" that lacks roots with the population they claim to serve or represent.[14] Karzai's political leadership would be very limited without the patronage networks and stakeholders that are necessary for him to have some influence and effectiveness.

Essentially, it is the central government's inability to extend these patronage networks and benefits of resources out to the rural populations that most defines corruption, since it is these sectors that see the central government and Karzai as illegitimate. When the central government is unable or unwilling to deliver basic services along with security to these segments of the population, then other actors step in to fill the vacuum in power.

Uncivil Society Actors: The "Wild Cards"

In Afghanistan, warlordism is an inevitable reality that permeates the very fabric of everyday life. What role these nonstate actors will play in an endgame strategy is not yet clear, but still pertinent. Their spheres of influence cannot be ignored in current planning and even in speculations about postwar stability and security operations. Traditional definitions of civil society would not take these illegitimate actors into account, but we argue that, in the case of Afghanistan, they are essential and have shaped the country's social, economic, and political environments throughout history.

Participation in informal economies, even illegal ones, is the only way people in some societies have to satisfy their socioeconomic needs. The more the state is absent from or deficient in the provision of public goods, the more communities become dependent on and support criminal entities and belligerent actors who sponsor the drug trade or illegal economies.[15] Marginal communities in Afghanistan, as a result of tribal feuds or simply their location in rural areas, have come to rely on physical security and economic survival at the hands of warlords, illicit drug traffickers, smugglers, and the Taliban. Strongmen who can command a militia and provide protection breed legitimacy because they can protect the local population. But also when necessary, they can form allegiances at the regional or national level. Uncivil society actors in Afghanistan have managed to co-opt vulnerable populations and monopolize power as well as resources, perhaps in a quicker and more efficient way than the central government, thus becoming representatives of larger constituencies.

Criminal organizations are vilified, yet they provide essential economic and social benefits. The unintended failure of legitimate civil society actors has created a vacuum for warlords and the Taliban to fill by delivering services to the population in ungoverned areas. Ironically, it is the presence of these uncivil society actors that has contributed to the short-term viability of the central government. It is partly the existing level of corruption that has allowed uncivil society actors to participate in civil affairs and contribute to maintaining a semblance of "stability" for the central government. Warlords as bureaucrats have contributed to the stability of the country through a system that requires only very basic adherence to the law in order for it to function and prevent the country from becoming a failed state.

There are unexpected benefits that come with corruption and crime. In some societies it is a way to gain status and honor without having to pay allegiance to the hierarchical and organic structure that is in place. It is human nature to want to be recognized and esteemed in some form or action. It has been argued that part of the reason the Taliban has been very successful, particularly in rural segments of the country, is due to the fact that, by killing many tribal elders, it has begun a process of reorganizing traditional power structures.[16] It has empowered those who wouldn't normally have access to that power structure, such as young males from tribal minorities and/or those who do not come from a traditional hierarchical lineage.

Therefore, Afghanistan's extended duration of conflict has allowed such "achieved status" actors to compete with, or in some cases to overcome, the traditional seat of power held by "inherited" power brokers. Those whose role in society comes from elite family/clan/tribal lineage have been overtaken by the Taliban, which has implemented a merit-based system, rewarding those who can craft quick solutions and deliver services demanded by the populace. This has hampered efforts by the central government to expand to the peripheries and build legitimacy. The Taliban has offered a more efficient, fast turnaround response to the needs and grievances of the population. Looking at the long-term development and governance needs of the country, we may be witnessing the seeds of future leaders being planted by the Taliban.

Illicit actors and their informal monopolies of power across rural areas of Afghanistan are not new. The historical roots that produced the current warlords stem back to the Cold War when many served as *mujahideen* commanders. After the Soviet withdrawal in 1989 and the collapse of the central government three years later, Afghanistan entered a period of civil war during which uncivil society actors competed for state control and monopolization of resources. Militia commanders competed for patronage access that could provide sources of revenue. These sources of revenue were largely derived from drug trafficking and smuggling. Warlords engaged in predatory and opportunistic behavior—extracting rents, taxing the usage of highways, and sadistically abusing the civilian population—which in many ways has continued under the Taliban through intimidation and bullying campaigns like the killing of tribal elders or anyone else who opposes Taliban presence in an area.

It is lucrative to be a warlord, because it provides a quick mechanism to gain local legitimacy by monopolizing power, status, and most importantly, access to and control over resources. Not all warlords are created equal. At the top of the hierarchy are the well-known tribal elders, former *mujahideen* commanders or local power brokers who command the loyalty of men beyond their ability to provide a paycheck. Providing security for the US and NATO forces is the latest iteration of long and colorful careers in a familiar setting of Afghanistan.[17]

For example, in Spin Boldak, a district in Kandahar province that borders Pakistan, warlords and their militias control access to trade routes as a way to generate revenue. In a *Washington Post* article titled "The Afghan Robin Hood," Afghan Colonel Abdul Razziq was profiled as a partner in helping to stabilize and secure areas otherwise inaccessible to US troops. The US military and Colonel Razziq forged a collaboration that required a delicate balance of tolerance toward corruption in exchange for security and stability in the border area. US officials say Razziq, who is illiterate in his early thirties, presides over a vast corruption network that skims customs duties, facilitates drug trafficking, and smuggles other contraband.[18]

It is clear that individuals like Colonel Razziq have access to a network of illicit traffickers who otherwise would pose a threat to US military interests in the region if it were not for the patronage arrangement that they have been able to agree upon. There are countless other warlords who have been able to reestablish themselves in this new reality. Another colorful character is Pacha Khan Zadran, also known as "the Iron Grandpa." His private militia is said to include around two thousand men. They control checkpoints and provide private security for US and NATO convoys. In an interview, he expressed his disdain for the term "warlord" by saying that they would kill anyone who refers to them as "warlords."[19] In order for security to be maintained at the border, tolerance toward corrupt individuals and illicit trafficking may have to be tolerated.

The role that warlords play in the current state-building process is undeniable. Theirs is a more organic legitimacy than that of central government, and in fact, the rejection of those warlords by the Afghan population usually only comes in situations where they are not checked by traditional governance structures and they have not bothered to provide public goods.[20] As long as they finance survival networks and assure local security, they have a legitimacy that the central government has yet to acquire in the eyes of many Afghans.[21] Of course, there is the danger that uncivil society actors could drive out legitimate civil society and create another terrorist safe haven, especially if they are stakeholders who are more ideologically driven. The difference between uncivil and civil society actors is that the former are not necessarily interested in ideas of national interest, nor in adherence to international guidelines and laws. Further, with the current reconciliation efforts under way, warlords and others who, until now, have been considered illegitimate actors, may end up being legitimized by the international community as viable actors in Afghanistan. It will be crucial that a sophisticated analysis of these actors is conducted in order to determine which warlord economies and their spheres of influence will be important to maintaining state stability.[22]

The challenges faced by civil society actors in Afghanistan require new paradigms for definitions and structures of governance, corruption, and civil society development. A careful assessment of who the uncivil society actors and their networks are will also be necessary in order to determine which actors can contribute to the greater good while serving their own interests. Until now, Afghanistan has learned to adapt and benefit from established illicit networks, but moving forward, a model that minimizes their negative impact and yet harnesses the power of informal stakeholders will be required. The absence of democratic governance in Afghanistan has not meant that there is an absence of governance altogether. Some warlords have delivered governing dividends and proved to be valuable assets in the absence of unlimited central resources, troops, and political will. The state does not grow strong as a result of their inclusion, but a period of hybrid governance "at the edges" may represent an inevitable stage in the project of state (re)formation in Afghanistan.[23]

The Periphery of Governance

The experience of Afghanistan suggests that, for historically weak states, a hybrid model of governance that draws on a mix of formal and informal power may be the only viable one. A hybrid model of governance would be comprised of formal and informal institutions and actors within that society.[24]

Making use of informal institutions may require a shift in the central government's view of how to build its power. Afghanistan, as we noted earlier, is quite fragmented, and in areas where the Taliban has been able to establish a presence, it has done so by co-opting and redefining organic social structures, but also by entrenching its organization and members through established networks at every level. Seth Jones reminds us that, after the Soviet withdrawal, the Taliban was able to move quickly and expand throughout the country, beginning in Kandahar, by co-opting groups through bribery and promises of power sharing. It has continued this bottom-up strategy to fight the Karzai administration and US and coalition forces.[25] Co-opting local leaders and grievances has been the modus operandi of the Taliban. Its evolution and resilience is a result of its ability to travel deep inside many parts of Afghanistan, collaborate with conservative clerical networks, and recruit the marginal, petty criminals and young unemployed of these areas.[26]

While this chapter has very briefly commented on the justice system as an aspect of civil society, it is important to point out that this is one area where the Taliban has been very successful and has worked within traditional institutions. These traditional institutions, while not formal, are effective and give the population quick results, as opposed to a top-down system forced upon the local communities from hundreds of miles away in Kabul. Through the establishment of shadow governments and a mobile dispute resolution system, the Taliban has been able to introduce order and consistency in villages where the local population is marginalized from central government authority. They have been able to gain legitimacy through this system and administer rule of law. This is a powerful prerequisite for establishing governance.

One could argue that, by placing commissioners at the local level, the Taliban has introduced a permanent presence that will outlast the war. These shadow governments are an aspect of the "formal" structure of the Taliban, but they also are an example of how it has been able to navigate through informal networks that foreign forces have had difficulty accessing. The insurgents's control over an area has not had to include territory. Rather, influence has been spread largely through informal means—mosques, family ties, tribal ties, connections from the 1990s, and so on. These channels are generally not available to foreign troops.[27] The Taliban has thus been able to make subtle yet strategically important moves.

Informal stakeholders such as warlords, their militias, and nonstate actors like the Taliban have historically played and are currently playing a role in shaping and influencing the Afghan social, economic, and political environment, along with the patronage networks that accompany them. In the same way that the Taliban has been able to expand and survive at the peripheries, Karzai's administration and the central government could also be strengthened by making use of a decentralized approach. This could include, as was mentioned in the previous section, working with established nonstate actors that have no political aspirations but have been able to maintain a presence in areas where the central government may need more time to establish roots. Allying with these networks at this crucial stage will determine whether a central government can stand on its own after coalition forces leave.

In countries where a strong central government is not in place, power is fragmented and segmented by local power brokers that monopolize force in certain areas. This is not unique to Afghanistan. Cycles in state formation, as seen in African countries that are primarily tribal and have been in conflict and have engaged in rapid change, have provided a strong incentive to decentralize in order to accommodate more participatory governance and networks of communities. Without considering structures at the local level and the interdependence of governance at the national and local levels, community actions and responsibilities cannot be properly addressed.[28] Furthermore, decentralization of the state is not a political phenomenon limited to Africa, but can be seen in other developing countries where this approach reduces ethnic tensions (Bosnia and Herzegovina, Ethiopia, and Russia), improves delivery of services to local populations, and keeps opposition factions at bay by forging countervailing federations.[29]

Providing local security has been another challenge that the central government has faced and one that it cannot master without decentralizing and forming allegiances that will allow it to shape the local security structures. There are many variables that define the security situation at the local level, each having its own social, economic, and political factors.[30] The central government will have to gain an understanding of the differences across provinces in order to leverage power brokers and the security architecture in which they function so as to begin to establish legitimacy in areas where it is less accepted. In the same way that the Taliban was able to expand by understanding local dynamics, the central government can harness the presence of local security forces to provide protection and reduce the signs of criminal activity. Programs like Village Stability Operations (VSO) that have included the engagement of elders and other stakeholders are a modest start in this direction. During the initial phase of the program, several experts were careful to point out that, throughout the history of Afghanistan, previous attempts at arming local security fighters have backfired against central rule. However, it is clear that without an initial perception of security by the population, particularly in areas where the central government has little or no presence, it would be very difficult to begin to build trust and acceptance of central governance by the population.

Security as a starting point is what will make the central government effective in areas where it is not present. Rather than view such local mechanisms as a threat to the monopoly of power by the central government, they can serve as a foundation for building from local to central structures, contributing to the management of power and governance throughout the country. In addition, the VSOs and community watch programs could be better exploited to strengthen state and civil society relationships. Further, they have also provided a process of engagement with local communities that the government, until recently, had not been able to engage beyond Kabul. A durable peace for Afghanistan will likely require a careful combination of top-down institutionalization and bottom-up co-optation of local leaders.[31]

Governance from the periphery can also go hand-in-hand with local, grass-roots development programs currently being conducted by civil society organizations, the State Department, and coalition forces. A decentralized approach to these programs is not a threat as long as the central government is able to manage local spheres of influence and balance corruption. Decentralized expenditures and sources of revenue generation ensure that corruption is managed at the local level. Local leaders should be held accountable by their local beneficiaries. In the case of Afghanistan, this model for controlling corruption at the local level works well since the stakeholder has to answer directly to his community and is depended upon to ensure that honor is maintained. Central government agencies that operate in central planning environments have a larger challenge in sustaining and maintaining local investments.[32] Community-driven development alongside local government structures is a model that has been tested and implemented, and one that could be further implemented in Afghanistan. The mantra "All Politics Is local" is not only true of the United States and other democracies, but of Afghanistan as well. Keeping in mind the history and social architecture of the country, governance and development from the periphery seem "organic."

Rethinking Civil Society—Youth

Youth may be the overlooked catalyst of civil society in Afghanistan. Despite their historic role in shaping the undercurrents of the country's social and political landscape, they have been an understudied and largely ignored variable. Sixty-eight percent of the population is under the age of twenty-five.[33] Some observers would argue that this a result of a high mortality rate and a history of protracted conflict, along with low health standards. However, it is important to remember that, like many of other developing countries, Afghanistan is but one example of the youth demographic bulge. Almost 85 percent of the world's youth live in developing countries, with approximately 60 percent in Asia alone. An additional 23 percent live in the developing regions of Africa, Latin America, and the Caribbean. By 2025, the number of youth living in developing countries will grow to 89.5 percent.[34]

It is no surprise that the recent calls for change throughout the Middle East have essentially come from disenfranchised youth.

In Afghanistan, youth have been participants and leaders in student politics. Their participation has shaped modern politics and elite group formation. As a result of expansion in university education during the 1940s and 1950s, the educated class started to grow numerically and a new intelligentsia was formed that would participate in competing for power in the 1960s and 1970s.[35] While political activism via student organizations is not new or unique to Afghanistan, it has largely been ignored as an important element of future politics. The student activists of the 1990s differed from their predecessors in that they entered a system largely influenced by Islamist or fundamentalist groups, leaving a significant cultural imprint on the current generation.[36] Today, student politics moves between two poles—patronage and rebellion. Disenfranchised, rural youth have found a way to raise their status and gain influence through membership in political parties that provide them with career advancement. Many of these parties are jihadist in nature, such as Jamiat-i-Islami and Hizb-i-Islami.[37] These political parties have created a mechanism for disenfranchised youth who are motivated to break out of their "silos" via patronage networks that extend to the peripheries of population centers. As mentioned earlier in this chapter, tapping into this segment of the population has proved effective for the Taliban. In a society accustomed to adapting to the forces of change, individuals maximize their potential and self-interest by aligning with those who will secure their survival. For youth, joining these groups has provided alternative options to the Taliban and, perhaps, secured protection under the umbrella of a political party.

Edward de Bono writes that creative thinking is often seen to be something that is better done by the rebels in society, since they like to break the rules and think the nonconformist thoughts.[38] In the case of youth, it may be that they have been the silent rebels in society who have been able to engage in creating solutions and alternative survival systems. They are potentially powerful catalysts for change. They continue to shape the social and political landscape. The patronage networks of student groups have provided options to the large segments of the male population. They have essentially introduced a new social order that provides the opportunity to gain honor, prestige, and resources, without being tied to traditional social and tribal structures.

Rather than focus on what has gone wrong in Afghanistan, policymakers should challenge themselves to think of alternative ways to analyze power dynamics in Afghan society by taking youth into account. Youth are significant not only in terms of demographics, but they also can perpetuate perceptions of grievances and can serve as spoilers in power structures.[39]

It is unfortunate that there has been less focus on the generational impact of conflict as an aspect of civil society programs. In thinking about civil society, what kind of *meme*[40] do actors want to leave in Afghanistan once US and coalition forces begin to leave? Have we thought of what kind of long-term strategy could help to sustain stability and prevent Afghanistan's future use as a sanctuary for international terrorists? How will it resonate with and be palpable to those segments of society, particularly youth, who have lived during an era of seemingly endless conflict? Will they become catalysts for peace or continued instability? Youth who have participated in combat will require different incentives in order to engage in reintegration, particularly when conflict has provided a dangerous, yet sustainable livelihood. If we can learn from the history of Afghanistan during the 1970s, it seems clear that student groups and patronage networks will be beneficial to those who harness the energy and motivations of youth. As legitimate civil society actors, they must have a role in shaping Afghanistan. Let the recent protests throughout the Arab world serve as an indication that youth can mobilize to introduce change.

The Endgame

A private contractor with experience in Afghanistan was asked to describe the main problem as it pertained to security and stability in the country.[41] He said the following: "People have friends, nations have interests and the US and Afghanistan have not defined a common interest." Unless the United States defines a long-term national interest in Afghanistan, it will not survive the domestic political reluctance to remain there beyond the Obama presidency. Our mission in 2001, to fight the "War on Terror," no longer resonates with most of the American population. Osama bin Laden's death makes it less clear what our purpose continues to be in Afghanistan.

Throughout this chapter we have highlighted how civil and uncivil society actors shape the landscape of Afghanistan. Civil society encompasses various sectors of society: social, political, and economic. A decade ago, mobile electronics usage in Afghanistan was almost nonexistent; now there are thirteen million subscriptions with an estimated annual growth rate of about 53 percent.[42] Challenges to future expansion include poverty, high illiteracy rates, corruption, an untrained workforce, and lack of security.[43] These are all issues upon which civil society actors have focused. They also strive to influence and have an impact on the lives of everyday Afghans, including youth. According to an Asia Foundation Report for 2009, up to 44 percent of rural households reported having a mobile phone. The more connected the marginalized areas and groups of society are, the greater the chance to have an impact; but this all depends on whether these channels are harnessed. US strategic interests need to be tied to these channels and networks throughout civil society, especially those that will shape the future of Afghanistan.

As we have seen throughout recent events in the Middle East, youth are drivers and channels of change. Much like in Afghanistan, the end result of current transitions is yet to be determined. However, it is undeniable that a new narrative led by young people and social movements is shaping reality, and this reality is being defined not by governments but by people. Similarly, in Afghanistan, young men have tasted power and influence, much like their *mujahideen* predecessors. How this power and influence are channeled will determine whether Afghanistan returns to being a breeding ground for extremist radical ideologies.

Economic aid has introduced a new set of problems. The traditional model of aid distribution and implementation of reconstruction programs across sectors of civil society is primarily a top-down approach. For that reason, it would be more efficient to promote community-based networks that bring aid to the rural and least-developed parts of the country where the Taliban and other uncivil society actors have a stronger chance of providing basic services. Grassroots- and locally-driven development projects tend to reflect the needs and priorities of a local population, particularly in places like Afghanistan where the majority of provinces are rural. There is also a history inherent in the tribal system of attending to and solving matters at the local level. The mantra would be: Buy local Afghan products; use local Afghan resources with proper oversight.[44] Rather than viewing this structure as a threat to central governance, it should be perceived and managed as a mechanism to strengthen stability from the edges to the center of government.

In a chapter that has argued about the importance of civil society and all that it entails, including investing in human and social capital, it would be a contradiction to say that an alternative (although less attractive endgame for Afghanistan) would be to leave the country to its own devices. While we do not call for precipitate withdrawal, ideas about free will and sovereignty make the case that Afghanistan should determine its own journey and future in the hope that civil society will evolve on its own course, under its own timeline. Who better to understand these ideals than the United States and other Western nations, whose early foundations were shaped by the Enlightenment and ideals about self-determination? Perhaps as part of an ongoing human evolution, the current trends in the Middle East, the growing youth bulge, and the global economic recession are challenging the United States to engage in the development of a new framework, not just for Afghanistan, but as a leader in the rest of the world and as one that is shaping a different sort of future, even for its own people.

Notes

1 Lisa Schirch, "The Civil Society-Military Partnership in Afghanistan," U.S. Institute of Peace brief, September 24, 2010: 5.

2 Susan Cornwell, "Factbox: A Look at the Costs of Afghan War to U.S. Taxpayers," *Reuters*, July 16, 2010.

3 Barnett R. Rubin, "The Political Economy of War and Peace in Afghanistan," *World Development* 28, no. 10 (2000): 1789–1803.

4 Linda Polman, *War Games: The Story of Aid and War in Modern Times* (London: Viking/Penguin, 2010).

5 Thomas H. Henriksen,"Afghanistan, Counterinsurgency and the Indirect Approach," JSOU report 10-3 (Hurlburt Field, FL: Joint Special Operations University Press, 2010), 27, 31.

6 Transparency International, September 2009, www.transparency.org/policy_research/survey_indices/cpi/2009/methodology, accessed 2010.

7 D3Systems and Langer Research Associates, Afghanistan Poll (Vienna, May 2010).

8 UNODC, Afghanistan's Opium Survey 2008, November 2008.

9 The UN estimates the number to be $125 million, while independent Afghan observers have put the number as high as $500 million a year. "Afghanistan's Narco War: Breaking the Link Between Drug

Trafficking and Insurgents," Senate Foreign Relations Committee, Committee Print, S. Prt. 111–29, 111th Congress, 1st Session, August 10, 2009; Gretchen Peters, *Seeds of Terror: How Heroin Bankrolls the Taliban and al Qaeda* (New York: Thomas Dunne Books, 2009).

10 Slobodan Lekic, "US Envoy: Most Taliban Funds Come from Overseas," *Associated Press*, July 28, 2009.

11 Canadian Department of Foreign Affairs, Kandahar City Assessment (Canadian government, 2009).

12 Pamela Constable, "Corrupt Leaders Trump the Taliban," *The Washington Post*, January 6, 2011, C1, C2.

13 Ibid.

14 Antonio Giustozzi, "'Good State' vs. 'Bad' Warlord? A Critique of State Building Strategies in Afghanistan," *Crisis State Programme Working Paper Series* No.1, October 2004, 1–17.

15 Vanda Felbab-Brown, "Conceptualizing Crime as Competition in State-making and Designing an Effective Response," Conference Report (Brookings Institution, 2010). www.brookings.edu/speeches/2010/0521_illegal_economies_felbabbrown.aspx

16 Panel of speakers, "Jamestown Foundation: The Future of FATA and the NWFP" (Washington, DC: Jamestown Foundation, April 15, 2009).

17 Commitee on Oversight and Government Reform. Warlord, Inc. Report of the Majority Staff (Washington, DC: U.S. House of Representatives, 2010).

18 Rajiv Chandrasekaran, "The Afghan Robin Hood," *Washington Post*, October 4, 2010.

19 Pratap Chatterjee, "U.S. Private Security in Afghanistan:Pay-off Warlords, Taliban," Inter Press Service (IPS) Washington, DC, June 23, 2010. http://ipsnews.net/news.asp?idnews=51927.

20 Felix Kuntszch, "Afghanistan's Rocky Road to Modenity: Non-State Actors and Socio-Political Entities in the Process of State and Nation Building," research (Quebec City: Universite Laval, 2008).

21 Rainer Glassner Conrad and Masood Karokhail Schetter, "Beyond Warlordism: The Local Security Architecture in Afghanistan," *Internationale Politik und Gesselschaft* [*International Politics and Society*], vol. 2 (June 20, 2007).

22 Felix Kuntszch, "Afghanistan's Rocky Road to Modernity." (Quebec City: Laval University, 2008) www.psi.ulaval.ca/fileadmin/psi/documents/Documents/Travaux_et_recherches/Afghanistan_s_Rocky_Road_to_Modernity.pdf

23 Dipail Mukhopadhay, "Warlords as Bureaucrats: The Afghan Experience," *Carnegie Papers* (Washington, DC: Carnegie Endowment for International Peace, 2009).

24 Ibid.

25 Seth Jones, "It Takes the Villages," *Foreign Affairs* (June/July 2010): 5–8.

26 Antonio Giustozzi, "The Resurgence of the Neo-Taliban" Open Democracy (London, December 15, 2007) www.opendemocracy.net/article/the_resurgence_of_the_neo_taliban.

27 Anand Gopal, "The Battle for Aghanistan: Militancy and Conflict in Kandahar," Counterterrorism Strategy Policy Paper (Washington, DC: New America Foundation, 2010).

28 James F. Hicks, "Community Driven Development and Good Local Governance," in Discussion Notes (Washington, DC: The World Bank, 2001).

29 Ibid.

30 Rainer Glassner Conrad and Masood Karokhail Schetter, "Beyond Warlordism: The Local Security Architecture in Afghanistan."

31 Jones, "It Takes the Villages."

32 Hicks, "Community Driven Development and Good Local Governance."

33 United Nations Development Programme, Afghanistan: NJYP, Annual Report (Kabul: UNDP, 2008).

34 United Nations, "Youth at the United Nations: Frequently Asked Questions," Youth and the United Nations, 2005, www.un.org/esa/socdev/unyin/qanda.htm, accessed January 14, 2011.

35 Antonio Giustozzi, "Between Patronage and Rebellion: Student Politics in Afghanistan," AREU Briefing Paper Series, (Kabul, Afghanistan: February 2010) www.humansecuritygateway.com/documents/AREU_StudentPolitics_Afghanistan.pdf: 1–7.

36 Ibid.

37 Ibid.

38 A. J. Richardson, R. C. Hupp, and R. K. Seethaler, "The Use of Lateral Thinking in Finding Creative Conflict Resolutions" The Urban Transport Institute (TUTI) (Australia: January 5, 2003). www.tuti.com.au/Publications/2003/2003ABA.pdf.

39 United States Institute of Peace, Youth and Post-Conflict Reconstruction, Questions and Answers, Assessment (Washington, DC: U.S. Institute of Peace, 2010).

40 Richard Dawkins coined the term "meme" in his 1976 book *The Selfish Gene*. "Meme" refers to ideas or beliefs transmitted from one person or group of people to another. Making use of the analogy of a gene, the idea can be said to propagate from one brain to another like a living organism.

41 Interview with Kevin Grose, DMDC, CTR, by Jade Rodriguez. Private contractor (July 2010).

42 Sheldon Himelfarb with contributions from Cecilia Paradi-Guilford, "Can You Help Me Now?" Special Report (Washington, DC: United States Institute of Peace, 2010).

43 Ibid.

44 SWJ Editors, "COMISAF's Counterinsurgency (COIN) Contracting Guidance," *Small Wars Journal (SWJ)* SWJ blog post, September 13, 2010. http://smallwarsjournal.com/blog/comisafs-counterinsurgency-coin-contracting-guidance.

PART IV

Conclusion

CHAPTER 12

Assessing the Strategic Alternatives

John Arquilla and Hy Rothstein

Helmuth von Moltke the Elder, whose military victories in the 1860s and 1870s did so much to make modern Germany, is perhaps best remembered for his insight that "no plan of operations extends with certainty beyond the first encounter."[1] Yet, for all the wide acceptance of this aphorism by soldiers and statesmen around the world, set "plans of operations" have all too often been adhered to in wartime long after being overtaken by events. For example, the suicidal massed infantry assaults of World War I persisted for years before changes were made. In World War II, the Germans kept relying on patented *blitzkrieg* battle plans long after their opponents had learned how to defend against such attacks, which led to catastrophic losses at Kursk, Falaise, and the Battle of the Bulge. And in these "conventional" wars of the past, identifying the critical targets for military action was relatively easy. Today, finding the enemy's pressure points is infinitely more difficult, thereby calling for more options and greater strategic flexibility from the start. What is clear in Afghanistan is that the status quo is untenable and therefore will not produce or sustain a stable equilibrium. Even changes at the margin that focus on troop withdrawals are unlikely to secure American interests, in the absence of significant policy and strategy changes.

It is troubling to note that the American experience—since long before the war in Afghanistan—has also reflected this tendency to stick with a plan in which much has been invested. This can be seen in the case of the Vietnam War, where the US military's stubborn devotion to its "big unit" plan of operations was the proximate cause of the debacle that ensued. Over the past decade, American field campaigns in Iraq and Afghanistan have also reflected a reluctance to depart from set plans. But in Iraq, a shift was eventually made from a latter-day version of the big-unit war concept to a network of small outposts that was nicely complemented by tens of thousands of now-friendly insurgents who had been induced to switch sides. This shift took too long to make, and war costs were far too high by then.

A shift of a similar sort is under way in Afghanistan today. Hy Rothstein notes, in chapter 4 on field operations there, that American, friendly Afghan, and other allied forces have become more "packetized" and more widely distributed throughout portions of the country and are becoming more effective. It is clearly an effort to rekindle the small-unit successes enjoyed by the US Special Forces teams at the outset of the war in Afghanistan and by conventional forces in Iraq in 2006 and after. But for all the innovativeness being shown in the military operational realm, the overall strategic aim of consolidating a strong, legitimate central government in Kabul seems to have remained mostly unchanged, even as evidence continues to mount regarding the high cost and low likelihood of achieving such an outcome.

This is not an uncommon situation, as larger strategic aims have often proved very hard to change—even in the face of highly problematic results in battle. Our own expectations of "right" often cloud our judgments regarding what can reasonably be achieved. And on occasion this sort of higher-level strategic stubbornness has led to terrible catastrophes. In ancient times, the Athenians, late in the Peloponnesian War, were offered peace terms short of their grander aims. They rejected the offer and subsequently lost, ending their golden age in ruin.[2] Something similar happened to the Germans during World War I, when they rejected compromise peace overtures and decided to "roll the iron dice" with a final offensive in 1918, in the hope of winning the victory that had eluded them in 1914. They failed, Germany fell, and the world careened toward a future cataclysm of even greater proportions.

To be sure, there are also some examples of winning by adhering to initial concepts of operations and larger strategic aims—but they are not predominant. Seldom is stasis the solution across the board. The Romans may have been quite single-mindedly devoted to destroying Carthage, but they could not have done so without first transforming themselves into a naval power, and then coming up with radical new battle tactics on land and sea. In more modern times, the steadfast Union aim during the American Civil War of bringing all the secessionist states back could not have succeeded without a willingness to shift from massed frontal assaults in a few areas to the strategic "cordon offensive" that Abraham Lincoln embraced—over the opposition of many of his senior generals, who viewed his ideas with what one historian has called "polite scorn."[3]

In pure operational terms, the war in Afghanistan should be seen as eminently winnable. In our view, however, the war, now over a decade long, surely falls into the category of conflicts that require military operational, strategic, and larger policy adjustments in order to avoid catastrophe. In chapter 2, Victor Davis Hanson has provided a compelling argument that Afghanistan is hardly the "graveyard of empires" that some have labeled it, noting that the ancient Greeks succeeded there for centuries by a skillful blending of innovative military action and systematic outreach to some selected indigenous tribal actors. Thomas Barfield, in chapter 3, has developed this notion further, focusing on the fissures in Afghan society between urban and rural populations and implying that a sufficient degree of security might be provided even in the absence of clear, countrywide order imposed by a strong central government. The ability to sustain control in urban areas might do well enough, and could even persuade recalcitrant tribal leaders to switch to what they might well perceive to be the "winning side."

That said, Rothstein's operational survey suggests that new military concepts of operations, that is, a shift toward more wide-ranging actions by smaller units, could even tame many of the rural parts of Afghanistan. And this sort of campaign can be pursued without the need to wait on, or even count on, the consolidation of a strong, legitimate, centralized political structure. In fact, undermining Kabul and strengthening local structures may be the best way to stabilize Afghanistan and secure American interests. This is a point that resonates with Scott Gartner and Leo Blanken (chapter 8) as well. They see the possibility of a downscale shift in military operations and a lessened effort at nation-building. What matters more to them is the emergence of a system that, while unable to prevent the continuance or recurrence of violence, does at least have the capacity to restore a well-functioning equilibrium once it has been disturbed.

In this regard, both of these previous views are consistent with Edward Luttwak's "minimalist" approach to the Afghan endgame outlined in chapter 7. The power and/or legitimacy of the Kabul government mean little to him. What matters more, in his view, is that enough power be used to fend off a military debacle, and he believes the best way to ensure this kind of "good enough" solution is to encourage (and perhaps even impel) other nations with interests in Afghanistan to end their free-riding and step in to keep minimal order. His is similar to a poker strategy in that there is some risk that an American disengagement from Afghanistan might *not* be followed by palliative actions taken by some mix of Russian, Chinese, and Indian—and perhaps Iranian—initiatives. Against this risk, Luttwak is willing to consider continuance of at least a special-operations-oriented American military effort with enough capability to keep the violence at an "acceptable" level, as Gartner and Blanken have argued.

But, in a larger strategic sense, the aforementioned operational changes and international gambits may signify either indefinite future politico-military involvement or renewed internal chaos, civil war, and terror in Afghanistan. In light of the possibility that this dark future might come to pass, Andrew Bacevich (chapter 5) has argued that American policy should focus immediately on capping off costs at their current levels and leaving the country. In the wake of Osama bin Laden's death, and in the knowledge that al-Qaeda actually plays only a small role inside Afghanistan, this line of argument is worthy of very serious consideration.[4] Indeed, the record of states that have continued interventions in the hope of coming out well in the end (like the Soviet Union in Afghanistan), but which have suffered costly defeats, is most sobering. That the United States withdrew from Vietnam and yet went on to win the Cold War suggests that giving up on some wars before the hour grows too late is essential when considering a nation's larger aims.

The critique of outright withdrawal, best articulated by Robert Reilly (chapter 10) and Fred Kagan (chapter 6) is largely based on the reputational consequences of such a move. For both of them, simply leaving Afghanistan to its fate would hand the Taliban and al-Qaeda a free, and huge, propaganda victory. This informational consequence aside, Kagan is also generally more reluctant to consider an outcome that would amount to something less than strong central governance and clear military victory. However, the costs of achieving such a result could prove quite high, depending on the kinds of military innovations introduced in the field that might allow counterinsurgent forces to do better with a much lighter "footprint."

Another complication faced by those contemplating a departure from Afghanistan arises out of the ethics of the situation, so thoughtfully studied by Russell Muirhead in chapter 9. The measure of *jus ad bellum,* the justice of going to war against the Taliban in the first place, seems clearly to have favored the intervening forces, given that the 9/11 attacks on America were plotted and supported from Afghanistan. The matter of *jus in bello,* fighting justly, has been generally conformed to as well, despite scattered violations of the principle of noncombatant immunity. But for Muirhead the great ethical challenge that lies ahead is that of meeting the requirements of *jus post bellum,* acting justly in the postwar period.

It is hard to see how an Afghanistan that could descend into bloody civil war once again, in the wake of the withdrawal of US and allied forces, would meet the ethical standard of *jus post bellum*. Whether postwar justice requires a great deal more than simply avoiding civil war—such as leaving behind a democracy, or a central government that can secure individual rights—is an open question. Muirhead argues for his own version of a "minimalist" ethical strategy that privileges legitimacy over democracy and stability over the full enforcement of rights. But in addition, he argues that we have special obligations to those who have helped our cause. These obligations direct us to provide refugee status for and take in those Afghans who fought as part of the anti-Taliban alliance. Much as, for example, both supporters of the Republic of Vietnam and friendly hill tribes like the Hmong were resettled, largely in the United States, after the fall of Saigon in 1975. For that matter, it would also be like the British embrace of the loyalist Tories at the end of the American Revolution, most of whom were allowed to settle in Canada. But even ethical palliatives of this nature might pale against the backdrop of an Afghanistan in perpetual flames after the final departure of American-led coalition forces, which is why a stable political order is of profound ethical importance.

To summarize the situation as we have assessed it thus far: Outright withdrawal from Afghanistan would certainly entail a significant "loss of face," and could result in massive new bloodletting. But staying there and trying to shore up strong, legitimate central governance appears to be a costly option, both in material terms and in the demands such a course would impose upon weary troops and their equally weary mass publics back home.

Perhaps one possible remedy would be to consider the legitimacy and centrality of government separately. In chapter 11, Jade Rodriguez and Rebecca Lorentz argue that a willingness to cede most governance tasks to the provincial, district, and village levels in Afghanistan might, within traditional, culturally accepted levels of corruption, convey a kind of "legitimacy at the edges." Over time, they continue, this sense of legitimacy could be expanded, eventually encompassing the whole country. Thus, they argue for a "periphery to the center" approach, one that is quite different from the "Kabul-centric," government-in-a-box strategy that has so clearly proved its inadequacy over the past few years.

For such a strategy to work, it would be necessary to provide a security structure that could keep the peace at the village level, hence General Petraeus's emphasis on "village stability operations" (VSO). And it is in this approach that it is possible to see a point of convergence between all the strategies proffered, save for the notion of immediate and complete withdrawal. For example, both Luttwak's and Gartner and Blanken's strategies clearly contemplate swift, sharp reductions in US forces. If residual troops are distributed widely among the VSOs, it is even possible to see how a much smaller quantitative presence would be more than offset by a significant *qualitative* improvement, for example, in presence; deterrent effects; in response time to any insurgent attacks; and in legitimate, localized capacity that allows self-determination. In this respect, the VSO concept of operations could also prove acceptable to those strategists, like Kagan and Reilly, who argue articulately about the imperative to avoid handing the Taliban a huge propaganda victory by unilaterally withdrawing from the country.

It is clear that, after the killing of Osama bin Laden, President Obama was given a political opportunity to make significant force drawdowns in line with his long-standing promise to begin them in July 2011.[5] That he generally affirmed this commitment and acted accordingly may not only make political sense, but also strategic sense, for the reductions under way do not imperil the VSO concept; instead, they will help provide a much-needed "rotation base" for tired troops, at last freeing American policy from the time pressure that accompanied keeping larger forces in Afghanistan for so many years. Additionally, drawdowns may also facilitate Luttwak's concept of attracting regional powers to play a greater role in Afghanistan's stability. Finally, the drawdowns also reinforce the "big bet" placed on building security and legitimacy "from the periphery to the center."

There is little chance of seeing any kind of new surge of US forces to Afghanistan in the future. But there are several ways to think about using the time granted by the VSO concept. First and foremost, this strategy affords the opportunity to support the democratic process in Afghanistan without backing a particular leader or faction, and without striving unduly to create a strongly centralized government in a country with little historical or cultural foundation for having one. In fact, nurturing competent, local capacity may produce the antibodies to thwart the corruption, incompetence, and rising anti-Americanism in Kabul. This may be the only mechanism to force Karzai to undertake real reform in order to survive.[6] Here, truly, is an opportunity to nurture grassroots, jirga-styled democracy.

If Gartner and Blanken are right, the Afghan polity that emerges will still face violent internal challenges from time to time. Their point is that we should not try to establish such a strong central government that no such challenges will ever arise; rather, their view is that the strategic fabric of Afghan society should simply be strong enough to mend the tears caused by such occasional violence. If Luttwak is right about the deep, enduring interests of Afghanistan's neighbors in fostering a stable environment, there is every reason to hope that the fledgling Afghan government will enjoy considerable international support from the outset—but most likely without a significant continuing US military presence. And it is in this manner that Bacevich's goal of complete withdrawal can be contemplated, perhaps not in the immediate future, but at a point perhaps sooner than even the 2014 deadline set by the members of the alliance participating in this campaign.[7]

In light of the range of strategic alternatives advanced in this volume, we feel strongly that senior policymakers can, and should, now free themselves from the strictures imposed by adherence to long-standing political and military practices that have directed, and sometimes misdirected, the intervention in Afghanistan over the course of so many years. If something less than a strong centralized government can be considered, and a military strategy different from the troop-heavy paradigm can be adopted, then a way ahead emerges that may take us successfully out of this thicket while assuring that our interests remain secured.

Practically speaking, we note that the "strategic truth" is not the sole property of any single perspective offered up in this volume. Each contributor's line of argument has considerable merit, and it is in the synthesis of these ideas that guidance for high-level policy is to be found. Bacevich's great insight is that there comes a point when costs must be capped, but this realization is bitter medicine indeed if it comes with a major propaganda catastrophe—and perhaps a renewed civil war—in the wake of our withdrawal, about which Kagan and Reilly have expressed concern. Their firmness about the importance of holding out for a good outcome, that is, a stable, reasonably secure Afghanistan, has much merit but does not adequately deal with Bacevich's concerns about mounting costs.

At this point, Luttwak enters with the key insight that several neighbors of Afghanistan have strong interests in seeing stability and security return to that sad land. And he is willing to call their bluff, that is, to end their "free-ride" at American expense by sharply and immediately drawing US forces down nearly to zero. There is some hedging built into his strategy, but not much. Yet Luttwak's approach can be strengthened, it seems, by adoption of the concept of operations that Rothstein argues for in chapter 4; and Gartner and Blanken's "resilience model" of having enough capacity to restore the societal equilibrium once it has been disturbed could prove very helpful as well.

With the interplay of these strategies in mind, something of a synthesis of ideas emerges. The goal should be complete American withdrawal, but not before hedging against handing the Taliban a propaganda coup, and ensuring against a bloody civil war ramping back up. New concepts of operations will help enliven this synthesis, but so will the scaled-back goal of seeking a resilient society that is able to deal with any renewed violence, versus the originally preferred outcome of an Afghanistan at complete peace.

In the end, we take much heart from Hanson's reminder that wars are winnable in Afghanistan—even with small numbers of troops—given that the right kind of military action, mixed with selective co-optation of local tribes, is undertaken. Afghanistan need not be, nor should it be, viewed simply as the graveyard of empires. From Barfield we draw the insight that Afghan culture has always been at least bifurcated, at times even more atomized, and that the disgruntled will align with a perceived winner. Ultimately, Afghans are much more practical than ideological. From Reilly we get a sense of the information strategy that should be followed to allow this sort of helpful "social virus" to spread. From Rodriguez and Lorentz we glean an accurate picture of the vectors by which the social virus can spread.

Thus, at this critical time in the long American intervention in Afghanistan, we conclude that a strategic review that cultivates a range of options is far more likely to point to a productive pathway ahead than adherence to originally preferred ends and means. And if there is a willingness to think in terms of an outcome that sees greater local capacity and control and a reduced role for the government in Kabul, and which contemplates smaller-scale, but "smarter," military actions, then it will quickly become clear that the answer lies not in a single strategy but in the skillful blending of several strategic elements.

It is with the foregoing in mind that we offer the following list of elements that should inform the development of sustainable policies and strategies for Afghanistan:

***Overall* theme: Much less is more**

- Demonstrate long-term US interest in Afghanistan by substituting qualitative, customized military approaches in place of today's primarily quantitative approach.
  - This will allow troop strength to fall dramatically, resulting in a minimized US presence.
- Go local. Go small. Go long.
  - Going local means that Afghan stability will depend on local political arrangements rather than control by the government in Kabul.
  - Going small means relying on Special Forces, probably numbering under five thousand, rather than on a conventional force presence of tens of thousands.
    - Forces will be distributed working by, with, and through legitimate local governments.
  - Going long means not publishing or announcing a withdrawal date—and being prepared to stay as long as necessary (i.e., indefinitely).
- Close most bases and downsize Kandahar and Bagram to the size of their 2002 "footprints." The large existing infrastructure fuels both the insurgency and corruption.
- Stop expensive development projects, including the one associated with building massive centralized security forces.
  - When investments are made, they must first be matched by some type of investment by locals.
- Identify and nurture young Afghan leaders who are committed to Afghanistan. Assist in pushing out the "old guard" (even by means of a civil/military coup if necessary).
- Drastically reduce efforts to build infrastructure and increase efforts to identify young, nationalistic, legitimate Afghan leaders who will cut deals that will lead to stability. Moderately reward individuals and locales for good governance ("Afghan style" governance is fine, probably preferred) and invest only in those areas where violence is neither tolerated nor exported.

- Downsize the Afghan National Army and develop security forces at the lowest practical level (VSO is a good example of the right level to emphasize).
  - Maintain moderately sized national security forces for external threats and for when interregional matters require intervention beyond Afghanistan's borders.
- Maintain very small US strike capability for high-value counterterrorist missions (like the Abbottabad raid on bin Laden) and to defeat insurgents who mass for an attack or otherwise present attractive targets.
- Drastically reduce funding to Pakistan ("Less is more" applies to Islamabad, too).
- Use all instruments of statecraft to persuade India to sharply reduce its footprint in Afghanistan, a presence that has done so much to antagonize and strike fear among Pakistanis.

In medieval times, the blending of elements was a central activity of alchemists. In our time, and for years to come, it seems clear that a new kind of "strategic alchemy" is called for. And just as alchemists did so much to inform what would become the field of chemistry, so too the kind of synthesizing undertaken here may, beyond helping to solve the problems of Afghanistan, point the way to a new approach to strategy.

Notes

1 Daniel J. Hughes, ed., *Moltke on the Art of War* (New York: Presidio Press, 1993), 45–46.

2 Donald Kagan, in *The Fall of the Athenian Empire* (Ithaca, NY: Cornell University Press, 1987), pp. 306–7 makes clear that Persian meddling also played a part in keeping Athens and Sparta from agreeing to a negotiated peace.

3 T. Harry Williams, "The Military Leadership of North and South" in *Why the North Won the Civil War*, ed. David Donald (New York: Macmillan, 1962), 54.

4 On this point, see Paul Pillar, "Spinning the al-Qaeda Threat in Afghanistan," *The National Interest*, April 18, 2011.

5 Ironically, the killing of bin Laden also provides the president an opportunity to keep some forces in Afghanistan.

6 Gary Anderson, "A Third Way in Afghanistan," *Small Wars Journal*, April 8, 2010, http://smallwarsjournal.com/blog/2010/04/a-third-way-in-afghanistan/, accessed May 15, 2011.

7 See Christi Parsons and Paul Richter, "NATO Sets 2014 Target for Afghan Pullout," *Los Angeles Times*, November 21, 2010.

CONTRIBUTORS

John Arquilla

Best known for his insights into information-age conflict (cyberwar, netwar, and swarm tactics), Dr. Arquilla spent several years at RAND before moving to the Naval Postgraduate School to help develop the special operations program. In the policy arena he advised senior military and political leaders during Operation Desert Storm and in the Kosovo War. In 2004, he argued publicly for entering into negotiations with Iraqi insurgents, an idea that was first resisted, but that proved to be successful when adopted in 2007. He is the author of seven books and over one hundred articles on a range of topics in military affairs. His latest study is *Insurgents, Raiders, and Bandits: How Masters of Irregular Warfare Have Shaped Our World*.

Andrew J. Bacevich

Dr. Bacevich is professor of history and international relations at Boston University. A graduate of the US Military Academy, he served for twenty-three years as a commissioned officer in the United States Army. He received his PhD in American diplomatic history from Princeton. Before joining the faculty of Boston University in 1998, he taught at West Point and at Johns Hopkins. Dr. Bacevich is the author or editor of several books, including *Washington Rules: America's Path to Permanent War* (2010); *The Limits of Power: The End of American Exceptionalism* (2008); and *The New American Militarism: How Americans Are Seduced by War* (2005). He is the editor of *The Short American Century, 1941–2008: A Postmortem* (2012); *The Long War: A New History of U.S. National Security Policy since World War II* (2007); and *Imperial Tense: Problems and Prospects of American Empire* (2003). His essays and reviews have appeared in a variety of scholarly and general interest publications, including *The Atlantic Monthly, The Wilson Quarterly, The London Review of Books, Foreign Affairs, Foreign Policy, The Nation,* and *The New Republic*. Dr. Bacevich is a member of the Council on Foreign Relations.

Thomas Barfield

Dr. Barfield first began his studies of Afghanistan as a student forty years ago when he traveled there by overland bus. Following nomadic migration trails on foot, donkey, and horse, he documented the lives of pastoralists in the country's northeast region (*The Central Asian Arabs of Afghanistan*, 1981) and later coauthored the most extensive study of traditional Afghan buildings ever published (*Afghanistan: An Atlas of Indigenous Domestic Architecture*, 1991). He expanded his studies to Mongolia to learn how nomads imbibing fermented mare's milk became the fast-moving cavalry archers that conquered and ruled large parts of Eurasia for more than two centuries (*The Perilous Frontier: Nomadic Empires and China,* 1989). Since 2001, his research has focused on problems of law and political development in Afghanistan. In 2007, Barfield received a Guggenheim Fellowship that led to the completion of his latest book, *Afghanistan: A Cultural and Political History* (2010).

Leo Blanken

Dr. Blanken's current research focuses on the impact of imperfect performance metrics on agent behavior in conflict, and theoretical issues surrounding conventional force structure planning. His most recent work includes *Rational Empires: Institutional Incentives and Imperialism Expansion,* forthcoming from the University of Chicago Press. He also has articles in the journals *Intelligence and National Security* and *Defense and Peace Economics*. In his spare time he is a DJ and collects rare 1960s soul records and trains amateur boxers.

Scott Sigmund Gartner

Dr. Gartner is professor of international affairs in the Penn State School of International Affairs and was previously professor of political science and director of the international relations program at the University of California, Davis. Gartner interned at the Federal Bureau of Investigation, the National Institute of Justice, and the Georgia Bureau of Investigation, and was once certified as an emergency medical technician. He holds an MA in international relations from the University of Chicago, and an MA and PhD in political science from the University of Michigan. His thesis won the American Political Science Association's award for the best policy dissertation, and he recently received the Thomas Jefferson Award for the best government resource. Gartner wrote *Strategic Assessment in War* and coedited *Historical Statistics of the United States* and *International Conflict Management*. He has published articles in the leading journals in political science, sociology, history, and international relations. His work has been widely reviewed, including in the *New York Times,* the *Washington Post, The Atlantic, Journal of Military History,* and *American Political Science Review*. He has frequently been interviewed on NPR and MSNBC, and has received funding from the National Science Foundation and the Folke Bernadotte Academy (Sweden).

Victor Davis Hanson

Dr. Hanson, a recipient of the National Humanities Medal (2008) and Bradley Prize (2009), was trained as a classical philologist at the American School of Classical Studies, Athens, and at Stanford University, where he received his PhD. Originally, he focused on classical Greek and Roman strategy, but soon explored both ancient and modern agrarianism as well as comparative military history in some twenty-one books that have been translated into over fifteen languages—among them the *New York Times* bestseller *Carnage and Culture: Landmark Battles in the Rise of Western Civilization*. He currently is a senior fellow at the Hoover Institution, Stanford University, where he directs the program in contemporary conflict and military history. He lives on his family's grape farm in central California, where he was born in 1953. Hanson writes weekly syndicated columns on culture and history for the Tribune Media Services and National Review Online. His historical novel, *The End of Sparta*, was published in fall 2011 by Bloomsbury.

Frederick Kagan

Dr. Kagan has had a profound influence on American military and security policy over the past decade. A trained historian with a doctorate from Yale, where his father is a renowned classicist, Kagan was a principal architect of the "surge strategy" that did so much to tamp down the insurgency in Iraq during 2007–8. He went on to serve as a senior advisor to General Stanley McChrystal, arguing for a similar surge in Afghanistan. Before this, Kagan was a principal voice in the late 1990s calling attention to looming threats to the national security, particularly in his book *While America Sleeps*. Dr. Kagan also taught military history at West Point from 1995 to 2005, and the following year he published his critical analysis of current military affairs, *Finding the Target*.

Rebecca Lorentz

Rebecca Lorentz is a research assistant in the Department of Defense Analysis at the Naval Postgraduate School in Monterey, California. She received a Masters of Public Policy degree from the Panetta Institute of Public Policy in 2010 and continues to study the subjects of terrorism and analytics. Using network and visual analysis, her research focuses on the sociological and demographic elements that affect domestic gang membership and gang-related crime. She has written on the complexity of these social issues as representative "wicked problems," and has served on the research team whose study, *Gangs & Guerrillas*, explores, the overlap between counterinsurgency doctrine and anticrime strategies. Previously, she served as editor of a county newsletter that focused on air quality, housing needs, and population shifts.

Edward Luttwak

Dr. Luttwak has pursued a career in military and strategic affairs that has spanned five decades. His academic achievements and his experience fighting insurgents in Borneo in the 1960s, as well as his involvement over the years in a range of classified operations worldwide, have given unique depth and breadth to his work. In fact, his book, *Coup d'État: A Practical Handbook*, has appeared in fourteen languages since its publication in 1968, and has been a guide to many who have overthrown their governments. He is the author of more than a dozen other books, most recently *The Grand Strategy of the Byzantine Empire*, and hundreds of articles on a wide range of topics in military and security affairs.

Russell Muirhead

Dr. Muirhead is a professor in the Government Department at Dartmouth College, where he teaches political theory. He writes on a wide array of subjects, including the work ethic, partisanship, American political thought, and the ethics of war. He is known among his students for giving two-hour lectures without notes and without a break. In the past, Muirhead has taught at the University of Texas at Austin, and at Harvard University. His study of the modern working life, *Just Work,* was published by Harvard University Press.

Robert Reilly

Dr. Reilly is a senior fellow at the American Foreign Policy Council. Most recently, he has taught at the National Defense University. He has served in the Office of the Secretary of Defense as senior advisor for information strategy and participated in Operation Iraqi Freedom as advisor to the Iraqi Ministry of Information. Before that, he was director of the Voice of America. Reilly has also served in the White House as a special assistant to the president (1983–85) and in the US Information Agency. In the private sector he spent more than seven years with the Intercollegiate Studies Institute, as both national director and then president. He is widely published on foreign policy, "war of ideas" issues, and classical music. He has contributed chapters to ten books and authored two, the most recent of which is *The Closing of the Muslim Mind*.

Jade I. Rodriguez

Jade Rodriguez has focused her professional career on the transformation and overall development of global civil society. She is a research assistant at the Naval Postgraduate School, specializing in issues relating to society and security in Latin America and the Middle East. Earlier, she served at the World Bank as a professional associate and was a youth advisor to the president of the bank, contributing to the development of a youth-engagement strategy and the creation of a global youth network. She has lived and studied in India, earning a postgraduate degree in software engineering and a diploma in advanced software technology from the Indian Institute of Technology. Her academic training also includes a master's degree in international policy from the Monterey Institute of International Studies. Ms. Rodriguez immigrated to the United States after fleeing the civil war in El Salvador during the 1980s.

Hy Rothstein

Dr. Rothstein has spent considerable time in Afghanistan since early 2002 observing, up close and in the most remote areas, the conduct of the war. He served in the US Army as a Special Forces officer for more than twenty-six years, spending much of his time in Latin America training and advising governments threatened by active insurgencies. Dr. Rothstein has written and edited books about Afghanistan *(Afghanistan and the Troubled Future of Unconventional Warfare)*, Iraq *(The Three Circles of War)*, and an anthology that explores the similarities between insurgency and gang violence *(Gangs & Guerrillas)*. He teaches courses and conducts research on the strategic utility of special operations, military deception, and psychological warfare.

INDEX